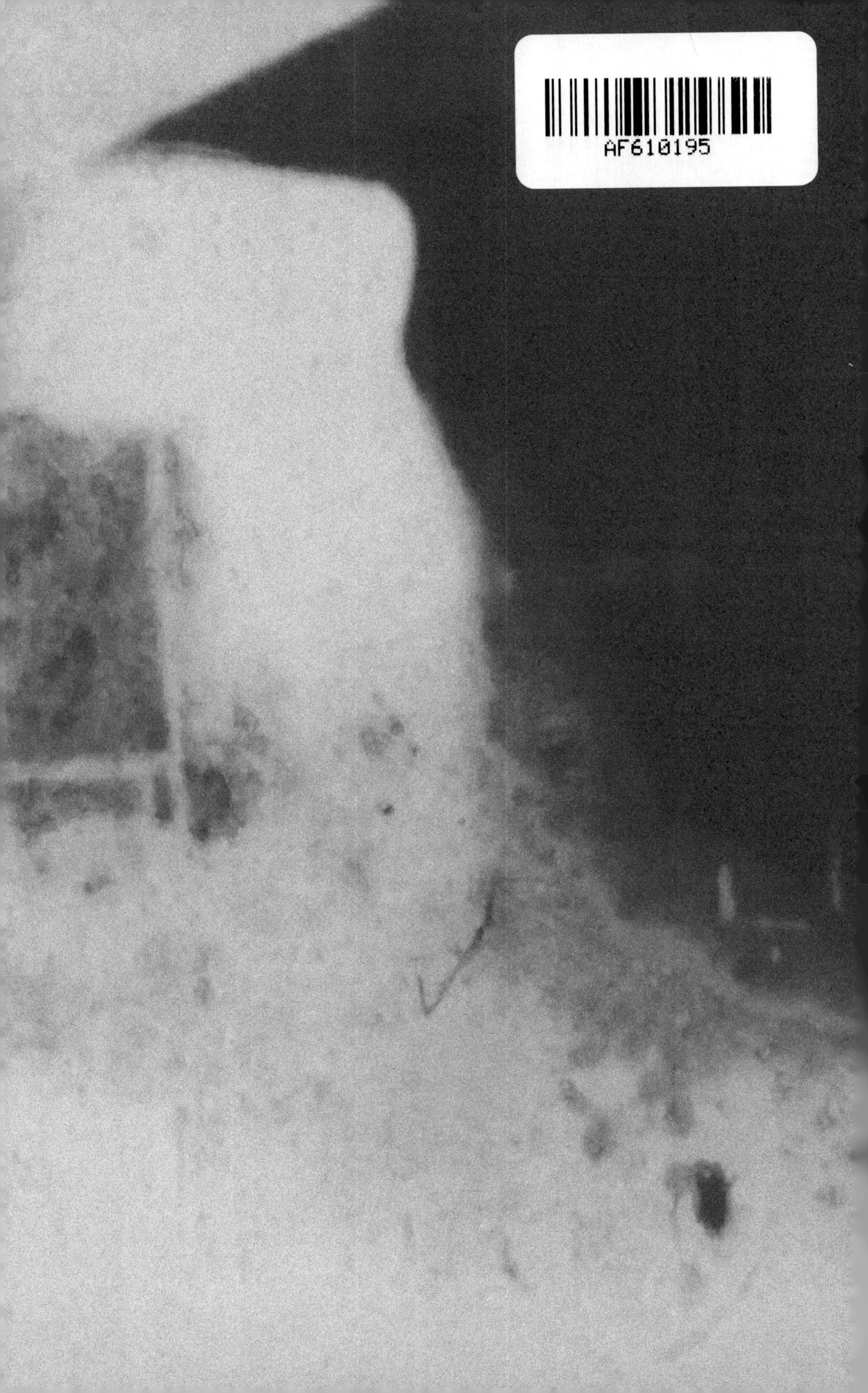
AF610195

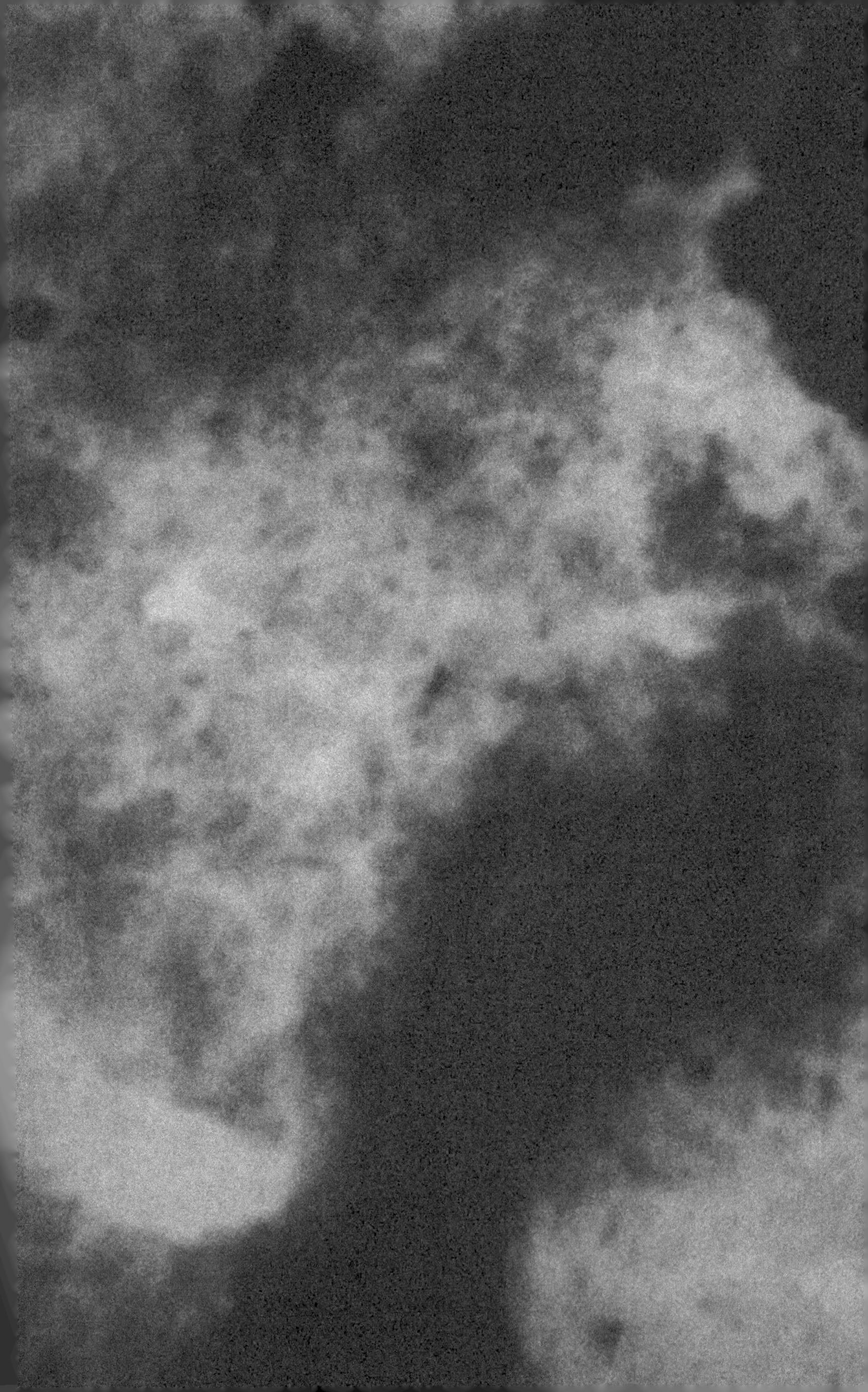

IMPRINTS

The Films of Louise Bourque

Imprints

The Films of Louise Bourque

Edited by
Stephen Broomer and Clint Enns

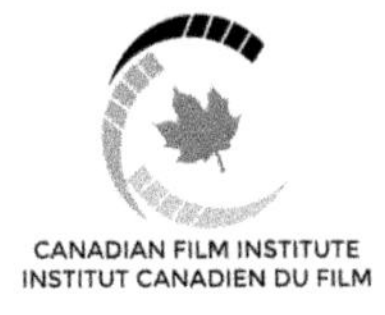

CANADIAN FILM INSTITUTE
INSTITUT CANADIEN DU FILM

Ottawa, Canada

Canadian Film Institute, 2021
Ottawa, Canada
www.cfi-icf.ca

ISBN 978-0-919096-55-4

Cover: still from Louise Bourque's *Imprint* (1997), courtesy of the artist.
Typesetting and design by Stephen Broomer.
Copyediting by Cameron Moneo.

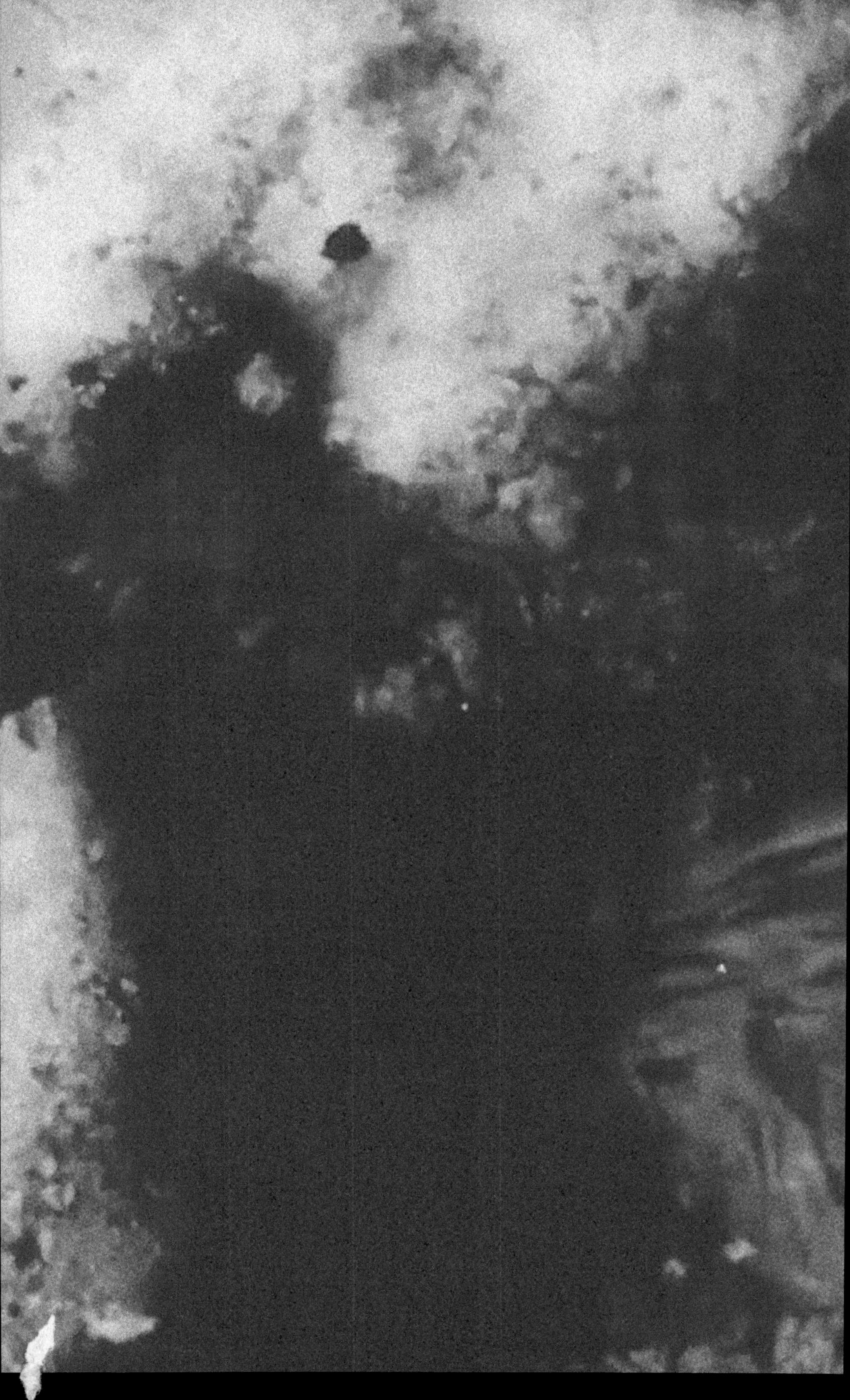

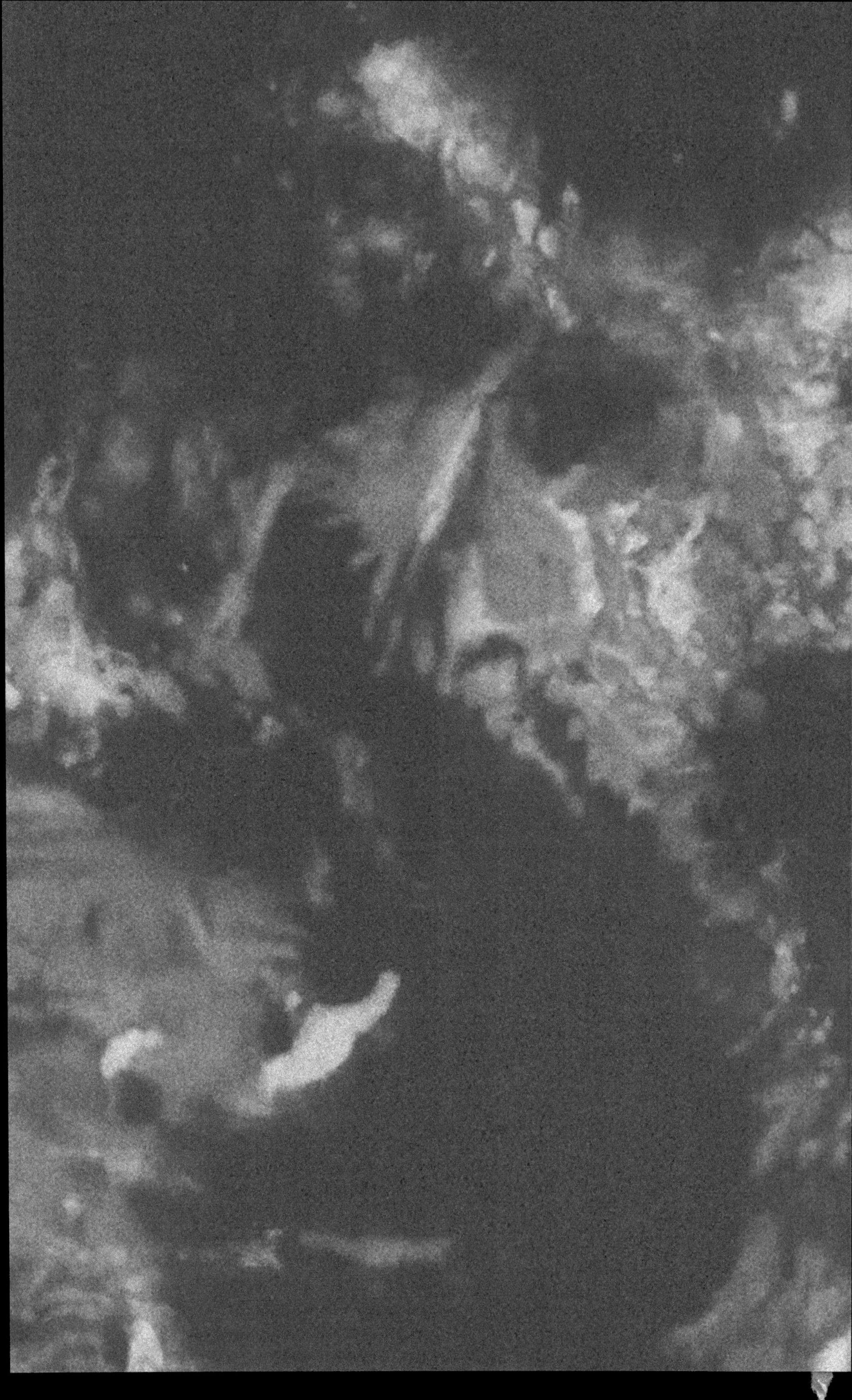

CONTENTS

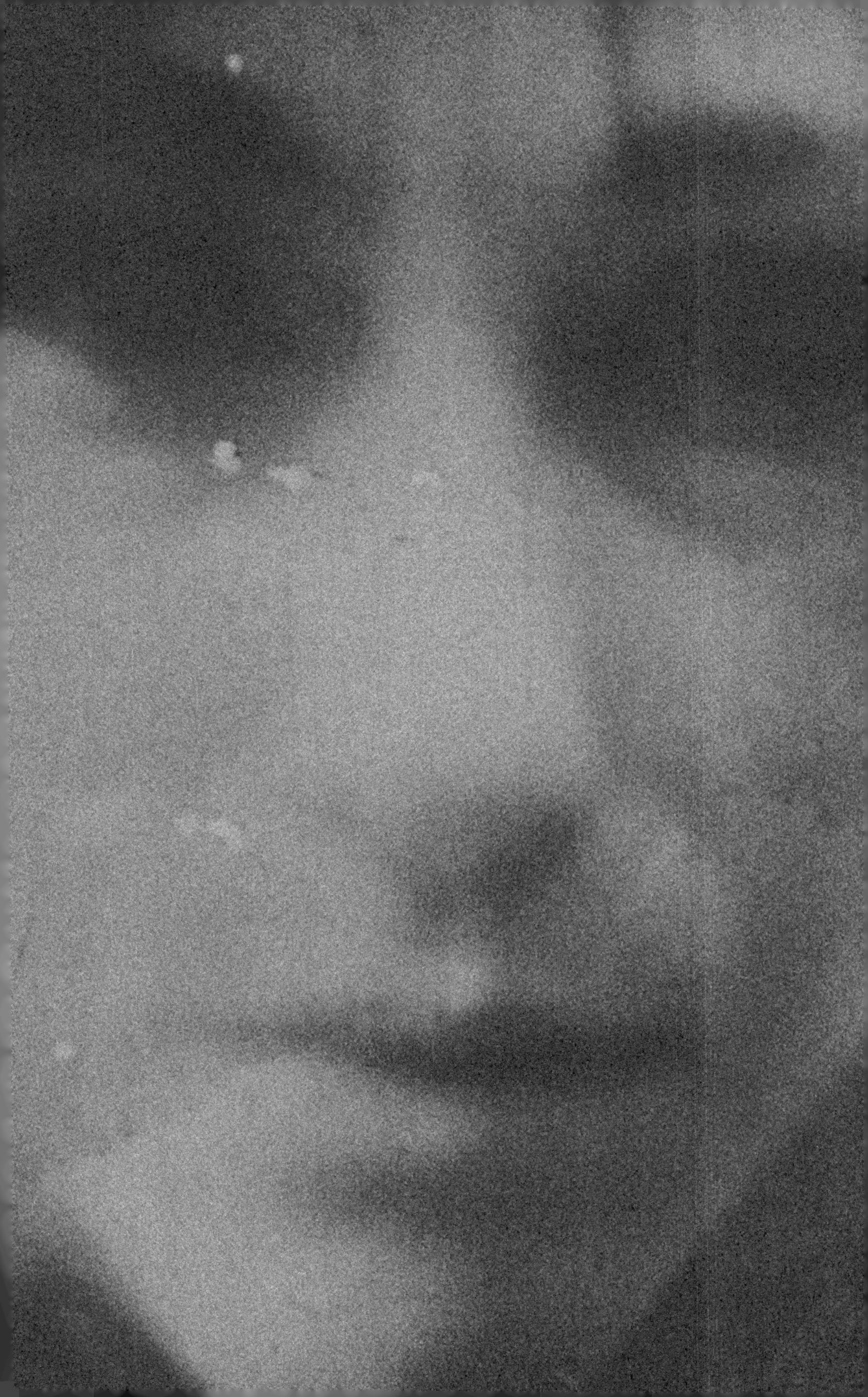

List of Ephemera

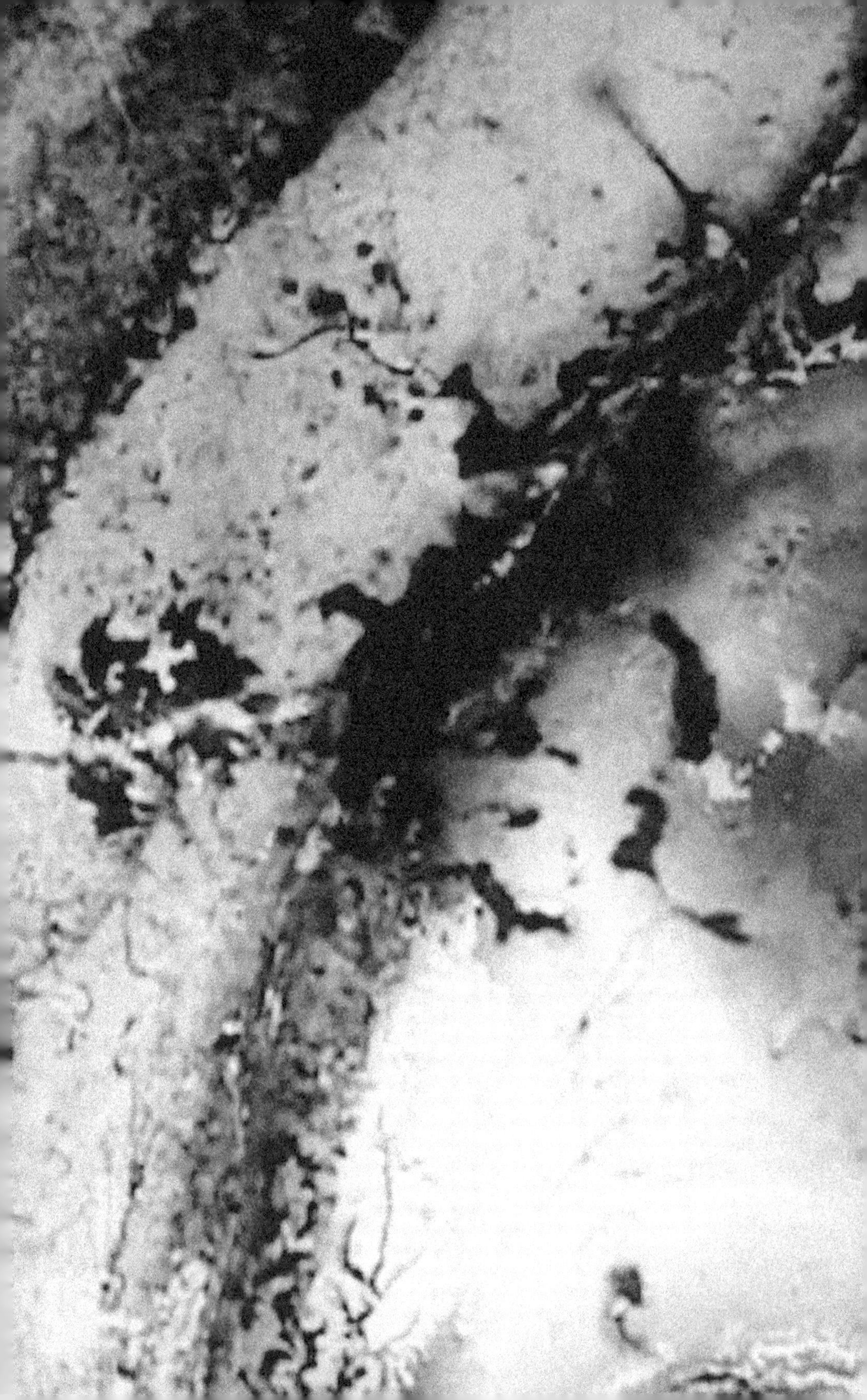

Introduction

Stephen Broomer and Clint Enns

Since 1989, Louise Bourque has made over a dozen films, crafting a body of work that has left a significant mark on Canadian experimental cinema. In addition to making films, Bourque has taught film studies and film production at Emerson College, Concordia University, and the School of the Museum of Fine Arts in Boston. She has mentored and influenced many artists, and her aesthetics are imprinted on the work of contemporary filmmakers dealing with memorial processes and abstract imagery. Her works often involve the physical manipulation of emulsion, with the content of the work stemming from a different type of imprint, namely, that of memory and trauma. *Imprints* collects essays, interviews, ephemera, and personal reflections that chart Bourque's life and work.

This book is informally divided into five sections. The first section of writing consists of overviews of Bourque's work. Stephen Broomer's essay was produced for this collection, Michael Sicinski's is an extension of an article produced to accompany a retrospective screening of Bourque's work at the 2009 Images Festival, and Nathan Lee's article was produced for the 2006 Whitney Biennial where Bourque screened *Jours en fleurs* (2003), *L'éclat du mal / The Bleeding Heart of It* (2005), and *The Producer* (2005), a collaboration with Joe Gibbons and Tony Conrad.

The second section consists mainly of essays addressing individual works. André Habib's essay is an extension of his previous scholarship concerning Bourque's work and explores her self-portrait films. Sébastien Ronceray takes a pedagogical approach to *Self Portrait Post Mortem*, demonstrating one way of teaching through the film. César Ustarroz explores Bourque's appropriation techniques in *Remains* (2011) and José Sarmiento-Hinojosa uses the concept of the palimpsest and the pentimento to further get under the skin of the film. Larissa Fan's article, a survey of Bourque's work written for *Take One* in

2005, explores the concept of home. Scott Birdwise takes this idea further by utilizing the Gothic concept of "otherness" in relation to the home and its use in *L'éclat du mal / The Bleeding Heart of It* and other experimental film practices. In a gem of an essay, originally published in French in 1992 and updated for this collection, Patricia MacGeachy relates her experience of playing the Mouth in Bourque's *Just Words* (1991). While MacGeachy provides an embodied experience, Dorottya Szalay provides a detailed reading of *Just Words*, working through Bourque's filmic interpretation of Samuel Beckett's play *Not I* (1972). Finally, Brian Wilson provides new insights into *Jolicouer Touriste* (1989). Sprinkled into this section are a poster and storyboards for *Jolicoeur Touriste* by Jean-Pierre Morin, a prop sheet from *The People in the House* (1994), prepared by the film's art director, Deborah Stratman, and Bourque's script for *Just Words*.

The next section of the book contains personal ephemera. The ephemera consists mainly of correspondence with other artists in the form of letters and artworks. They are extremely personal to Bourque and remain a source of inspiration for her work. Contributors include: Martha Colburn, Bruce Baillie, Ken Jacobs, Craig Baldwin, Luther Price, Brittany Gravely, Robert Breer, Mark Bain, Tony Oursler, and Joe Gibbons. The fourth section of the book consists of a different type of correspondence—interviews with Bourque. The first, conducted by Micah J. Malone, was produced for the Boston-based online magazine *Big Red & Shiny* after the 2006 Whitney Biennial; the second is conducted by Todd Fraser and Clint Enns and was produced for this collection.

The final section contains personal responses to Bourque's work. Mike Hoolboom provides a poetic reading of *a little prayer (H-E-L-P)* (2011), and Guillaume Vallée discusses his experiences working with Louise on her latest film, *Bye Bye Now* (2021). In "Dialogues imaginés : Spectroscopie générationnelle / Imagined Dialogues: Generational Spectroscopy," Bourque and Acadian artist Herménégilde Chiasson discuss their experience working with each other on a 4 × 4 assemblage of digital images. Amanda Dawn Christie provides a reading of *Going Back Home* (2000) that cleverly blends personal anecdote, film criticism, and disability studies, while Clint Enns attempts to establish a few facts about Louise Bourque.

Acknowledgments

The editors would like to thank the following people for their help in putting together this collection: the beyond-patient Kathryn Michalski, who translated articles and whose kind-hearted spirit brought warmth to this project through insightful conversations, acute observations, and the occasional car ride to Edmundston; our copyeditor, Cameron Moneo, for his keen eye and attention to detail; Guillaume Vallée, who helped compile some of the archival material; André Habib, who has been extremely supportive of Bourque and her work; the Bourque family, in particular Jean-Claude and Simone Bourque who braved the extreme summer heat to dig through boxes of Louise's archival material and even supplied muffins; Guillaume Lafleur and the Cinémathèque québécoise, who are favourably disposed towards Louise's work and who are currently housing archival elements of her films; the Double Negative Collective/le collectif double négatif for providing us with space and equipment for viewing *People Shoot - "Home Movies"* (1991); Jesse Brossoit and Genne Speers of the Canadian Filmmakers Distribution Centre, who distribute Bourque's films and who provided us with access to her work; Joe Gibbons for his insightful feedback and for supplying us with copies of his collaborations with Bourque and Conrad; and Tom McSorley and the staff of the Canadian Film Institute for their support of this book.

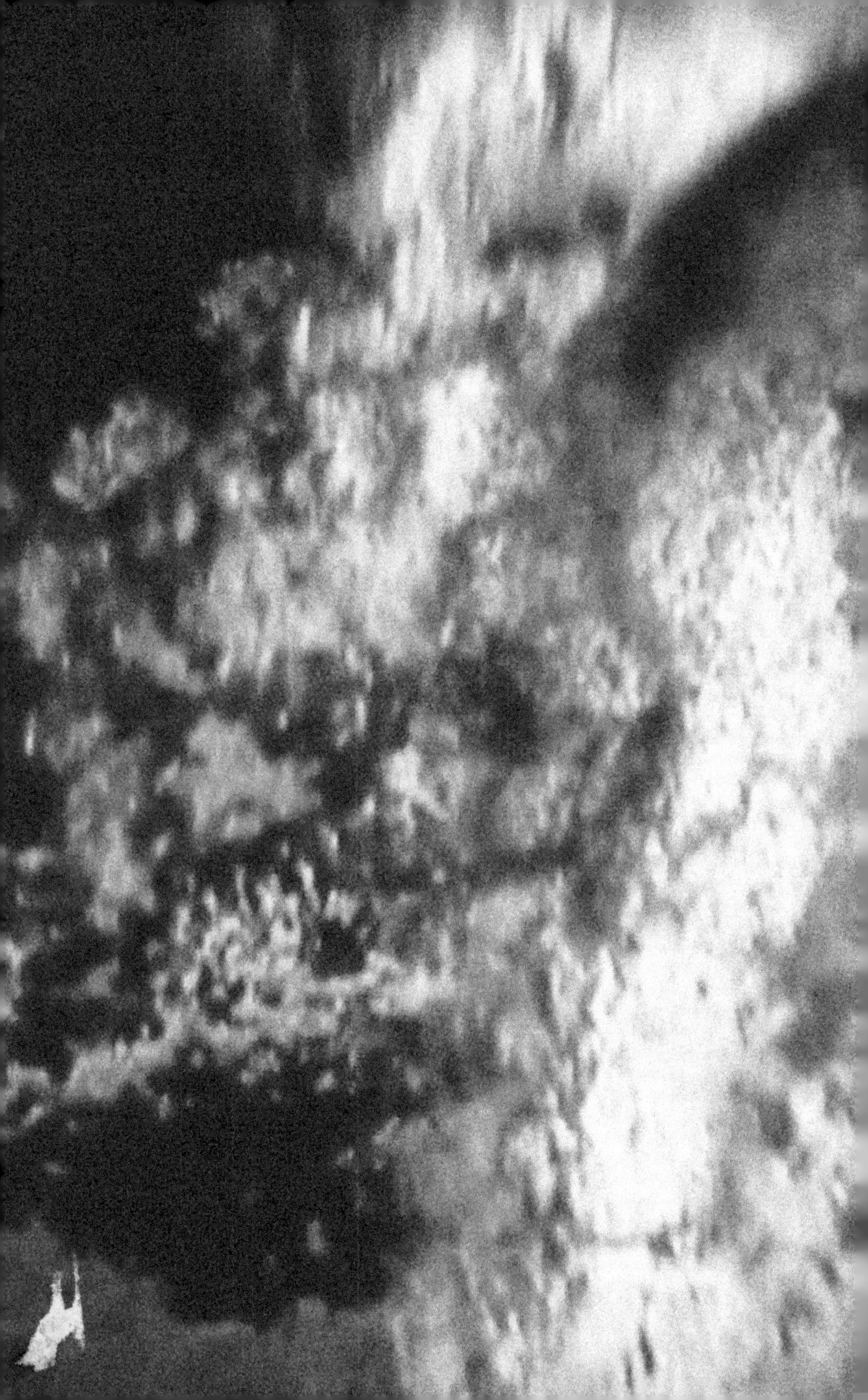

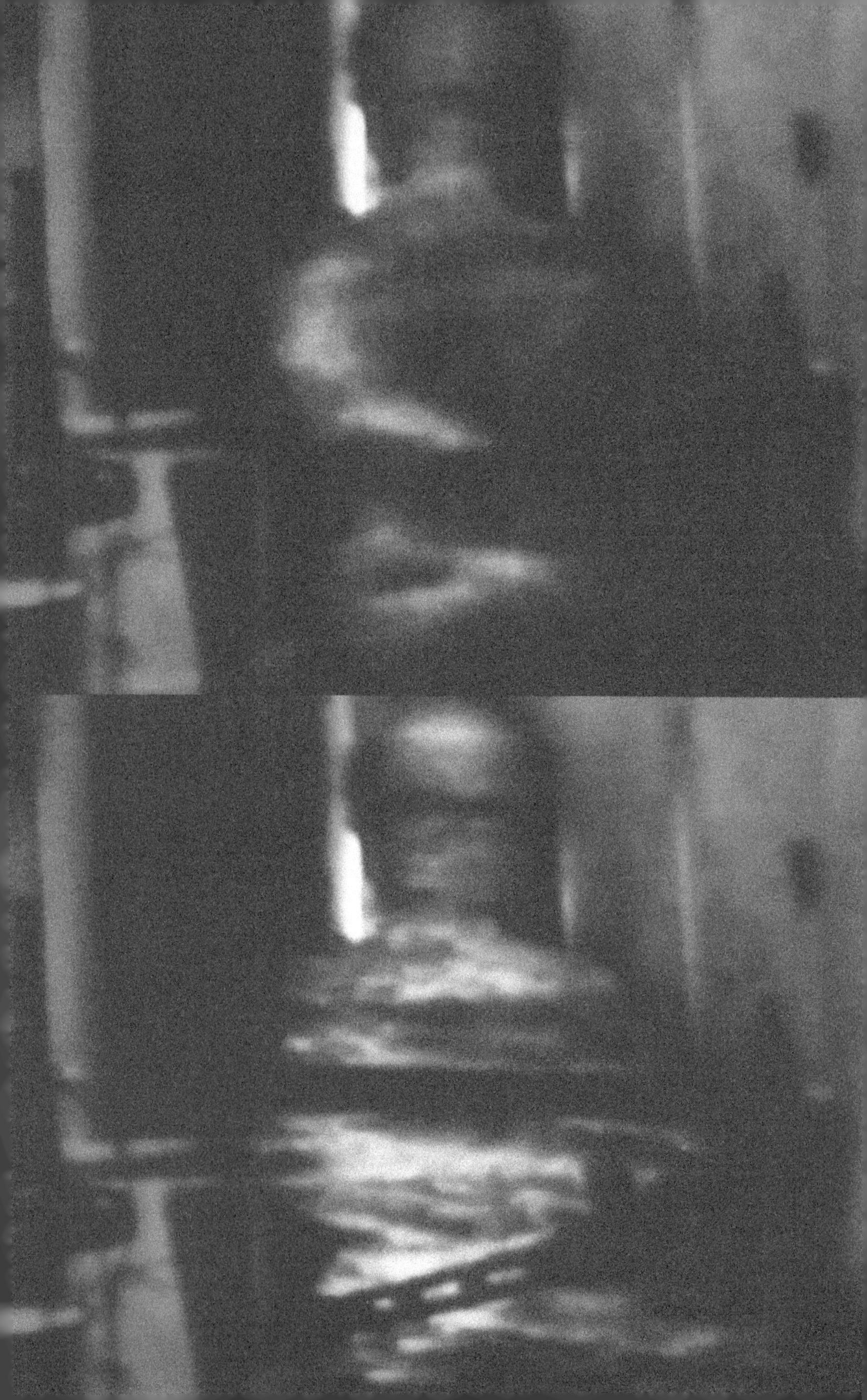

Imprints

Stephen Broomer

Born in Edmundston, New Brunswick, Acadian filmmaker Louise Bourque began to make films in the late 1980s while a student at Concordia University in Montreal. The bulk of her films were made while living in Boston, Massachusetts, where she also taught at the School of the Museum of Fine Arts and Emerson College. From the mid-1990s onward, Bourque's films have dealt with plastic manipulation of the film plane, in the form of scratches, chemical alteration, contact printing, and tricks of time created by re-photography. In 2010, she returned to Canada, where she now lives in Montreal, Quebec.

Bourque's first film, *Jolicoeur Touriste* (1989) combines themes of interstellar travel, televisual signals, and a monologue about journeys taken in childhood. The monologue is repeated and with each repetition becomes stiffer and more self-consciously performed. In a hostel, a man (Johnny Chouinard) repeatedly grabs a beer from a nearby fridge, slumps in his chair, turns the radio dials, watches late-night dial-flipping television broadcasts, all in tones of unnaturally saturated colour (the blue of the television, a green lamp near the fridge and radio, a red lamp hanging over the figure's armchair). Like the monologue, the sequence is repetitious, as if the man is suspended in the interminable attention of space travel. At the end, after recounting a visit to the planetarium, the figure is seated, his form optically removed and filled with scenery of movement from the television broadcast and super 8 footage of landscapes in Ireland. The theme suggested by this final image, of the self riddled with the dust of the past, is one that would persist throughout Bourque's work. Her next film, *Just Words* (1991), uses a monologue by Samuel Beckett (*Not I*, 1972, historically performed, as it is here, by an illuminated mouth) as a backdrop to home movies of her mother, sandwiching the menacing undercurrent of home movies to the mouth's declarations and denials. In this film, Bourque continues the theme of the past occupying the present, if we are to take the mouth as the present—as a surrogate for the filmmaker—and the home movie, inevitably, as a past that interrupts and illustrates or provides counterpoint.

The People in the House (1994) is the sole continuation of the style of *Jolicoeur Touriste*, in its use of primary-coloured light to develop a stylized, alien atmosphere. Otherwise the film is a psychodrama in the tradition of Maya Deren: a house is occupied by a number of figures who perform rituals—dancing, sleeping, gathering to tearfully read a letter, potting a gift of flowers—the routines that are performed by these figures, for the most part in slow motion, turn menacing with a sad-eyed patriarch carrying the seemingly lifeless body of a woman in formal dress and long gloves up a turning stairwell. Montage renders all of these events discontinuous, overlapping, and Bourque's optical effects include a slowed shutter that makes the space of the house all the more alien, staggering time, casting trails through corners and scenery in such a way as to create even more stylized colours and textures. These effects render the figures as spectral. The "people in the house" are ghosts of an inexplicit past.

Bourque's work had, from its start, engaged with elaborate optical effects, but she had also balanced these effects with dramatic content in the forms of monologues and the presence of actors. With *Imprint* (1997), these traits are shed in favour of a plastic experience. The film draws from footage of the edifice of a home seen, primarily, in photographic negative, first in a pale blue colour cast, which changes as Bourque's method of experimentation changes. Early in the film, Bourque's plastic manipulation involves cutting out a circle in the middle of the frame, leaving in the punched-out image so that it vibrates in place, replaced with different footage; later sections of the film use a photographic negative unconstrained by tints, the house surrounded by bleeding black forms. Finally, the windows are etched out, and with the image now in photographic positive, the faces of children running around the lawn become more visible. As the soundtrack shifts from gritty, restless noise to the sounds of Enrico Caruso singing "A Dream," a distant pastoral anthem of bygone days, the emulsion is rent from the frame, refiguring in quick bursts the shape of the house and making visible an underlying blue and pink of the filmstrip. These colours become more violent, more autumnal, as the section repeats, until the image is finally fully abstract, pulsating forms of cyan and magenta.

The themes and stylistic traits of this work—this newly plastic, abstract direction—would continue in *Fissures* (1999), in which home movies are cropped, their frame lines shifting, their sprockets providing a continuous rhythm coursing through the frame, the image smearing, bleeding light and solarized, passing in a single composition from positive to negative and fading into darkness. *Going Back Home* (2000) likewise uses images of home, here in traces of catastrophe: in a sequence of eight shots we see a derailed train car, a sunken house, a dog on a roof, a raging inferno in a window, the controlled collapse of buildings, all in a golden hue. With the comic aplomb of a mellifluous, jangling toy piano on its soundtrack, *Going Back Home* offers a series of homes to which no one can return. The film repeats for a second look. Bourque would revisit the footage used in *Imprint* in *L'éclat du mal / The Bleeding Heart of It* (2005), this time with a soundtrack in which the filmmaker narrates the content of a terrifying dream of wartime that seems to be illustrated by the decay, the plastic décollage of the home. In her accompanying annotation, Bourque describes the role of such scenes in her trauma explicitly: "the house that bursts; the scene of the crime; the nucleus." Between this description and the terrors described by Bourque on the soundtrack, the images of the family become deeply unsettling, even threatening. Bourque would revisit this same footage again in *Bye Bye Now* (2021).

Self Portrait Post Mortem (2002) is the first of two self-portraits, this one made from an image of Bourque as a young woman. She occupies the centre of the frame, in a sequence slowly advancing frame by frame. Her eyes are shut at first, then she stares into the camera. Each frame is eaten away at its edges by mold, each abstraction advancing manually through the shadow of the preceding

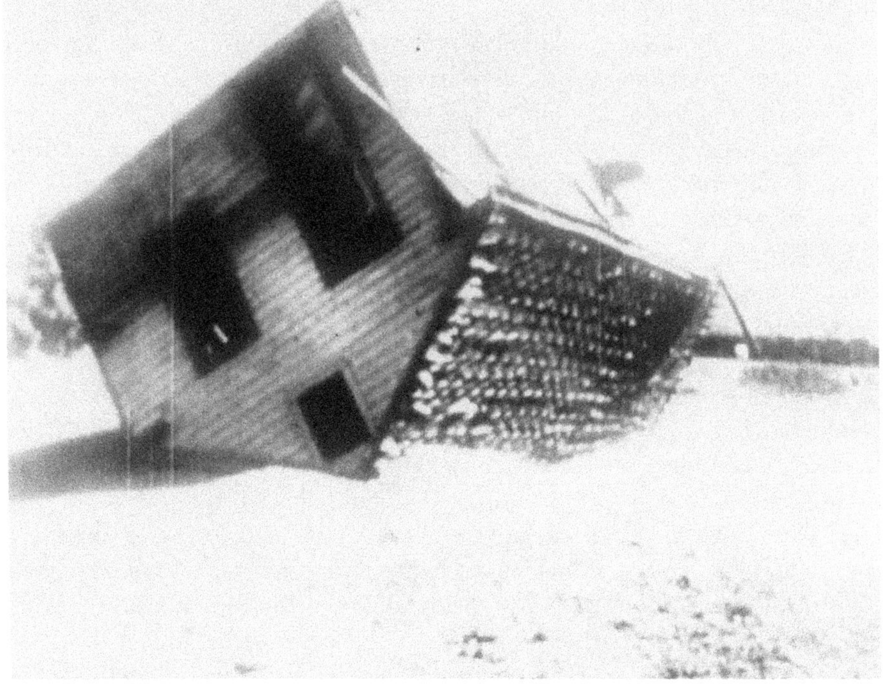

one. Bourque would repeat this gesture, the manual advancing of decayed frames, in *Jours en fleurs* (2003) and *Remains* (2011), films that largely eschew representational imagery in favour of non-objectivism and the experience of colour. In the case of *Jours en fleurs*, made using images incubated in menstrual blood for nine months, there are rich blues and browns, the patina of time achieved by way of her blood; in the case of *Remains*, yellow and white pair with a brief glimpse of the maternal figure from *The People in the House*. The second of Bourque's self-portraits, *Auto Portrait / Self Portrait Post Partum* (2013) hosts a three-part structure: following a prologue, of speech taken from a love letter, the first part begins: it is a long-take self-portrait, in a blue cast, trained on Bourque's tearful face, with closeups on her eyes and lips, accompanied by songs ranging from Neil Young to the Supremes. The second part, in a red cast, involves the distortion of found scenes from movies and scratched texts and attributions; the scenes she has selected suggest violence inflicted by a man on a woman. The final sequence involves a further act of self-portraiture, of Bourque underwater, floating ethereally towards liberation from mourning and from yearning. Throughout, text communicates a devastating separation, in this case, from her former longterm partner, confessional filmmaker Joe Gibbons (who is credited as co-editor). *Auto Portrait / Self Portrait Post Partum* is an ultimate work for Bourque that lays bare one of her primary themes: catharsis, and the achievement of catharsis through objects (be they home movies, records, love letters).

In 2011, Bourque made *a little prayer (H-E-L-P)*, distinct from her prior work in the speed and aggression of its editing. It uses the rolling of a shutter, its opening and closing, to glimpse fragments of found and abstract (scratched) black and white footage of magician Harry Houdini trying to free himself from chains. The stroboscopic effect shuttles us from representation to non-objective imagery, mixing the shot of Houdini, scenes from Niagara Falls, lines of men in uniform, with images resembling the black and white slashes of Franz Kline paintings. The quick roll of the shutter leaves us in a state of unstable vision that cannot glimpse the whole of any single composition, such that the edges of each image are glimpsed only at the moment when the shutter rolls back, to close and open again on a new image. This is an opposite strategy to the one employed by Bourque in *Self Portrait Post Mortem*, *Jours en fleurs*, and *Remains*, where the slow advance of a shutter allowed each image to be seen in full and to overlap with what preceded and followed. Bourque's work has always played with what was not visible, from her earliest use of the home movie and its surfaces, to her photochemical abstraction of the image; here that tactic achieves its apotheosis, demanding an engagement that tunes the eye, and through it the whole organism, to the flicker of the image.

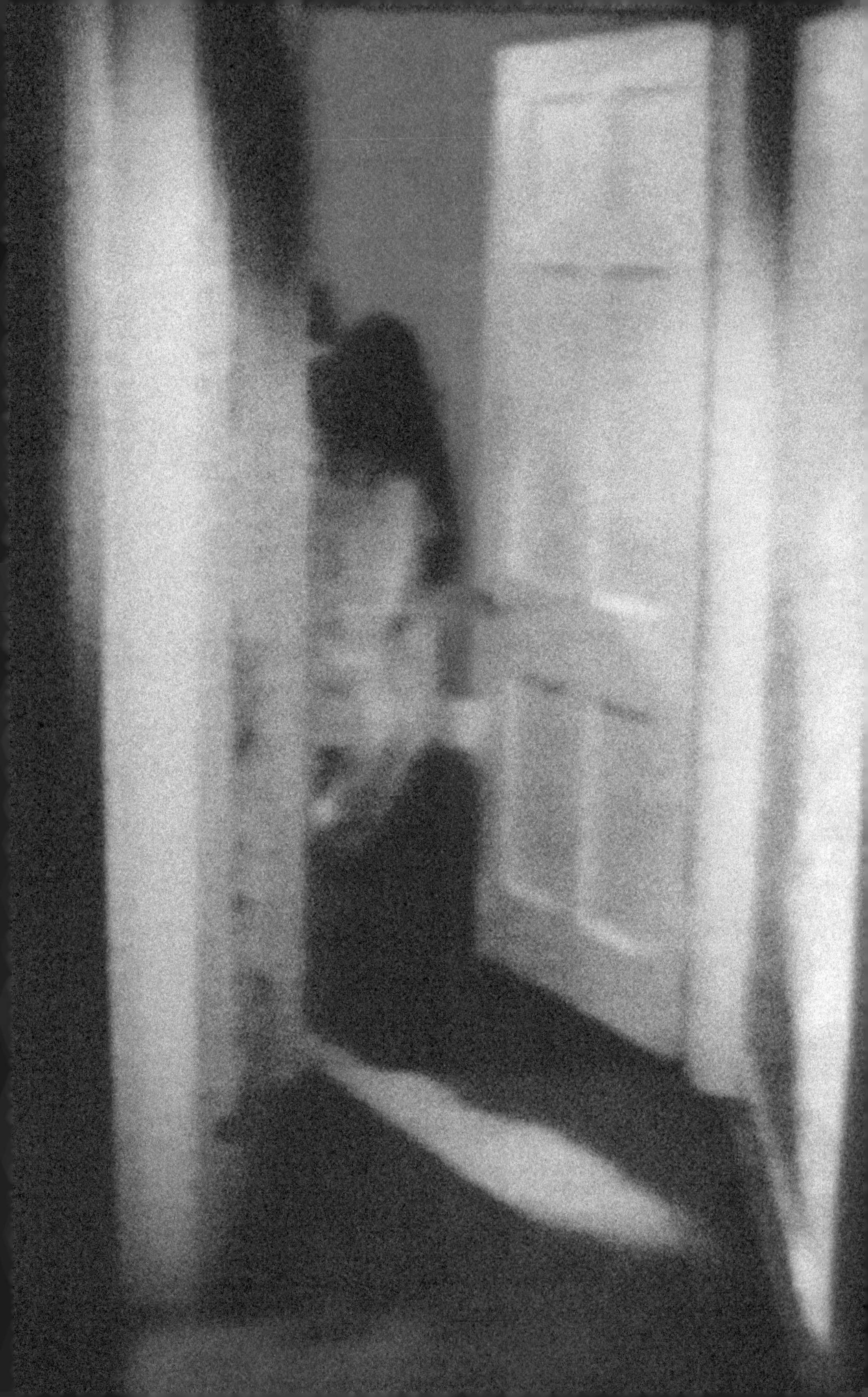

Impossible Trips Back Home

The Films of Louise Bourque

Michael Sicinski

Revised from a text originally published in *Images Festival Catalogue* (Toronto: Images Festival, 2009), 41–43.

Apart from the varied textures of physical decay and worry on the filmstrip, or the fractured swaths of pain, or the saturated hues that result from tinting or partially cameraless exposure, the single most characteristic aspect of Louise Bourque's cinema, the iconic image to which she returns again and again, is the house. Bourque's houses are complicated precisely because she places them at a juncture, or within a blended, liminal space, with respect to the iconography of the domestic. These houses hover at a dense twilight of representation. Bourque's films usually involve some form of found footage that is then subjected to compositional processes and tactile manipulations, so we never get "the house" as a straightforward image. But we know from statements about her work, and sometimes from her brief end credits, that several of her key films work with home movies from her childhood, excavating poetic resonances and unseen emotional valences from her personal history.

Familiarity with this history and its particulars is in no way necessary for accessing Bourque's work. These are not esoteric films, and it seems to me that knowing specific details about the meanings evoked for Bourque by her childhood home would only serve to impoverish these rich works. But more than this, that house, that façade, always keeps us on the outside, and on that representational cusp. After the early, rather Lynchian dramatic work *The People in the House* (1994)—which spends a leisurely twenty-two minutes exploring the home as an architectural and psychological interior—Bourque shuts us out for much of the rest of her career. The "house" is now closed.

This is a zone where we must not only access our own visceral attachments as the iconicity of the works call them forward; we must also attend to Bourque's activation of a social dialectic that speaks beyond the ken of individual longing. After all, the inside of that house is the domestic sphere, where historically defined gender codes are learned and transmitted (or hopefully subverted), where power relations are naturalized (or decentred), where desire is implanted in the individual psyche through the Freudian family romance (or short-circuited in some unforeseen way). But aside from a few brief glimpses in 1999's *Fissures*, the later works never allow us inside Bourque's house. These are not films about "home."

Instead, the majority of Bourque's works—*L'éclat de mal / The Bleeding Heart of It* (2005), *Going Back Home* (2000), *Fissures*, and most significantly *Imprint* (1997)—maintain the exterior space of the private residence as a boundary, both spatial and ideational, between the public and the private. The various ways in which our personal histories inevitably inform our reactions to Bourque's works, charged as those works are with the affective memories of a collective childhood, earlier recording modes, a lost suburban promise, and other generational signposts, are also framed by the social and historical legacies the films depict.

Some are fairly broad, such as the inscription of gender. Throughout Bourque's work, including her admirably incriminating *Self Portrait Post Mortem* (2002), we witness girls and women learning how to behave in front of a camera lens, particularly one wielded by Daddy. Bourque's thicket of re-photographed effects pulled from the jostled, off-track filmstrip in *Fissures*, for example, offers a perfect formal correlative to the subtle game of seduction and peek-a-boo that the home movie's subjects play with the camera-eye. *Fissures* is a brief but riveting articulation and disarticulation of profilmic space (the domestic sphere of the amateur films) with film as space, its twisting movement across the Z-axis, framelines, sprocket holes and all. In some respects *Fissures* resembles the work of Austrian neo-structuralist Peter Tscherkassky, but Bourque goes spelunking for signs and wonders right in her own backyard.

The windowed façade of the Bourque family home recurs as a barrier between a social understanding of ideas like "the family," "domesticity," or "the heartland," and the radical specificity with which each viewer confronts the films themselves. As such, it's possible to read certain of Bourque's own specificities back into the films. The large house is both anonymous and somewhat imposing, implying the large family it contained and the rather traditional, family-first ideologies it may well have fostered in its suburban atomization. Bourque's films, especially in terms of their thick, gritty manipulations of colour, surface, and superimposition, operate on a dramatic, at times even rhapsodic plane, which could speak to her own background as well.

A film such as *L'éclat du mal* takes the front of the house and, through painterly alteration, vivifies it, turns it into a damaged body. Bourque's primary procedure in this film is to overlay colour fields via optical printing, and although her palette is quite varied, a mottled coagulation of blood reds and bruised blues are the dominant tones. The skin of the film (to borrow Laura U. Marks' critical category) is a fragile envelope, practically an open wound. Bourque's sound mix, in which the filmmaker recounts a complex, troubling dream, conflating Christmastime and a battleground, adds to the density of *L'éclat du mal*'s corporeal memory mix.

Bourque's treatment of the house, the home space, as a site of drama, trauma, and a fragmentary struggle waged both on the personal (female) body and the social body, all place her work in a unique position with respect to experimental film history in Canada. While it would be far too easy to make broad claims regarding Bourque's New Brunswick Acadian background, the artist herself has expressed that the religious element in her upbringing has had a significant impact on her imagery. At any rate, Bourque's full-bodied visions are quite removed from the dominant threads of English-Canadian avant-garde production—the jaunty visual jazz of Norman McLaren, the paranoid style of Arthur Lipsett, the cerebral conceptualism of Michael Snow, the wry elegance of David Rimmer, or the hesitant cosmologies of Jack Chambers.

In early efforts, such as Bourque's Samuel Beckett adaptation *Just Words* (1991), one can see the fairly direct influence of Joyce Wieland's work, particularly her lips-only political treatise *Pierre Vallières* (1972), but at the same time, even Wieland's offbeat humour and language play is somewhat foreign to Bourque. Like certain other French-Canadian experimentalists (such otherwise disparate artists as Vincent Grenier, Donigan Cumming, and Sylvie Laliberté come to mind), Bourque fuses formalist investigations with explicitly dramatic gestures, a full-throated Expressionism that, placed against the better-behaved Conceptual lineage in Canadian art, can seem downright jarring.

If any taxonomy might prove useful for understanding what Bourque's films do (and of course, this is an open question—tags and labels are a critic's bread and butter but frequently a fool's game and of dubious value either to those who watch or those who produce cinema), it may pertain to Bourque's intersectional identity. At present a true cinematic "co-production," Bourque has been living and teaching in Boston for years, and so her work, while

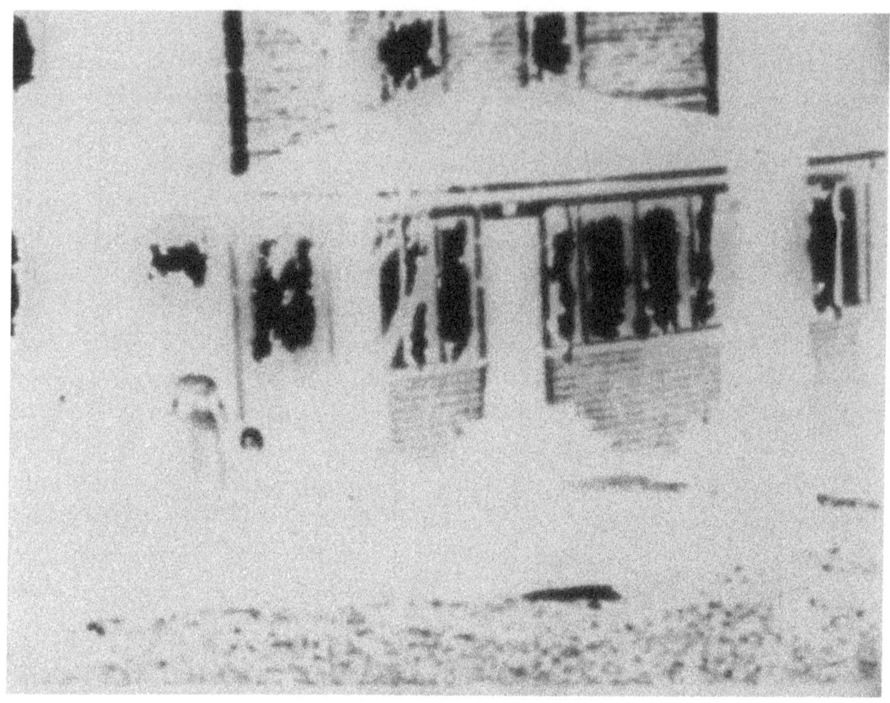

retaining its concrete connection to the image of home and the circumstances of her Acadian heritage, has been affected by hybridity and distance.

On the one hand, the spatial as well as temporal distance may well have provided the necessary remove that allowed Bourque to treat her own geographical history as raw material. But even more than this, her work seems less tied to a trend or scene, and more indicative of one of the most interesting and most productive tendencies in recent experimental film and video practice. This "tendency" (for lack of a better word) has to do with a general renunciation of austerity for its own sake, often in favor of explicitly theatrical effects. This is a cinematic mode that has internalized the lessons of Brakhage and the Structuralists but taken them in fundamentally new, unexpected directions. Bourque's work seems to share in this "certain tendency" in many ways, connecting her films to those of Phil Solomon, Lewis Klahr, Jennifer Todd Reeves, Jeanne Liotta, David Gatten, and others who have taken formal procedures into emotive, evocative, and occasionally even operatic realms.

Bourque's films are exacting in their construction, but unrelenting in their willingness to argue their case on the basis of mystery and presence, anxious to vibrate before you like tuning forks for the unconscious. No film exemplifies this better than *Imprint*, in some ways Bourque's simplest film but also, in my opinion, her finest. The façade is there again. It hovers and trembles, we see a little girl on the right-hand side of the screen running up to the porch, and a klatch of girls huddled in a family pose just in front of the house, not quite dwarfed by it but clearly in its shadow. Bourque loops this passage, whites it out, prints it in negative, sandwiches positive and negative, subjects it to scratches and dust, and scrapes the emulsion out of the house's windows, rendering this space metaphorically "blind," Oedipalized.

The shot, handheld by the taker of this home movie (presumably the paterfamilias), pans up, left, and around, into the trees and sky, as if trying to avert his gaze from this space. But the camera circles back, down and to the right, into position once more, again and again. The sequence ends with a medium closeup of two indistinct children, one clearly a girl and the other most likely a girl judging from her hat. Then, cut. Bourque hole-punches this and other scenes and affixes them to other passes of the loop, resulting in a kind of microscopic iris within the scene. (Freud's remark about children as "little detectives" regarding the private world of adulthood comes to mind.) On the soundtrack: the ch-chow, ch-chow of a skipping record, although it is only apparent in retrospect that that's what it is. (On first viewing, this repetitive sound seemed like white noise from the projector's sound head, not unlike the materialist sounds one finds in many structural films.)

By the middle of *Imprint*, Bourque is optically printing the blurred imagery of the original strip moving free of the sprocket holes, bending and twisting in much the same manner as in *Fissures*. Framelines slip, the image goes in and out of the frame altogether. Movement within the image is redoubled or halted by the filmstrip's movement within the frame. Figures and space merge into an indistinct set of compositions in cobalt blue, pure white, and rounded black. Eventually, developer spots and thrashed yellow leader obliterate the image completely, only for it to return in numerous hand-tinted configurations. By this point, Bourque is clearly examining the multitude of ways that a single set of images can be manipulated, reconfigured, and re-presented, and how the close proximity of these iterations will affect the viewer's apprehension of the image's denotative contents—a set of manoeuvres well within the parameters of structural experiments, such as those conducted by Ken Jacobs or Owen Land.

But then, as the image is nearly broken apart by collaged fragmentation and bulbous white areas, and the "home" and "family" are on the verge of total disintegration, Bourque introduces a new, final element. We hear an old record of Enrico Caruso singing "A Dream." By this point in *Imprint*, Bourque's work on the surface of the image has become feverish and more agitated, evoking Brakhage's hand-painted films, Solomon's molten alchemy, as well as Gatten's environmental-distress filmstrips such as *What the Water*

Said. But *Imprint* is different from all of these.

Bourque's painting style is scratchier and more weatherbeaten than Brakhage's, giving *Imprint* the raw feel of an excavated artifact. Unlike Solomon's cine-metallurgy, Bourque's impastos and physical accumulations are perceived as existing on the surface of the filmstrip, and not somehow "inside" it. *Imprint* is clearly a work of additive and subtractive sculpture, not a wholesale chemical reconfiguration of the object. And, unlike Gatten's films, Bourque employs clear photographic images. What's more, she maintains control over the elements that affect *Imprint*, and most of her other films as well. (*Self Portrait Post Mortem*, which Bourque left buried for a period of time, is an exception.) Nevertheless, *Imprint* shares an urgency and a willingness to explicitly engage with the plangency of song, the density of recorded memory, and the unconscious glitch of repetition in the viewer's psyche, in order to attain a transportive experience, an "elsewhere" or an outside to the film's internal time.

And this, I think, sums up what is special and valuable about Bourque's films as a whole. Like the other filmmakers I've discussed above, Bourque has moved through numerous strands of experimental film and video history, grounded herself in practices and traditions that once may have seemed incompatible, and is now pointing the way towards something new. Watching *Imprint*, *Fissures*, or *L'éclat du mal*, we are allowed to exist in the here and now, with the concrete materiality of the filmstrip and the film image. That is, we can satisfy the formal injunctions to attend to film's own parameters best summed up by Ernie Gehr: "film is a real thing and as a real thing it is not imitation."

But at the same time, Bourque's works allow us to move away from the surface of their own making, to enter zones of emotive contemplation, metaphorical connection, and yes, even narrative desire. She no longer insists that films actively prevent spectatorship that moves you to another time and place, nor does she succumb to the simple gratifications of conventional, non-materialist story cinema. Instead, Bourque's films split your consciousness, toggling you back and forth between where you are and where you suspect you once might have been.

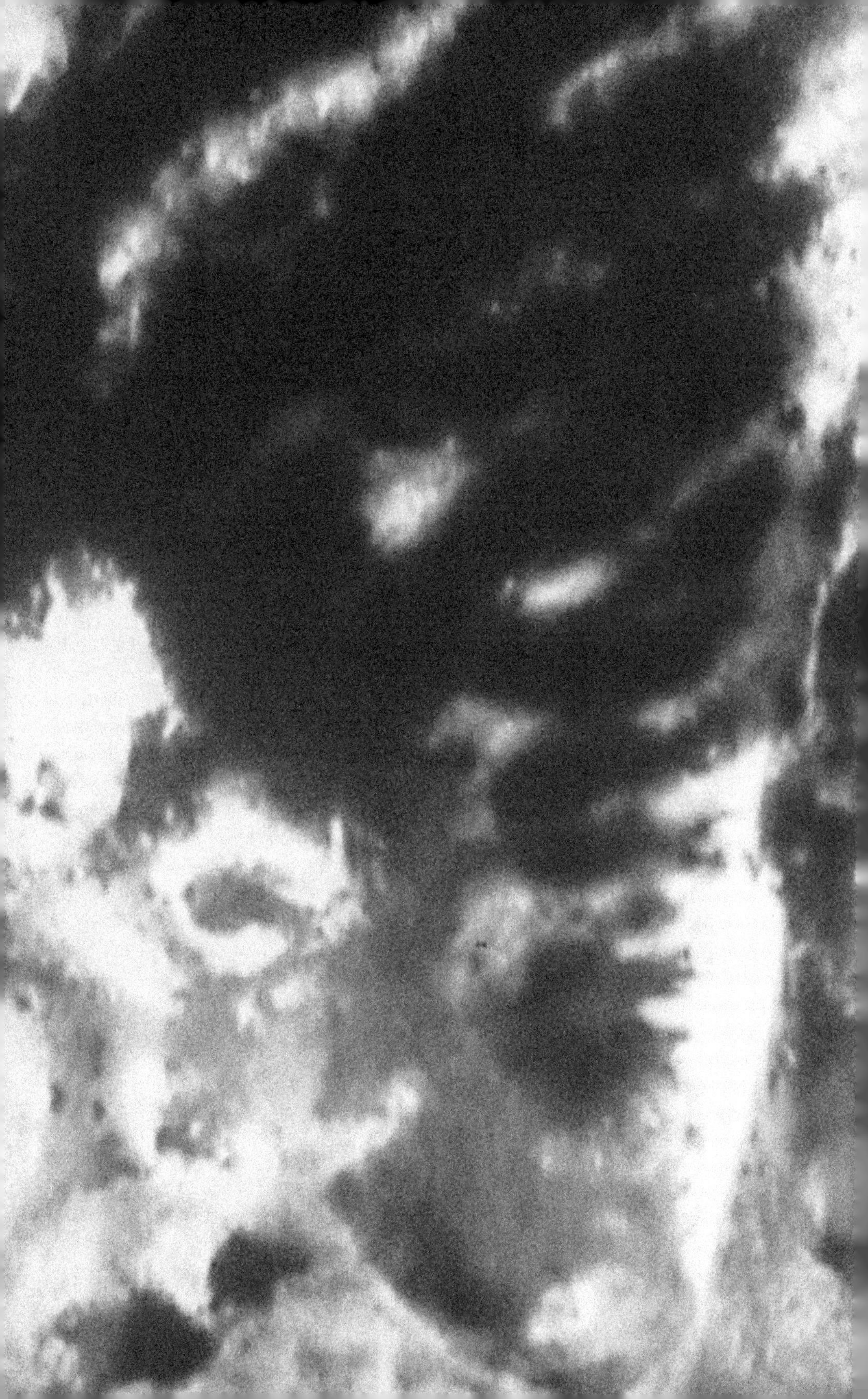

"It's dark in the tunnel but I'm heading towards the light ..."

Nathan Lee

Originally published (with poster) in Chrissie Iles and Philippe Vergne, eds. *Whitney Biennial 2006: Day for Night* (New York: Harry N. Adams, 2006), 182.

Process is both meaning and method for filmmaker Louise Bourque. Her films reckon with the instabilities of identity, family, and home. Traces of the past (home movies, found footage, childhood memories, dream imagery) are processed in every sense of the word. Though she has worked in a more traditional mode of production (involving actors, set lighting and design, mise en scène, and narrative structures), for the past ten years Bourque has focused on a process-oriented approach. Manipulation of materials is the essence of her technique, whereby filmstrips are scratched, bleached, buried, punctured, soaked, solarized, and specially printed, resulting in rich layers of abstraction and ambiguity.

"All the techniques I use," Bourque has explained, "are about finding ways to imbue the materiality of film with a metaphorical quality." *Self Portrait Post Mortem* (2002), constructed from an outtake from Bourque's first film, shows traces of decay effected by a three-year burial of the image in the Bourque family backyard. The floral and arboreal imagery in *Jours en fleurs* (2003) was chemically altered by several months' immersion in the artist's menstrual blood. *Imprint* (1997) and *Fissures* (1999) assault the surface of home movies with everything from hole punching to the use of lip balm as a stopping agent in a multicolour toning process akin to batik. Through such treatments Bourque seeks to "tease out new means and ... call attention to image-making as manipulation and construct. In doing so," she writes, "I hope to prompt a questioning of representation (inherent to the vernacular material I appropriate as well as in my own images) and claim a space for other expression wherein the poetical and political meet."

Home, war, and the dark truth of the unconscious fuse in Bourque's new film *L'éclat du mal / The Bleeding Heart of It* (2005). "In my dream there's a war going on," the artist gently intones over faint images of members of her family gathered outside their house. Shot by Bourque's father before she was born, this archival memento is submerged in thick, painterly blotches of colour and shadow that reflect the anxious lyricism of the voiceover: "There are all kinds of obstacles ... there's debris everywhere, and bombing ..."

"It's dark in the tunnel but I'm heading towards the light ..."

XX Louise

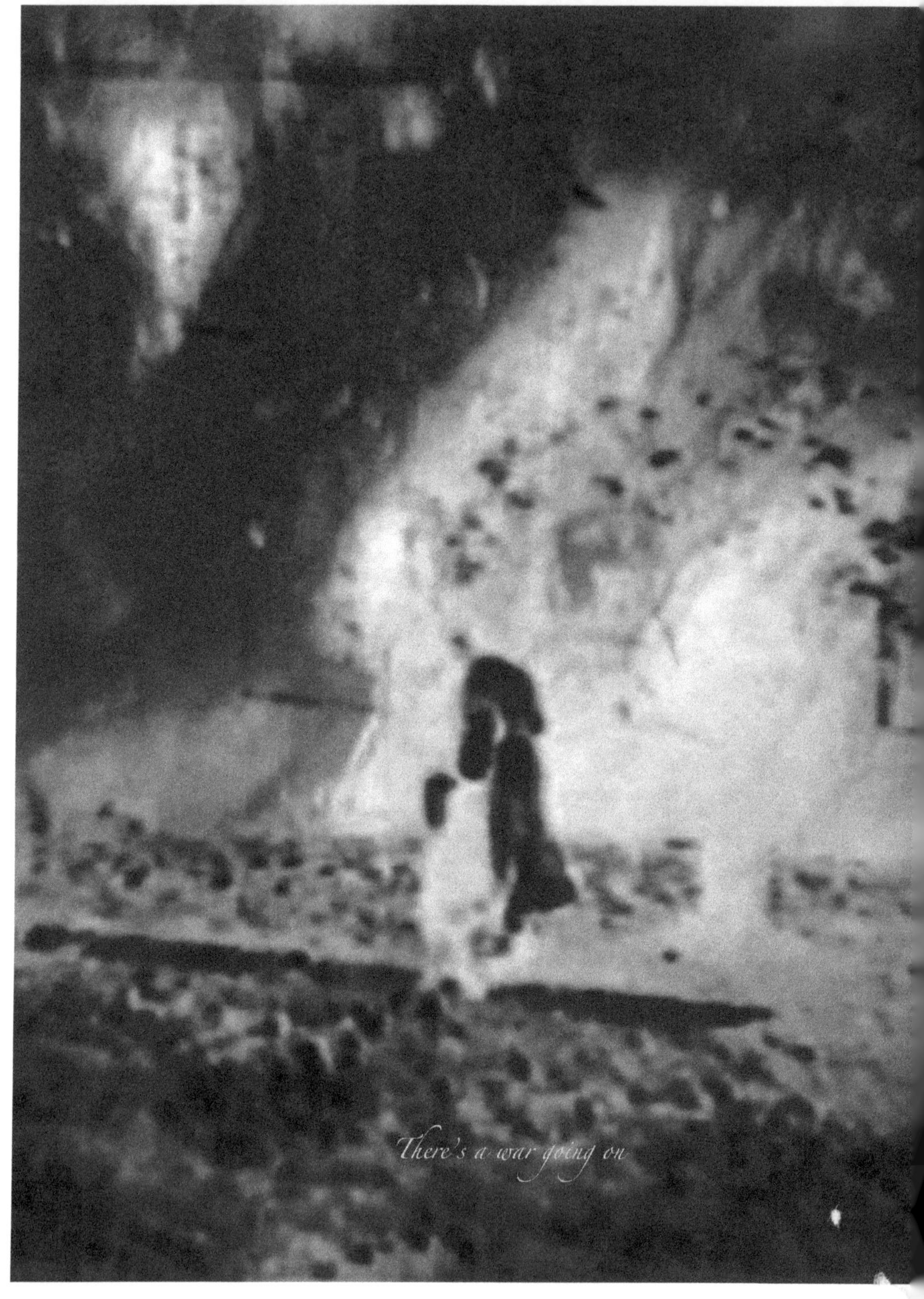
There's a war going on

This image originated as a still from my 35mm film "L'éclat du mal / The Bleeding Heart of It". I personally print each image one at a time in a limited edition using archival inks on Premium Glossy photographic paper. This paper is specifically chosen because of its luminous appearance and its vulnerability to scratches, which evoke film emulsion. The print should be handled with care but any scratches on its surface should be considered part of its fragile nature and aesthetic character.

Louise A. Bourque

L'autoportrait et autres ruines

Quelques réflexions sur Self Portrait Post Mortem et Auto Portrait / Self Portrait Post Partum

André Habib

Ce texte est issu d'une conférence donnée le 4 mai 2018, dans le cadre de la journée d'étude « Autofilmage(s) » organisée par Marion Froger, Viva Paci, et Lucie Szechter, en collaboration avec le Vidéographe, le labdoc de l'UQAM, et l'Université de Montréal. Pour une série de raisons, je n'ai pas cherché à effacer le contexte de rédaction et de présentation du texte initial, qui conserve donc par moments un caractère oral.

Je voudrais dire un mot du contexte dans lequel j'ai accepté de participer à cette journée. Lorsqu'on m'y a invité, assez intuitivement, assez aveuglément, je me suis dit que je parlerais du travail de Louise Bourque dont j'avais découvert, quelques mois auparavant, le dernier film, *Auto Portrait / Self Portrait Post Partum* (2013) au FNC [Festival du nouveau cinéma], une œuvre qui faisait écho à une autre de ses œuvres sur laquelle il m'était arrivé d'écrire, *Self Portrait Post Mortem* (2002), et qui sont deux bons exemples des abymes que la question de l'autofilmage permet de poser et faire miroiter. Pour répondre à l'injonction qu'on nous impose de devoir fournir un titre, comme un droit de passage pour apparaître au programme de ces colloques, j'avais décidé de voler un titre à Jacques Derrida, « L'autoportrait et autres ruines », me disant que je repartirais de ce texte, et de ce que j'avais pu écrire sur les ruines et l'autoportrait (en pensant par exemple au célèbre *Autoportrait devant le Colisée* de Maerten van Heemskerck, 1553). Fort de cette réserve bien garnie, la conférence était à toute fin pratique déjà écrite.

Mal m'en pris, bien évidemment, car tout s'est avéré plus complexe et enchevêtré. Et tout ceci, qui va suivre, que je vais vous lire, ne sera donc qu'un aperçu du désordre passionnant devant lequel je tâtonne depuis des jours (en aveugle davantage que dans un champ de ruines). Et peut-être que vous arriverez à y voir plus clair que moi.

Pour ne pas trop se perdre quand même — ou bien alors mieux se perdre justement — je dirais peut-être quelques mots à propos de l'histoire de ces films et de la cinéaste qui les a conçus. Louise Bourque est originaire du Nouveau-Brunswick, à la frontière avec le Maine, elle a étudié à Concordia à la fin des années 80/début 1990, elle a déménagé aux États-Unis où elle a fait une maîtrise, puis enseigné de nombreuses années avant de revenir s'installer, il y a quelques temps, à Montréal (notamment en raison de problèmes de santé, qui hantent implicitement, je le dirai dans un moment, ces deux films, de même qu'ils hantent souvent les autoportrait filmiques, si on pense à Alain Cavalier, à Johan van der Keuken, à Boris Lehman entre autres, mais aussi à bon nombre d'autoportraits peints ou dessinés, de Rembrandt à Van Gogh à Artaud, etc.). Louise Bourque est connue dans le milieu du cinéma expérimental pour des films comme *L'éclat du mal* (2005), *Jours en fleurs* (2003), *Fissures* (1999), *Imprint* (1997), *Going Back Home* (2000), frappants pour leur travail sur la matérialité de la pellicule, les manipulations à la tireuse optique, le travail de réemploi (souvent à partir de ses propres images), les techniques de développement à la main et de décomposition photochimique (comme beaucoup de sa génération, comme Carl Brown, François Miron, Phil Solomon, Peggy Ahwesh). J'avais découvert pour ma part son travail avec ce film, *Self Portrait Post Mortem*, qu'elle était venue présenter au FNC, en 2002, projeté en 35mm.

La genèse de ce film en est aussi le programme et l'abyme. En 1996, alors qu'elle s'apprêtait à déménager de façon définitive aux États-Unis, elle décida d'enfouir sous terre les chutes 16mm de ses trois premiers films [*Jolicoeur Touriste*, 1989, *Just Words*, 1991, et *The People in the House*, 1994], trois films qui tournaient autour de la famille, des liens familiaux, de la maison. Ne voulant s'en départir, et dans la crainte, me disait-elle, que ces images tombent entre les mains de quelqu'un d'autre qui aurait pu les réutiliser, elle décida donc de les enterrer dans le jardin de la maison familiale ancestrale (construite par son grand-père), maison qui jouxte une église et un ancien cimetière (en creusant quelques années auparavant, non loin de là, pour faire une clôture, on avait retrouvé des ossements). Ses bobines de pellicule furent donc ensevelies, à peine emballées de papier journal, se disant — sans savoir, pour voir — qu'elle en ferait peut-être quelque chose un jour, dans un geste où se noue un désir de conservation et une certaine pulsion de mort, de destruction (et les deux sont bien souvent liés, comme dans la conception de l'archive derridienne). Ces bobines, ces chutes, cette cendre échouée de ses premiers films, se trouvaient confiées à la terre, à la merci des éléments, dans le jardin de la demeure familiale, au moment de sa vie où elle quittait son sol natal, qu'elle se déracinait en quelque sorte (même si la maison continuait à appartenir à la famille, et qu'elle allait revenir y habiter). La « maison » est d'ailleurs un motif qui revient dans plusieurs de ses films en particulier *Going Back Home* et *Imprint* [comme il aura été question dans cet ouvrage] — et jusque dans *Self Portrait Post Partum* dont je parlerai plus loin, même si c'est de façon plus confidentielle, voire sublimiale.

Cinq ans passeront au courant desquels elle contractera la maladie de Lyme — une maladie dormante, latente, très violente, qui surgit des mois ou parfois des années après l'infection —, qui la laissera clouée à son lit pendant près d'un an et demi, de 2000 à 2001 —, et dont elle ne se débarrassera qu'en 2009. C'est donc après cette quasi-mort que, revenue à la vie, elle déterra ses bobines dans le jardin de la maison familiale. La première chose qu'elle découvrit, quand elle déroula le premier rouleau de pellicule 16mm qui lui tomba sur la main, après quelques pieds d'amorce, fut son propre visage, les yeux clos, cerclé par les scories, les éclaboussures de décomposition, dorées, ocre, vertes, violacées, qui avaient rongé les bords de l'image mais en laissant le centre plus ou moins intact.

Sachant qu'elle ne pourrait envoyer son film dans un laboratoire pour en tirer une copie, qu'aucune tireuse contact ne pourrait entraîner le film dans son mécanisme (les perforations étaient trop abîmées), elle décida de refilmer ses images au ralenti — comme elle les avait visionnées elle-même — à partir de l'écran d'une visionneuse sur table, une Cinemonta (l'équivalent d'une Steenbeck), qui fait défiler la pellicule latéralement et en réfractant l'image à travers un prisme à 12 côtés (la Steenbeck, en a 18), un peu comme celui d'un praxinoscope. Ceci explique cet effet de glissement par surimpression (qui descend et s'élève), ce miroitement sans obturation (et qu'il s'agisse d'un tournoiement-chevauchement d'images-miroirs entrouvre une porte fascinante pour les questions qui nous intéressent). Ces images (les toutes premières donc qui se trouvaient sur cette bobine retrouvée) ont été refilmées d'abord en numérique, avant d'être reportées, réimprimées, sur une pellicule 35mm. Le son fut produit en ralentissant à l'extrême un matériau sonore brut, tiré de la fameuse *sound effects library* de la BBC (il s'agissait d'un son de machinerie, mais qui ralenti revêt des sortes de qualités telluriques, comme un cri provenant des profondeurs de la terre). Il y aurait long à dire d'ailleurs sur ces multiples remédiations de supports, mais je n'ai pas la place ici.

Après avoir elle-même en quelque sorte traversé la mort, elle se retrouvait, se revoyait dans ces images rescapées, morte et enterrée et en même temps revenue à la vie, sorte de figure lazaréenne, sortie de son tombeau, conservant les stigmates de son passage sous terre, et nous fixant d'outre-tombe ; elle se retrouvait, se revoyait dans des images tournées durant le tournage de son premier film, *Jolicoeur Touriste*, en 1989 (sorte d'*arché* originaire de son propre parcours de cinéaste), dans des images dont elle ne se souvenait pas, dont elle n'avait aucune connaissance, qui n'avaient pas laissé de traces en elle avant d'être redécouvertes, et qui lui revenaient par une sorte d'anamnèse paradoxale, puisque l'image réveille un souvenir qu'elle ne savait pas qu'elle portait en elle, comme une maladie dont on ne pouvait pas soupçonner qu'on pouvait en être le « porteur ». Ces images — je viens de l'apprendre, et c'est sans doute là pour moi, et pour quelques-uns d'entre nous ici dans cette salle, où l'abyme se creuse douloureusement — avaient été tournées par son amie et directrice artistique sur le film, Élène Tremblay — une amie et une collègue décédée il y a deux ans d'un cancer fulgurant, dont elle a cru un moment s'être débarrassée, et qui l'a emportée en 2016. Il y a donc beaucoup de fantômes, de revenants, d'apparitions autant que de disparitions, logées dans la douleur et la beauté de ce film.

Parmi les nombreuses choses qui me fascinent et me troublent dans ce très court film c'est ce jeu sur le regard — qui hantera également *Post Partum*. En regardant bien, on voit que ce visage apparaît, tout d'abord, surgissant de l'ombre, de la nuit, avec l'apparence d'un masque mortuaire, les yeux clos, quasi-immobile, cerclé de terre, de matière organique tournoyante ; suit un geste de la main, furtif, qui remonte vers le visage (comme on imagine un ressuscité avancerait en tâtonnant, avant d'ouvrir les yeux) — puis la tête se tourne et les yeux s'ouvrent et on nous fixe à partir d'un point lointain, qui semble être à la fois un temps passé et un temps à venir (comme si la cinéaste nous fixait depuis le passé d'où nous l'avons déterrée, et, en même temps, nous observait déjà, par avance, depuis la mort qui l'attend, qui nous attend tous). Et je ne sais pas pourquoi, mais j'ai toujours eu le sentiment que — tout comme dans la performance de Guy Sherwin, *Man with a Mirror* (1976), tout comme, à un autre niveau, *Self Portrait Post Partum* —, qu'avant de *me regarder*, moi, qui regarde ce film, que *ce regard est dirigé vers la cinéaste elle-même* — comme si, avant toute chose, ce que l'on voit dans ce film, c'est la mise en scène du regard de la cinéaste qui se regarde se voyant. C'est comme si c'était son propre regard qui la hantait, d'outre-tombe, d'outre-temps, mais peut-être aussi qui lui disait continûment, qu'il y a moyen de renaître, de dessiller les yeux, de remonter à la surface de la terre, à la surface de l'eau, de survivre. « Je suis une apparition », me disait-elle.

La ruine du film, ici, est bien ce qui ronge la vie, mais elle est aussi l'écrin qui la conserve, ne fût-ce que comme spectre vivant. Mais n'est-ce pas ce que fait déjà tout autoportrait ? S'il faut suivre Derrida lorsqu'il écrit : « ruine est l'autoportrait, ce visage dévisagé comme mémoire de soi, ce qui reste ou revient comme un spectre dès qu'au premier regard sur soi une figuration s'éclipse ».[1] Cette citation, fascinante et cryptée, fait un bel écho avec le film : elle semble dire à la fois ce qui revient et ce qui fuit, s'éclipse ; elle nomme cette part de lumière aveuglante et de nuit obscure, d'où ce film nous vient et nous parle, *de près et de loin*.

Je dirais que toutes ces questions, ces problèmes apparaissent sous une autre forme dans l'autre *autoportrait* réalisé par Bourque, plus récemment, sur lequel je voudrais brièvement m'attarder. Cet *Auto Portrait / Self Portrait Post Partum* a été complété en 2013 mais ne circule que depuis quelques temps seulement. Le film part et nous parle d'une rupture amoureuse. Il fut en partie tourné lors d'une retraite au fameux Film Farm du cinéaste canadien Phil Hoffman, un lieu où des cinéastes et des artistes se retrouvent pour s'initier en communauté à des techniques cinématographiques artisanales, découvrir des films, partager des connaissances, etc.

Le film se divise en trois sections : les deux premières parties réutilisent une même série d'images tournées sur un 100 pieds de pellicule où l'on voit en une succession de gros plans (de plus en plus rapprochés, sur ses yeux, sa bouche) le visage de la cinéaste, adossée à un arbre, la nuit, sanglotant, en larmes. Les bobines noir et blanc (Tri-X) ont été développées à la main (dans un sceau, avec une lampe de poche) ce qui vient accentuer les accidents, les taches, les égratignures, les variations d'exposition. Dans la seconde section, cette même série d'images, de gros plans, a été teintée par imbibition, en bleu nuit. La troisième partie, teintée d'un halo bleu somptueux, nous montre le visage de la cinéaste, filmée de face, nageant sous l'eau, retenant son souffle, les yeux ouverts, avant de refaire surface, à la toute fin du film, baignée dans une nouvelle lumière (on pourrait dire, pour filer la métaphore, qu'elle s'immerge, qu'elle se plonge dans l'eau, comme elle plonge la pellicule dans le bain fluidifiant du révélateur, pour tirer au bout du processus un positif de tout ce négatif accumulé).

Chacune des parties est entrecoupée de citations grattées sur la pellicule, sur la chaire du film, comme des phrases mantra venant d'amis, d'auteurs rencontrés par hasard, des sortes de « clichés » qui aident à comprendre, à guérir et qui lui permettent au final de faire le deuil, d'écrire sa propre douleur, sa déchirure mais aussi sa suture, de parvenir à graver à son tour son nom sur l'écorce du film. À cela s'ajoute enfin des brefs extraits manipulés d'un film de série B (trouvé par Louise dans une archive à Boston) où un homme inquiétant étrangle une femme, et où on entre-aperçoit, très rapidement,

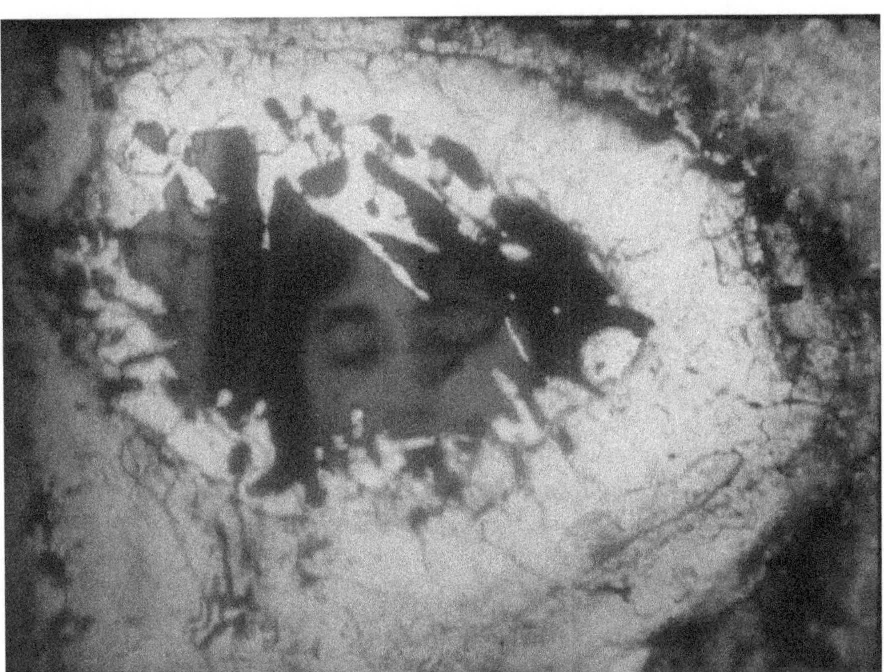

une photographie de maison qui semble crépiter sous les flammes. Sur la bande-son, on entend au début et à différents moments du film, la voix de la cinéaste, s'adressant à son amant (à qui le film s'adresse sous forme de lettre et de supplique), puis diverses musiques, des chansons populaires qu'on cherche à syntoniser sur un poste de radio, un peu kitsch, jouant volontairement du cliché, allant de Neil Young à Louis Armstrong aux Supremes et à Doris Day, la ramenant à sa jeunesse ou à sa relation avec celui qui la plonge dans la folie et la dépression. On entend aussi des sons qui lui rappellent sa maison (le son familier du chemin de fer, l'harmonica de son père, les huards, les cris d'oiseaux), etc. Tout ceci fait évidemment partie des secrets intimes du film que j'ai pu recueillir en parlant avec la cinéaste, même si on devine sans peine la teneur affective et biographique de ces musiques et de ces sons. Dans le même ordre d'idée, il peut être bon de souligner que tout le traitement de la pellicule à la main — ce n'est pas innocent sans doute — s'est déroulé dans l'atelier de la maison familiale, au Nouveau Brunswick.

À l'image inconsciente de *Post Mortem* (une image qu'elle ne connaissait pas, sur laquelle elle n'est pas intervenue personnellement, qu'elle avait oubliée et retrouvée), on trouve ici une image délibérée, voulue, jouée, travaillée à la main. On y trouve ce désir de se filmer, pleurant, pour objectiver sa douleur sans doute (c'est le propre du travail du deuil), de se voir ne plus être capable de voir, les yeux ouverts mais aveuglés par les larmes, même si comme le rappelle Derrida (et comme nous montre le film), les larmes aussi peuvent voir, « *These Seeing Tears* » [en anglais dans le texte]… du moins nous aident à voir.

Ces deux autoportraits sont inséparables d'un processus de guérison, d'un travail de deuil, d'un certain arrachement à la cécité, qui passe par une forme de corrélation matériologique entre le film et la vie, la pellicule et le corps, le développement photochimique et la révélation à soi. Ce travail présuppose et assume une part d'aveuglement, aveuglement volontaire, ou aveuglement créatif ; admettre en tout cas qu'il faut tâtonner, travailler dans le noir, se terrer, s'enterrer, laisser des forces obscures agir, pour voir. C'est ce que font d'ailleurs les cinéastes expérimentaux en général : ils expérimentent, ils essaient des choses, comme on dit, juste pour voir. Enterrer un film, pour voir ; développer la pellicule dans un seau en éclairant à la lampe de poche des portions de film, en variant la température des bains, etc. Et je dirais que la force créatrice, ainsi que la beauté plastique de ces œuvres se loge précisément dans ce travail de délégation à la nature, au hasard, par le surgissement des aléas matériels du support, mais qui font signe, qui font figure, qui font image. Dans *Post Partum*, les taches, les rayures, les scories sur la pellicule apparaissent comme le flot heurté et accidenté de sa conscience qui l'assaille, l'aveugle, la font cligner des yeux ; dans *Post Mortem*, la matière ectoplasmique qui enveloppe son visage, est un voile, un linceul, mais aussi une danse de la matière, à la fois florale et mortuaire.

Peut-être une des curiosité de ce dernier film — pour finir — est son

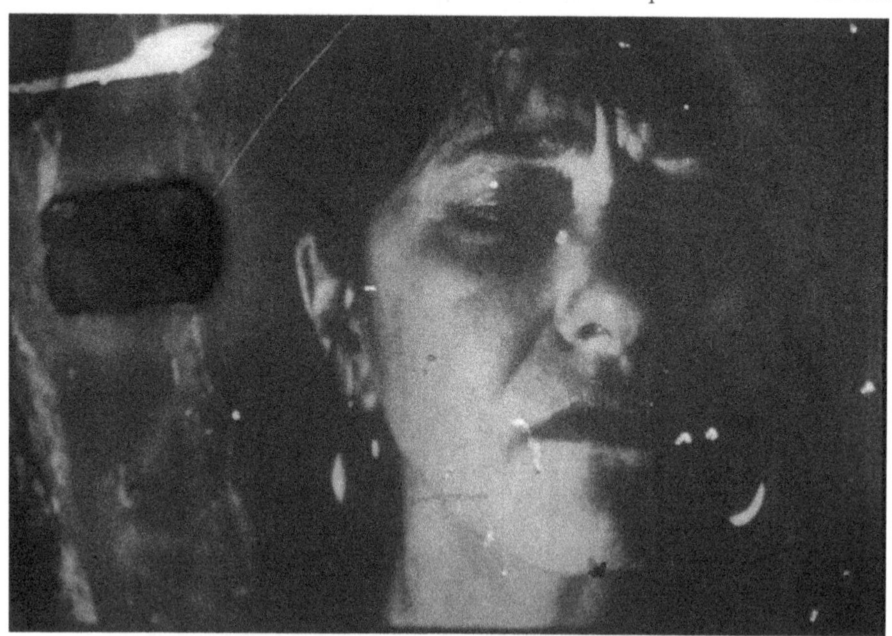

appropriation libre du terme latin *partum*. Le *post-partum* renvoie comme vous le savez normalement à la période de dépression qui suit l'accouchement, et non la séparation amoureuse, pour laquelle le latin a d'autres mots… ceci dit, n'importe qui a vu le film, *comprend et accepte* le principe. Mais peut-être y a-t-il une fécondité à cette confusion, à cet aveuglement révélateur — qui force le rapprochement entre le post-*Mortem* et post-*Partum*. C'est comme si, devant ces deux films, l'autoportrait pouvait servir paradoxalement à mettre en scène sa propre mort (une mort au travail, le travail de la mort), la possibilité de la mort et, en même temps, à représenter une sorte de naissance, de nouvelle naissance, de renaissance, en tout cas de traversée initiatique ou alchimique qui transforme à la fois le matériau et la cinéaste. Ça nous permet de placer du coup la question de l'autoportrait sur un terrain complexe où se joue la filiation, l'engendrement, mais aussi la déchirure et sa suture symbolique, le deuil qui suit tout processus de séparation avec celui ou celle avec qui on avait l'impression de ne former qu'une seule et même personne.

Chaque autoportrait, à sa manière, ouvrirait la question, le problème, l'abyme de sa propre création, et peut-être de toute gestation créatrice ; mais aussi de la mort et de la ruine, qui lui est coextensive : chaque œuvre s'offrant alors comme une réponse, provisoire, à cette question, ce problème, cet abyme aveuglant, en guise de *post-scriptum*.

NOTES

1. Jacques Derrida, *Mémoires d'aveugle : l'autoportrait et autres ruines* (Paris: Editions de la Réunion des musées nationaux, 1990), 72.

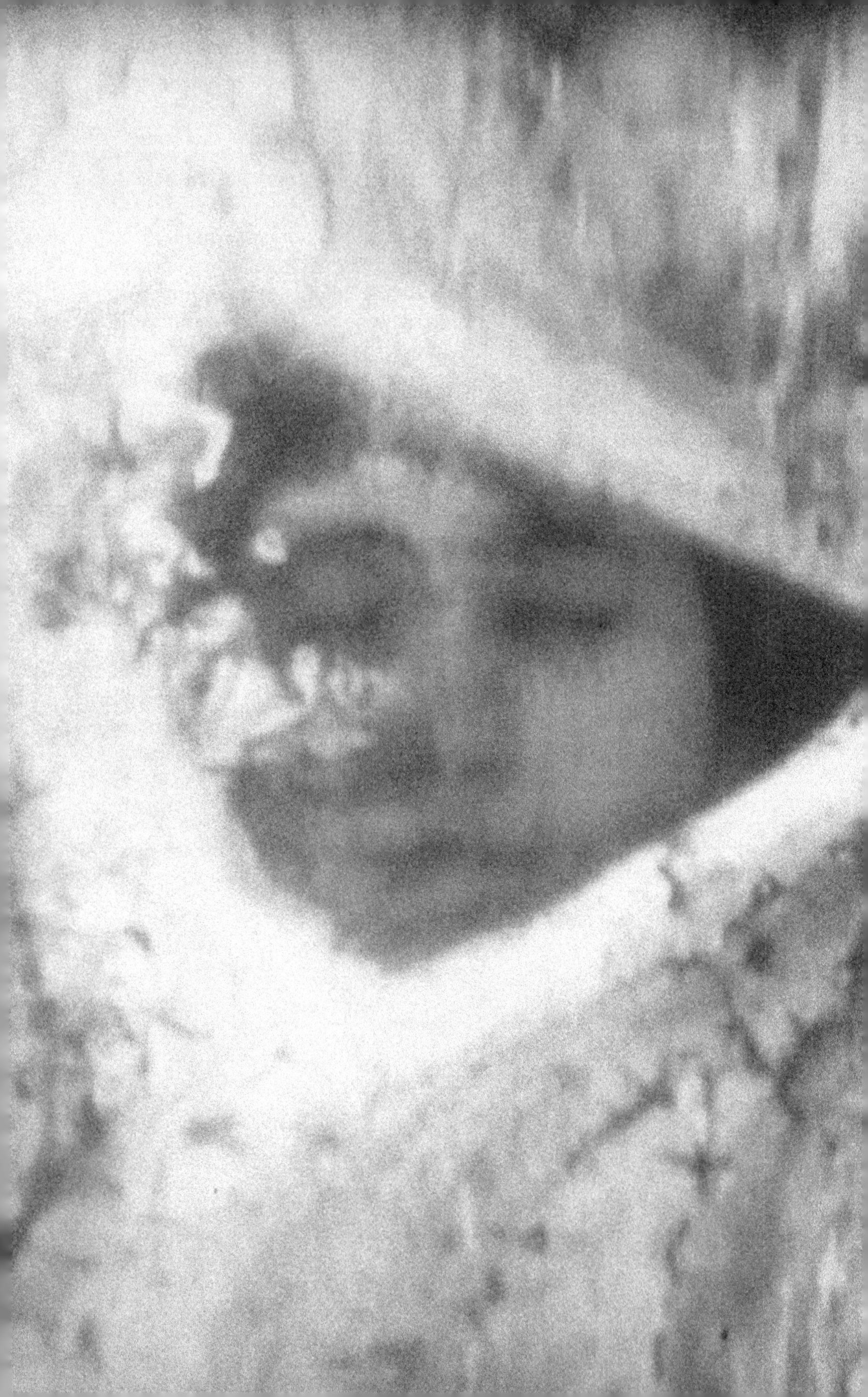

The Self-Portrait and Other Ruins

Reflections on Self Portrait Post Mortem and Auto Portrait / Self Portrait Post Partum

André Habib

Translated by Kathryn Michalski

This text was written for a conference given on May 4, 2018 as part of "Autofilmage(s)" ("Cinematic Self-Portrait(s)") organized by Marion Froger, Viva Paci, and Lucie Szechter, in collaboration with the Vidéographe, the Labdoc of UQAM, and Université de Montréal. For a variety of reasons, I chose to maintain the context in which the initial text was written and presented, therefore retaining an oral, audience-oriented voice.

I would like to begin with a few words about the context in which I had agreed to participate in this event. Upon being invited, rather intuitively, rather blindly, I told myself that I would speak about the work of Louise Bourque, whose last film, *Auto Portrait / Self Portrait Post Partum* (2013) I had discovered a few months earlier at the FNC [Festival du nouveau cinéma]; a piece that echoed another of her works that I had written about previously: *Self Portrait Post Mortem* (2002), both being excellent examples of the abysses that cinematic self-portraiture can unearth. When asked to provide a title for my talk, I had opted to steal one from Jacques Derrida, "The Self-Portrait and Other Ruins," rationalizing that I would then build upon both this text and my existing knowledge of ruins and self-portraits (thinking, for example, of the famous *Self-portrait with the Colosseum* by Maerten van Heemskerck, 1553).

Well equipped, I felt the lecture was, in every practical sense, already written.

Alas, of course, everything turned out to be far more complex and tangled than I had previously anticipated. And this journey, which I shall now share with you, will therefore be but a glimpse of the exciting disorder that I have toiled with over the last few days (lost in a field of ruins). Upon accompanying me on this journey, perhaps you shall emerge with a deeper understanding than I.

In order to stay on course—or better yet, to get lost entirely—I wish to share a few words about the history of the films and the filmmaker who made them. Louise Bourque is originally from New Brunswick, bordering Maine. She studied at Concordia University in the late 1980s and early 1990s, and later moved to the United States to complete a master's degree. She later taught for several years before coming back to settle down in Montreal notably due to a health issue, which implicitly haunts, as I'll demonstrate in a moment, these two films (just as they often tend to haunt cinematic self-portraits such as those of Alain Cavalier, Johan van der Keuken, and Boris Lehman, to name but a few examples, as well as a number of painted or drawn self-portraits, from Rembrandt to Van Gogh to Artaud, etc.). Louise Bourque is known in the experimental film scene for her moving-image works such as *L'éclat du mal / The Bleeding Heart of It* (2005), *Jours en fleurs* (2003), *Fissures* (1999), *Imprint* (1997), and *Going Back Home* (2000). These artworks stand out for their treatment of the materiality of film, manipulations with the optical printer, use of recycled images (often her own), hand-developing techniques, and photochemical decomposition (similar to others from her generation, such as Carl Brown, François Miron, Phil Solomon, and Peggy Ahwesh). I discovered her work for myself in 2002 at FNC when she came to present *Self Portrait Post Mortem*, projected in 35mm.

The genesis of this film functions both as its essence and its abyss. In 1996, about to move to the United States permanently, Louise decided to bury the 16mm rushes of her first three films (*Jolicoeur Touriste*, 1989, *Just Words*, 1991, and *The People in the House*, 1994); three films focusing on family, family ties, and the idea of home. Not ready to part with them, and fearing, as she shared with me, that these images could fall into the hands of someone else who could appropriate them, she decided to bury these scraps in the garden of her ancestral family home (built by her grandfather), a house built next to a church and an old cemetery (where bones had once been found while the land was being dug up to build a fence). Bourque then buried her reels of film, wrapping them scantily in newspaper, thinking—without knowing, just to see—what she might do with them one day, a gesture in which the desire for conservation and a certain fascination with death and destruction were intertwined (as the two often are, such as in the conception of the Derridian archive). Her reels, her scraps, the stranded ashes of her early films, were entrusted to the earth, at the mercy of the elements, in the garden of the family home, at the moment in her life when she left her native soil, and was herself uprooted (even if the house remained in the family, and she would come to live there again one day). "Home" is a recurring motif in several of her films, particularly in *Going Back Home* and even more so in *Imprint*, but also in *Self Portrait Post Partum*, albeit more subtly and subliminally, as we shall touch upon later.

Over the next five years, Louise contracted Lyme disease—a dormant, latent, very violent disease that can emerge months, or sometimes years after infection—which left her bedridden for almost a year and a half between 2000 and 2001, and from which she did not fully recover until 2009. This brush with death is what ultimately brought her back to life, inspiring her to unearth the film previously buried in the garden of her family home. The first thing she discovered, upon opening the first roll of 16mm film that her hand touched, upon unrolling the first few feet of leader, was her own face, eyes closed, surrounded by the slag, splashes of decomposition, golden, ochre, green, purplish, that had gnawed away at the edges of the image while leaving the centre more or less intact.

Knowing, as she did, that the film could not be sent to a laboratory to be copied, as no contact printer could securely attach the film into its mechanism (the perforations were too damaged), she decided to re-film the images in slow motion—as she had watched them herself—from the screen of a table-top viewer, a Cinemonta (the equivalent of a Steenbeck), which scrolls the film laterally and projects the image through a twelve-sided prism (the Steenbeck has eighteen), much like that of a praxinoscope. The result of this is a gliding superimposition effect (shifting up and down), a shimmering, a swirl of mirroring images that open a fascinating door into the questions we are scrutinizing. The scrolling of these images (the very first ones, therefore, that were on this found roll) were first digitally re-filmed before being transferred and reprinted on 35mm. The sound was then produced by drastically slowing down the raw sound material, taken from the famous BBC sound effects library (the sound of machinery, slowed down, produces an earthy quality—a desperate cry coming from the depths of the abyss). There is a lot to say about these various remediations, but I don't have space here.

Having herself experienced a brush with death, Louise later found herself, rediscovered herself, in these surviving images, dead and buried while at the same time coming back to life, like Lazarus, emerging from her tomb, preserving the stigmata of her passage underground, and staring at us from beyond the grave; she found herself, saw herself, in the images of her first film, *Jolicoeur Touriste*, in 1989 (a sort of archaic figure from her own journey as a filmmaker), in images that she no longer recalled, of which she had no knowledge, and that left no traces of herself prior to being rediscovered. Suddenly, these images rushed back in a kind of paradoxical amnesia, like a disease that had long lay dormant, awakening memories she no longer knew she carried. It's probably here that I too, as with most of those in the room, felt the deeply painful abyss of these images. These images were shot by her friend and art director on the film, Élène Tremblay—a friend and colleague who has since passed away from an aggressive cancer, which for a moment she believed she had overcome, but which ultimately took her life in 2016. There are many ghosts, apparitions, and disappearances, all of which are captured in the pain and beauty of this film.

Among the many things that both fascinate and disturb me in this very short film, as with *Post Partum*, is the use of the gaze. If you look closely, you can see a face appear, emerging from the shadows at first, from the darkness, the appearance of a death mask, eyes closed, almost motionless, surrounded by earth and swirling organic matter; followed by a furtive hand gesture, rising towards the face (as one could visualize a resurrected person grasping for life, prior to opening their eyes). Suddenly the head turns and the eyes open, staring at us from far away, from both a time passed and a time to come (almost as if she is staring at us, watching, both from the past that we are digging up, and from the present we are unearthing, foreseeing the death that awaits her, and that ultimately awaits us all). I don't know why, but I've always had the impression that—just as in Guy Sherwin's performance, *Man with a Mirror* (1976), but on another level than *Self Portrait Post Partum*—before looking at me-the-viewer, this gaze is directed at the filmmaker herself, as if, above all, what we see in this film is the staging of the filmmaker's gaze as she looks at herself. It is as if it were her own gaze that comes back to haunt her, from beyond the grave, from beyond time, but perhaps also to tell her, to tell us, continuously, that there is a way to be reborn, to open our eyes, to rise to the surface of the earth, to the surface of the water, to survive. "I am an apparition," she told me.

The ruins of the film gnaw at life, while at the same time conserving it, if only as a living ghost. But isn't that what every self-portrait already does? If one were to follow Derrida's perspective: "ruin is the self-portrait, this face looked at in the face of memory of itself, what remains or returns as a spectre from the moment one first looks at oneself and figuration is eclipsed."[1] This sentiment, both fascinating and cryptic, is echoed beautifully within the film, highlighting that which returns, and that which flees and eclipses; defining

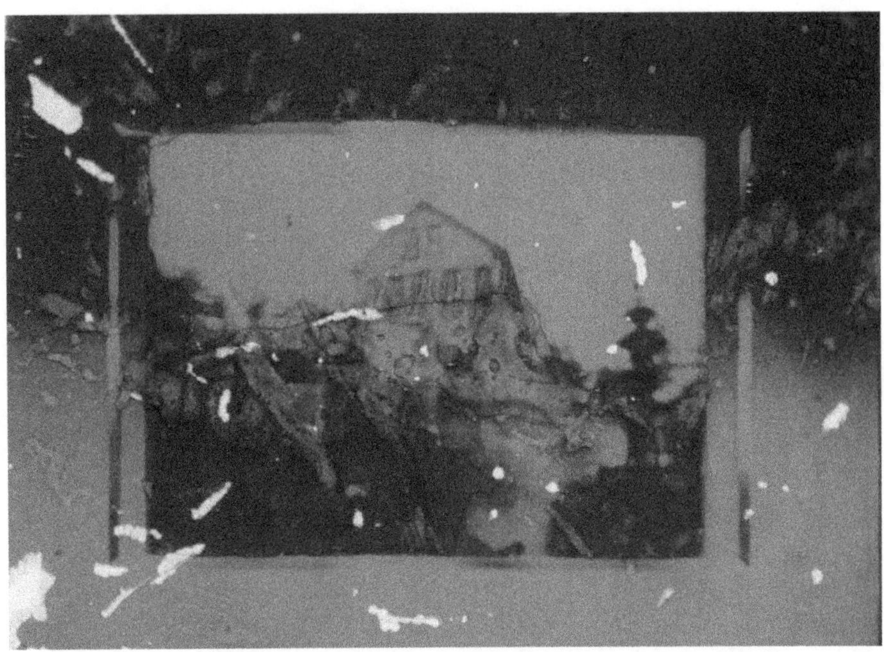

both the blinding light and darkest of nights, from which this film comes and from which it speaks to us, *from near and from far*.

All of these questions, these problems appear once again in a more recent self-portrait by Bourque, which I would like to touch upon briefly. This *Auto Portrait / Self Portrait Post Partum* was completed in 2013 but has only recently been released. This is a film that shares with us the story of a romantic breakup. It was partially shot during a retreat at the famous Film Farm, organized by Canadian filmmaker Phil Hoffman, a place where filmmakers and artists alike meet to exchange and learn about traditional filmmaking techniques, discover films, share knowledge, and so on.

The film is divided into three sections: the first two parts reuse the same series of images shot on 100 feet of film where we see in a succession of closeups (slowly closing in on her eyes, her mouth) the filmmaker's face, leaning against a tree, at night, sobbing, in tears. The black and white reels (Tri-X) were hand-processed (in a bucket, with a flashlight), accentuating faults, stains, scratches, and variations in exposure. In the second section, the same series of images and closeups are tinted to midnight blue by imbibition. The third section, now tinted with a blue halo, shows the filmmaker's face, swimming underwater, holding her breath, eyes open, before resurfacing, at the very end of the film, bathed in a new light (one could say, to spin the metaphor, that she plunges into the water, submersing herself, just as she immerses the film in the fluidizing bath of the developer, to draw at the end of the process a "positive" from all of the accumulated negative).

In each of these parts, phrases have been physically scratched onto the emulsion of the film. Mantras from friends and authors encountered by chance, clichés of sorts meant to help one to understand, to heal, to help, and in the end to mourn, to share one's personal pain, to both destroy and suture one's self, to manage to engrave one's self and one's name onto the film itself. Finally, there are short, manipulated excerpts from a B-movie (found by Louise in an archive in Boston) in which a disturbed man strangles a woman. We also, very quickly, catch a glimpse of a photograph of a house that seems to crackle beneath the flames. For the most part, the filmmaker's voice dominates the soundtrack. At the beginning, as well as at different moments throughout the film, she can be heard addressing her lover (to whom the film is addressed in the form of letter and plea). A mix of music is incorporated as well: popular songs that we may try to tune into on the radio, slightly kitschy, waxing cliché. From Neil Young and Louis Armstrong to the Supremes and Doris Day, bringing the filmmaker back to her youth or back to the relationship with the one who ultimately thrust her into madness and depression. We can also hear sounds that remind her of home (the familiar sound of the railway, her father's harmonica, loons, bird calls, etc.). These were some of the intimate secrets shared with me in my talks with the filmmaker, even if it is easy to piece together the emotional and biographical content of these songs and sounds. In the same vein, it may be worth pointing out that the hand-processing of this film—intentionally no doubt—all took place in the workshop of her family home in New Brunswick.

Unconsciously in the images of *Post Mortem* (images that she did not construct, but that were forgotten and discovered once again) we find a deliberate, wanted, performed, and hand-crafted image. We witness here a desire to film oneself crying, to objectify one's pain (characteristic of a labour of mourning), to see oneself while no longer able to see, with open eyes that are blinded by tears, even if, as Derrida reminds us (and as the film demonstrates), tears too can see, "These Seeing Tears" ... at least help us to see.

These two self-portraits are works of mourning and are therefore inseparable from the healing process. They carry with them a withdrawal from blindness and can be seen as a material correlation between film and life, film and body; a photochemical development and self-revelation. The work both implies and embodies blindness, voluntary blindness, or creative blindness; admitting, in any case, that it is necessary to grope, to work in the dark, to bury oneself, to let dark forces take over, in order to see. In general, this is what experimental filmmakers do: they experiment, they try things for the sake of seeing what happens. Burying film, just to see; developing film in a bucket by lighting portions of the film with a flashlight, varying the temperature of the baths, just to see. And I would posit that the creative force as well as the visual beauty of these works emanate from this relationship between nature and chance, the random material resulting in the creation of signs, figures, and images. In *Post Partum*, the stains, the scratches, the slag on the film appear as the bumpy and uneven flow of consciousness that assails her, blinding her, making her blink; in *Post Mortem*, the ectoplasmic matter that envelops her face is a veil, a shroud, but also a dance of matter, both floral and unearthly.

To conclude, perhaps one of the curiosities of this last film is its liberal use of the Latin term *partum*. *Postpartum*, as you know, normally refers to a period of depression that can follow childbirth. It is not an actual separation from love, for which Latin has other words. That being said, anyone who sees the film *understands and accepts* the principle. Perhaps there is a method to the madness, to the revealing blindness—a reconciliation of post-*Mortem* and post-*Partum*. It is as if, within these two films, the self-portrait could paradoxically serve to stage one's own death (death at work, death's work), the possibility of death, while at the same time representing a kind of resurrection, a new birth, a rebirth, in any case an initiatory or cosmic crossing, transforming both the material and the filmmaker. This allows us to place the question of self-portraiture on a complex terrain where our designations are symbolically torn apart, forcing us both to mourn and to confront the one whom we had the impression of being.

Every self-portrait, in its own way, opens up the question, the problem, the abyss of its own creation, and perhaps of any creative gestation; but also of death and ruin, which is coextensive within it: each work would then offer itself as a response, provisional, to this question, this problem, this blinding abyss under the guise of a *postscriptum*.

NOTES

1. Jacques Derrida, *Memoirs of the Blind: The Self-Portrait and Other Ruins*, trans. Pascale-Anne Brault and Michael Naas (Chicago: University of Chicago Press, 1993), 68.

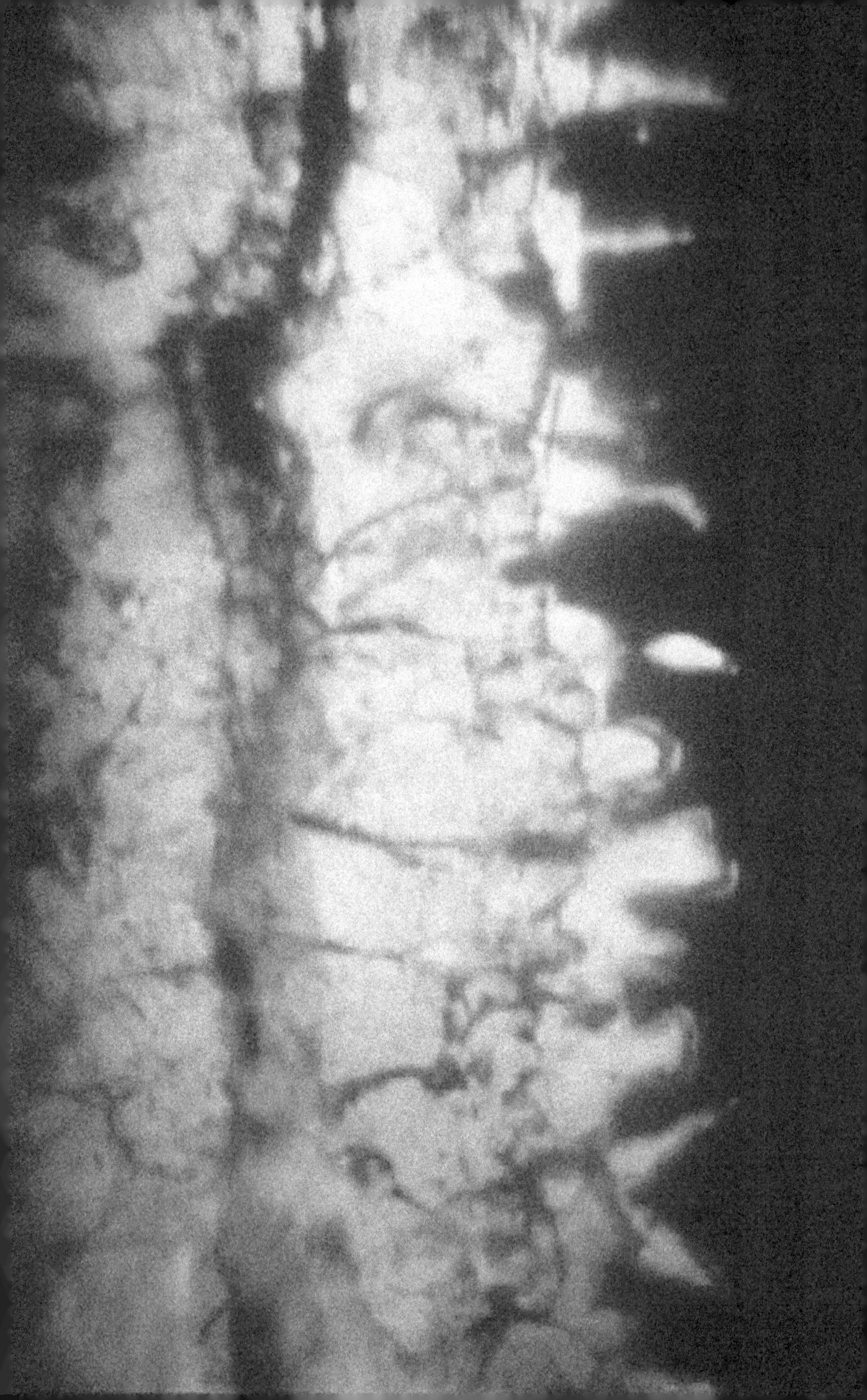

Décrire une sensation

Sébastien Ronceray

Une section de "Exploration du cinéma expérimental," un parcours pédagogique, publiée à l'origine sur le site du CICLIC, UPOPI (Université populaire des images), en 2015.

La rencontre avec les films est indispensable dans le cadre d'une approche du cinéma. L'important est avant tout de créer les conditions pour ressentir, comme le souligne Alain Bergala : « L'art, cela ne s'enseigne pas, cela se rencontre, cela s'expérimente, cela se transmet par d'autres voies que celles du discours seul, et parfois même sans discours du tout ».[1] Face à des films expérimentaux, souvent sans histoire, voir sans personnage, ou composés d'images abstraites, comment exprimer notre sensation ?

L'exercice consistant à décrire des films expérimentaux en classe n'est pas toujours simple, mais il suffit de s'affranchir de nos habitudes, et de voir les films comme ils sont pour éprouver des sensations. La recherche de (dé)figurations, l'aspect de purs collages générant des images inconnues et étranges, les transformations qu'elles subissent, invitent à considérer la composition de ces films comme des jeux d'images. Ils s'encrent dans des formes propices à la sensation, à la réaction : alchimies de couleurs, effets rythmiques, dislocations, mouvements de caméra inventifs, accidents créatifs. Tout cela entraine aisément des remarques, des questions ... Ces films, qui s'ouvrent alors volontiers aux commentaires, laissent aux élèves la place à la projection comme sensation.

Self Portrait Post Mortem (2002) s'organise autour d'un rythme lent, autant dans le son que dans les images. Le son s'assimile à une respiration, à un battement doux. Quant aux images, elles dessinent au début une ligne colorée serpentant aléatoirement au centre de l'image. Puis apparaît une sorte d'interstice sombre encadré de granulations brunes et rougeâtres. De cette obscurité centrale apparaît enfin un visage. On peut se questionner sur le titre de ce film, qui annonce un autoportrait après la mort. De quel portrait et de quelle mort s'agit-il ici ? Avant de montrer ce film de Louise Bourque, il est intéressant de questionner les élèves sur ce qu'est un autoportrait. Ce terme semble trouver facilement des échos picturaux avec la peinture et la photographie. Mais qu'en est-il du cinéma ? Le cinéaste retourne-t-il sa caméra vers lui ? Que choisit-il de nous raconter de lui ? Quelle utilisation va-t-il faire du son ? Comment le mouvement des images est-il utilisé ?

Le film de Louise Bourque nous plonge dans une matière organique accompagnée par des bruits corporels. Les couleurs brunes ajoutent une sensation d'intériorité, les formes ressemblent à un grossissement de tissus humains, à des matières observées à l'intérieur d'un corps. Leur défilement pourrait évoquer des écailles, ou une carapace d'où émerge un visage. C'est celui de la cinéaste jeune : ce portrait a été filmé par ses parents alors qu'elle était adolescente. Il semble jaillir d'un ensevelissement organique, comme s'il était enfoui sous de la lave. Ce film nous plonge dans un voyage à l'intérieur d'un corps d'où ressort un visage. Le corps en question peut bien sûr être celui de la cinéaste (comme la vision métaphorique d'une renaissance), mais il est aussi celui de la pellicule, matière vivante, vibrante, soumise aux variations de la lumière, des opérations de développement des images. La pellicule (et ses composants : les émulsions photosensibles) réagissent au passage du temps et aux effets chimiques qu'elle subit. Techniquement, pour obtenir cette dégradation de l'image, la cinéaste a enterré ce film de famille pendant plusieurs mois. Cet autoportrait tisse un lien très étroit entre la cinéaste et la matière même de l'image cinématographique.

Atelier autoportrait

Après la diffusion de ce film, il est judicieux de laisser les élèves évoquer leurs sensations personnelles. Ils peuvent noter cela sous la forme d'une liste regroupant les différentes sensations que ce film a produit sur eux. Le jeu des couleurs dans ce film peut aussi évoquer une saison. Quelle serait-elle ? À partir de là, on peut demander aux élèves de réaliser un autoportrait en lien avec les couleurs d'une saison de leur choix. On peut s'appuyer bien sûr sur des peintures (Arcimboldo, Frida Kahlo, Vincent van Gogh, Pablo Picasso, Francis Bacon, Gustave Courbet, Andy Warhol ...), des photographies ou des films.

NOTES

1. Alain Bergala, *L'Hypothèse cinéma. Petit traité de la transmission du cinéma à l'école et ailleurs* (Paris: Cahiers du Cinéma, 2002), 30.

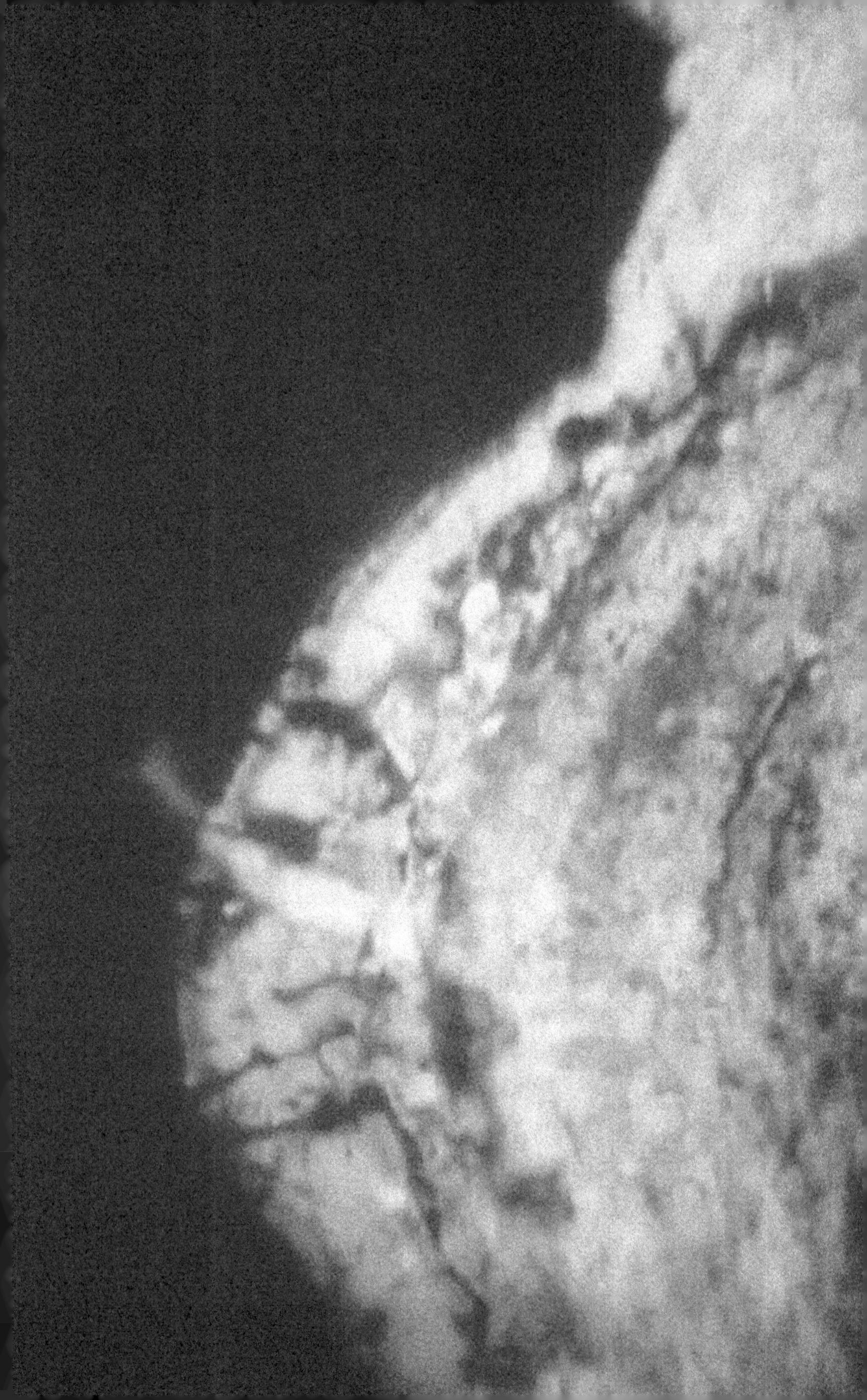

Describing a Sensation

Sébastien Ronceray

Translated by Kathryn Michalski

An excerpt from "Exploration du cinéma expérimental" ("Exploring Experimental Cinema"), a pedagogical journey, originally published on the CICLIC website, UPOPI (Université populaire des images), in 2015.

In order to approach cinema, it is important to have an understanding of film. Setting the proper conditions for feeling is also an essential part of the process. As highlighted by Alain Bergala: "Art cannot be taught, but must be encountered, experienced, transmitted by other means than the discourse of mere knowledge, and even sometimes without any discourse at all."[1] With that said, how does one express their feelings and reactions when faced with works that are experimental; films that are often without narrative, characters, or that can consist solely of abstract images?

The presentation and discussion of experimental films in a classroom setting is not always easy, but it is important to let go of any preconceptions and to allow ourselves to experience the films for what they are, inviting in any new sensations. The process of (de)figuration, the pure collages that generate strange and unknown images, as well as the transformations they undergo, invite us to consider these films as images at play. The films are embedded with forms that are conducive to sensations and reactions: alchemies of colour, rhythmic effects, dislocations, innovative camera movements, and creative accidents. All of these elements stimulate reactions and questions. Although these films are open to commentary and analysis, they leave room for the students to experience the sensation of watching in and of itself.

Self Portrait Post Mortem (2002) is structured around a slow rhythm, both in sound as well as image. The sound is reminiscent of a breath, a gentle beat.

The images initially form a coloured line randomly weaving its way through the centre of the image. This is followed by a type of dark interstice, framed by brown and reddish granulations, a darkness from which a face eventually appears. One may question the title of this film, which announces itself as a self-portrait after death. Which portrait and whose death are we talking about here? Prior to showing Louise Bourque's film, it is interesting to ask the students to discuss the concept of a self-portrait. It is easy to find echoes of self-portraiture in painting and photography, but how is it used in cinema? Is the filmmaker turning the camera towards themselves? What are they telling us about themselves? How is the sound used? How is the movement of the images used?

Bourque's film plunges us into an organic matter that is accompanied by bodily sounds. The brown colours add a feeling of interiority, the shapes resemble a magnification of human tissue, all materials that are found inside a body. The movement of the images resembles scales, or a shell from which the face of the young filmmaker emerges (this portrait was filmed by her parents when she was a teenager). It seems to spring out from an organic burial, as if it were buried under lava. This film takes us on a journey inside the body from which the face emerges. The body in question can, of course, be that of the filmmaker (a metaphorical vision of rebirth), but it could also be that of the film itself: a living, vibrating matter, subject to variations in light and the developing process. The film (and its components: photosensitive emulsions) physically reacts to the passage of time and the chemical process it undergoes. Technically, the filmmaker buried her family film for several months in order to obtain this image degradation. This self-portrait weaves a close link between the filmmaker and the physical material upon which the image was created.

Self-Portrait Workshop

After showing the film, it is a good idea to let the students share their personal feelings. They can write these feelings down, listing the different sensations that the film triggered. The play of colours in this film can also remind one of a season. What season would it be? Students can then be asked to make their own self-portrait in relation to the colours of a season of their choice. Of course, this can be based on paintings (Arcimboldo, Frida Kahlo, Vincent van Gogh, Pablo Picasso, Francis Bacon, Gustave Courbet, Andy Warhol ...), photographs, or films.

NOTES

1. Alain Bergala, *The Cinema Hypothesis: Teaching Cinema in the Classroom and Beyond*, trans. Madeline Whittle (Vienna: Austrian Film Museum, 2016), 22.

Remains

César Ustarroz

Before *Remains* (2011), there was another movie, an ascendency in images. Of course, anybody could think that a movie always leads to another, and one is in all, and all is in one. The latter could also be said about a daughter and a mother. But such aphorisms of cinema and life have a literal value in this respect, sensitive to the physical nature that joins two works made by the same flesh. That is because Louise Bourque assembled *Remains* out of the remaining pieces of a film she previously made, or rather, never-used outtakes from *The People in the House* (1994). Those fragments buried in the backyard, these decayed bones, are not quite the same thing. Therein lies a tiny miracle: to see how in *Remains* the exhumed celluloid serves a different purpose and takes on an extraordinary character.

But what was there, so fierce, in *The People in the House*? A striking anguish, heated emotions, fear of losing ourselves in sin and blame. It is therefore necessary to continue speaking more in detail on *The People in the House*, since *Remains* takes us back to a domestic sphere that conspires with the sacred to live under strict precepts. The beings who inhabited that house, the inner demons, the guardian angels, lamentations, love and disaffections coming from within and without, they are all intensities of will and conscious belief in which a family exists at the mercy of moral conventions. And what are those constraining webs? They are many. The most absolute: the ones imposed by religion when the walls of reason crumble. Bourque has translated these powerful forces in *The People in the House* to measure them in their influences. Bourque, who wants to overcome an intangible catechism, definitively breaks the doctrinal rope that God as accomplice dropped from heaven to tie our hands and vilify us. This idea was similarly explored by Simone Weil in *Gravity and Grace* (1947); she implored Him, and Us, to "do our duty at the prescribed time in order to believe in the reality of the external world."

Both in *The People in the House* and *Remains*, Bourque exorcises the hours of wrath that pervert the family environment every single day. Neither film has a straight explanation nor realistic façade. But *Remains* is even more confusing. Here, there are no characters who play a role in a battle of moral edicts. Here, in *Remains*, there are indeed diluted pigments, anarchic movements, permission for enchantment with its dancing, abstract frames ravaged by mold and stain. In *Remains*, dissolved by time, the old feelings give way to new ones. That they are a complement to the earlier ones seen in *The People in the House*; perhaps. That they are contaminated with the mysteries that concern Bourque's whole filmography; absolutely. Bourque has been poking around in the erosion of time, no matter whether she takes a camera to the scene or she opts for a cameraless cinema. Dauntlessly, she is always looking for autobiography. She wants to expurgate memories from bitterness to find a relieving image, to grasp it as a shipwrecked sailor embraces a rock in the sea.

Now to examine something concrete. What image is distinguished in the aged celluloid of *Remains*? From all the visible and invisible substances, from those moving forms dwelling in *The People in the House*, only one, the beloved one, can be recognized in *Remains*. It is the redeeming image of a mother, to Bourque, "a ghost that we won't let go." It is the representation of a surviving image that won't stop beating, the heart of an extant film full of regret. Listen carefully: to recover such a holy image, Bourque had to regenerate it, in its wholeness, from old material. By means of a ritualistic gesture—death, burial, and a numinous return to light—Bourque makes mementos rise from their rest to suspend them within a mythical space of yearning where past blends with present. Does it not sound like an eternal return? There is no doubt that, from such a return, only illusion remains. What I see through the corrupted glass of *Remains*, tarnished with shapeless spots, is a maternal aura, resurfacing again to be restored in the memory thanks to the pious chant of a daughter.

It can be argued that *Remains* announces a new presence. Bourque finds it by transforming reminiscences through a regeneration process. Thus, in *Remains*, recycling images imply physical and spiritual transmutation, entropy, creative destruction, and the medium's dematerialization: that which Pavle Levi calls "cinema by other means." This is how the passing of time has helped bring us a pure presence, one cleansed of reproaches. But it is pointless to paint Bourque's works with words. Try yourself, try to bring these distant images to mind; now try to retain them. They remain at the limits of interpretation, a lightning flash of joyous signification.

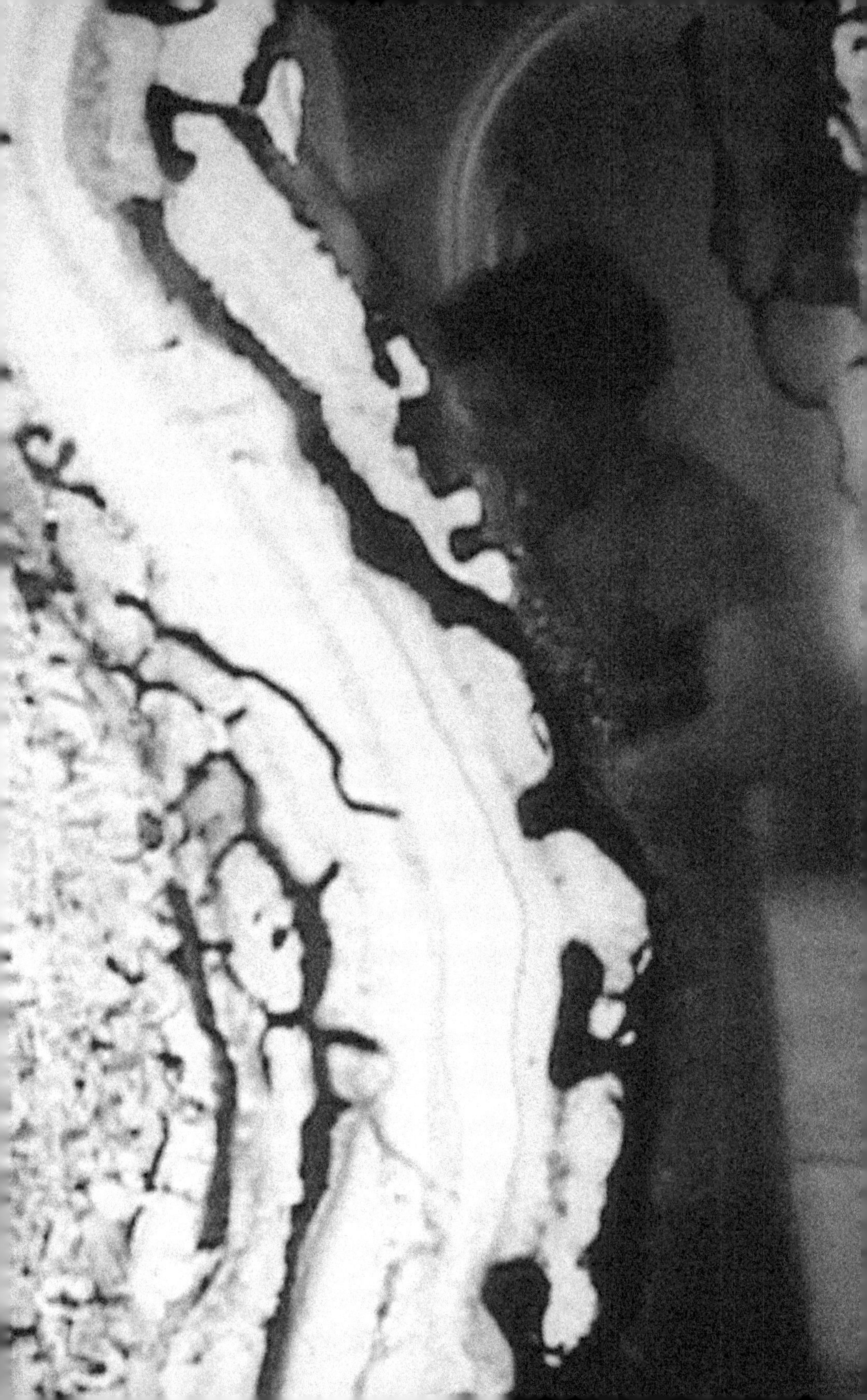

Palimpsests/Pentimenti

On Louise Bourque's a little prayer (H-E-L-P) and Remains

José Sarmiento-Hinojosa

> ... pondering the elusive meaning of what we constantly search for, meaning, attempting to unravel the mocking, enigmatic cryptography of dreams, love, passion, ghosts, murder, madness, trying to calm the tempest within our bodies, minds, and souls; the ebb and flow of disintegration of the self and its reconstitution ...
>
> Peter Whitehead, *Terrorism Considered as One of the Fine Arts*

Louise Bourque's hand-processing of footage burrows under the emulsion to find a hidden truth. It is not a universal truth, nor the inescapable truth of existence and death. It is a personal one that is etched beneath the layers of meaning, of material discourse, which turns tangible in several unveilings; the decoding of permanent trauma, fear, and imminent danger. In the closed compartments of the dark box that is experimental cinema—where everything is alive and dead, pulsating constantly between two immanent realms of existence—the intervention of found footage solves this Schrödinger equation over and over, working in strata, writing over or erasing, like a palimpsest.

Escape, memory, release: to scratch the material as an archaeological impulse, to find certainty among the intricate geography of the *mind* over the *material*, or to let time—the intrinsically natural chemical process of time—to act as an agent on it, still bearing visible traces of its earlier form, like a pentimento. The impending appearance of danger, the image of the mother as persistent *hauntology*; all of these documents on Bourque's psyche appear in different configurations, permeating all of her work, but particularly in two films from

2011, *a little prayer (H-E-L-P)* and *Remains.*[1]

Harry Houdini's ghost appears as an allegory in *a little prayer*. His image is exposed in high contrast, its phantasmagoric presence enhanced by the pulsating light emanating through the projector, searching for a state of transcendence, a scratched surface whose scars we only see for a moment, as if seeking passage to the subconscious mind. These images, the images of danger, of fear, appear to the naked eye as instants, gravity pulling Houdini's body to the void, a nervous twitch that accentuates the imminent. "View in total darkness to appreciate full flicker effect."[2]

This flicker effect induces a state of trance and a violent reaction, a fight-or-flight response that can be traced back to impulses of anxiety and terror. As Houdini is strapped to a wheel, or falling constantly, the passage of these instances, the scarring of the celluloid is the mimesis of a primal idea of threat. As a mimetic instrument, Bourque's film works in layers, accentuating the effect of this filmic palimpsest to get closer to its final instance: "to evoke the violence of a tortured soul in search of escape."[3]

Through treating archival memory as a substitute for personal memory and mental trauma, the author is imprinting their own impulses on the original material. As such, Bourque's personal experience is etched onto the scenes of Houdini's own passage through danger, amplified by abstraction and by the acceleration of the shutter effect. It is a haunting, spiritual, and liberating instance of filmmaking, a cathartic exercise through the recreation of spiritual strain. The complex soundscape creates an eerie atmosphere, where the sound of menacing wind, falling water, and the cracking of a whip further link the original footage to the author's personal struggle.

Revisiting the words of Dante at the beginning of the film—"O sun which clears all mists from troubled sight, / such joy attends your rising that I feel / as grateful to the dark as to the light"—the image of a tortured soul graced by illumination acknowledges both the temporal feebleness of the mind and spirit, and the experience of cathartic recovery. *a little prayer (H-E-L-P)* is particularly powerful as a ritual of liberation through the decoding of the material presence of mental and spiritual strain, a stroboscopic instrument of healing, and an exorcism of sorts.

One of the stronger elements of Bourque's work is the physical presence of synaptic manifestation through the materiality of film. In its early stages, it manifested itself through spoken word, veiled faces, and the ghostly images of her mother's presence (*Just Words*, 1991). Her own image became ghost-like in her self-portrait films, *Self Portrait Post Mortem* (2002) and *Auto Portrait / Self Portrait Post Partum* (2013). *Remains* is somewhere in the middle of this journey—the author's passage through personal, inner turmoil.

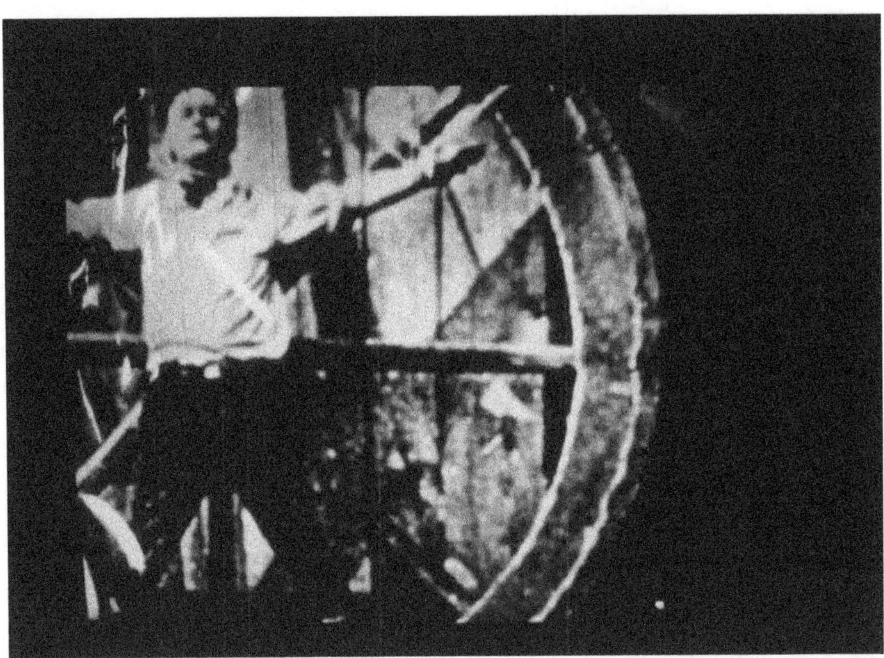

Whatever is left of the image of the mother in *Remains* has survived the excruciating process of time. For Bourque, the pivotal experiences and the people in our lives follow us past our own existence and into the ether—memories that never let go. The de-layering of filmstrips through erosion over time works as an analogy of post-traumatic negation, but again, recalls the strenuous effort Bourque goes through to let go of trauma, delivering herself to the liberating energies of art, even if her own emotional patterns bleed through in the exercise. Watching this litany go through what looks like an archaeological survey of strata, or the slow layering of brain images in a CT scan (there's a metaphor hidden somewhere between images of rock being stripped to its core and CT images surveying the human brain), brings us back again into the realm of spiritual presence as a manifestation in film.

These ideas, used again in the self-portrait films, denote the interest of materiality and decomposition. These *filmic pentimenti* revealed through the process of deterioration present an abstract configuration of the image where brief lapses of visual elements peek through the gaps. The leakage of the image is accompanied by what appears as an echoey chant and a childhood whistle, which slowly mutates into a muffled wailing, the dripping of voices that join a ritual chant in constant crescendo, until the appearance of the mother's figure and the presence of the filmstrip itself, the container of this phantasmagoria.

"The mocking, enigmatic cryptography of dreams," the dealings of methods of enlightenment, of personal discovery, of mitigation of hurt, of personal ritual against the haunting, form the backbone behind the strategies of Bourque's work throughout her filmography. This method opens up a space of discussion for the personal, a method of filmmaking akin to a séance, or a psychoanalytic session, a process in which the mind hunts for a prey that doesn't seem to be there, but whose presence is constant and at times becomes the hunter; a constant ballet of synapses, an endurance session of liberation. Palimpsests and pentimenti act as a melting pot of information to be decoded/analyzed/apprehended/experimented with, as a ritual initiation for the personal battles of the spirit, as guidance documents or codices for our own personal trauma.

NOTES

1. These configurations are also paramount in both *Self Portrait Post Mortem* and *Auto Portrait / Self Portrait Post Partum*, which, alongside *Remains*, complete a trilogy of sorts.
2. "*a little prayer (H-E-L-P)*," Canadian Filmmakers Distribution Centre (CFMDC), catalogue entry, <https://www.cfmdc.org/film/3689>.
3. Ibid.

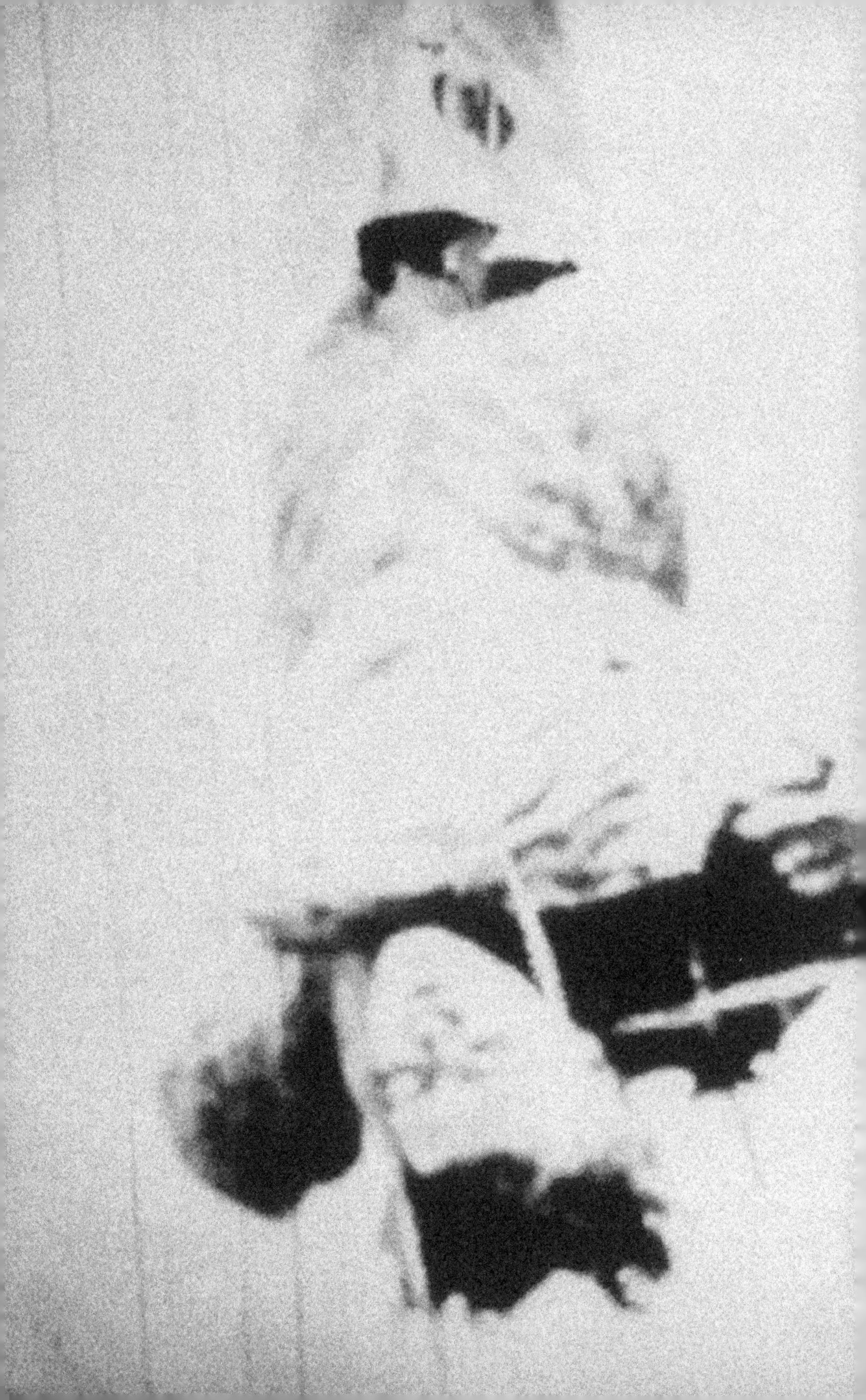

Beyond the Fringe: Louise Bourque

Larissa Fan

Originally published in *Take One*, Issue 48 (December 2004 / March 2005): 54.

A home with its windows scratched out; buildings collapsing; houses on fire; a street submerged in flood water; images of a family that slide in and out of focus are scratched, degraded and covered in cracks and fissures—in Louise Bourque's films, the world is an uncertain place and home is most definitely not a safe haven. A Quebec filmmaker who has been working since the 1980s, Bourque studied at Concordia University in Montreal and at the School of the Art Institute of Chicago and now works and teaches in the U.S. at Emerson College in Boston and the School of the Museum of Fine Arts. Her films have screened at festivals around the world, including the Rotterdam International Film Festival, Osnabrück European Media Arts Festival, TIFF and Switzerland's Viper Festival.

I first saw *Going Back Home* (35 mm, 2 × 30 seconds, 2000) three years ago at Toronto's Images Festival, and in 30 seconds (played twice so that you don't miss it) it neatly encapsulates the concern with home that infuses almost all of her work. Scratchy, hand-processed and bathed in shades of fiery oranges and yellows, *Going Back Home* consists of scenes of destruction culled from found footage—of buildings falling and collapsing, engulfed in fire or surrounded by floods. Ironically accompanied by the sound of a tinkly music box tune, it warns that you are on shaky footing in this world and had better not count on home as a refuge.

Throughout Bourque's body of work, this concern with the idea of home borders on obsession, like a dark memory that reasserts itself over and over again, and won't release either her or the audience. In *Fissures* (16 mm, 2.5 minutes, 1999), home-movie footage is contact printed then hand-processed

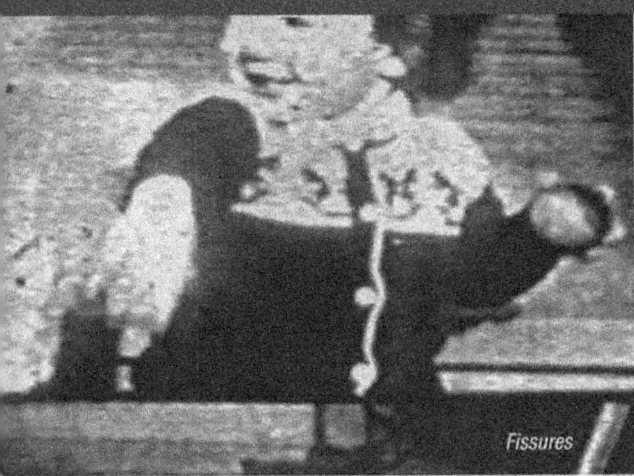
Fissures

By Larissa Fan

BEYOND THE FRINGE

Louise Bourque

A home with its windows scratched out; buildings collapsing; houses on fire; a street submerged in flood water; images of a family that slide in and out of focus are scratched, degraded and covered in cracks and fissures—in Louise Bourque's films, the world is an uncertain place and home is most definitely not a safe haven. A Quebec filmmaker who has been working since the 1980s, Bourque studied at Concordia University in Montreal and at the School of the Art Institute of Chicago and now works and teaches in the U.S. at Emerson College in Boston and the School of the Museum of Fine Arts. Her films have screened at festivals around the world, including the Rotterdam International Film Festival, Osnabrück European Media Arts Festival, TIFF and Switzerland's Viper Festival.

I first saw *Going Back Home* (35 mm, 2 x 30 seconds, 2000) three years ago at Toronto's Images Festival, and in 30 seconds (played twice so that you don't miss it) it neatly encapsulates the concern with home that infuses almost all of her work. Scratchy, hand-processed and bathed in shades of fiery oranges and yellows, *Going Back Home* consists of scenes of destruction culled from found footage—of buildings falling and collapsing, engulfed in fire or surrounded by floods. Ironically accompanied by the sound of a tinkly music box tune, it warns that you are on shaky footing in this world and had better not count on home as a refuge.

Throughout Bourque's body of work, this concern with the idea of home borders on obsession, like a dark memory that reasserts itself over and over again, and won't release either her or the audience. In *Fissures* (16 mm, 2.5 minutes, 1999), home-movie footage is contact printed then hand-processed and toned so that the images are warped and fractured, emerging from and disappearing into passages of darkness. Together with the pulsing, repetitive soundtrack, *Fissures* creates a strong feeling of struggle and dread that is almost unbearable for the film's short two-and-a-half minutes.

Imprint (16 mm, 14 minutes, 1997) visits similar territory, this time focusing on home movie images of her family house that are relentlessly examined and manipulated. Hand-processed, solarized, toned, bleached, scratched and cut up, she treats the footage, as Fred Camper, noted American critic of the avant-garde, describes it, "as if attacking the place." The house is a large and ominous presence, its windows often scratched out so that it appears alternately as if it is on fire or as a place of dark foreboding. The family gathers in front of the house, the mother in her wasp-waisted dress a picture of 1950s domesticity as she repeatedly leads a child down the walk. The scratchy soundtrack of a record skipping reinforces the obsessive quality of the imagery. *Imprint* is the embodiment of an inescapable memory; a childhood experience imprinted on the adult.

An earlier work, *The People in the House* (16 mm, 22 minutes, 1994), is an experimental narrative that examines the dynamics of a 1950s Catholic household in crisis. Filmed in "a highly-stylized and surreal style, the drama is played out within the confines of the house, its four walls becoming increasingly oppressive as the family members struggle to cope. The film breaks down idealized visions of family and religion, for in this house, they offer not consolation but despair.

Bourque's most recent film, *Jours en fleurs* (35 mm, 4.5 minutes, 2003), is quite possibly the first of her works that does not deal with family and memory. It's a beautiful work of abstract colour and texture, of contrasting dark and light. Here Bourque plays with the phrase *jours en fleurs*, which in Quebec refers to a woman's menstrual cycle. A truly process-based work, footage of flowers was soaked in menstrual blood for several months, which degraded the image and resulted in crystalline patterns and colours of gold, emerald, magenta and black. At a solo show at Cinematheque Ontario earlier in 2004, Bourque said "Disintegration is also transformation." Perhaps *Jours en fleurs* signals a new chapter for the artist, one in which despair has been transformed into something like hope.

Larissa Fan is the finmaker liaison at the Canadian Filmmakers Distribution Centre and a regular contributor to Take One.

Background image *Going Back Home*

and toned so that the images are warped and fractured, emerging from and disappearing into passages of darkness. Together with the pulsing, repetitive soundtrack, *Fissures* creates a strong feeling of struggle and dread that is almost unbearable for the film's short two and a half minutes.

Imprint (16 mm, 14 minutes, 1997) visits similar territory, this time focusing on home-movie images of her family house that are relentlessly examined and manipulated. Hand-processed, solarized, toned, bleached, scratched and cut up, she treats the footage, as Fred Camper, noted American critic of the avant-garde, describes it, "as if attacking the place." The house is a large and ominous presence, its windows often scratched out so that it appears alternately as if it is on fire or as a place of dark foreboding. The family gathers in front of the house, the mother in her wasp-waisted dress a picture of 1950s domesticity as she repeatedly leads a child down the walk. The scratchy soundtrack of a record skipping reinforces the obsessive quality of the imagery. *Imprint* is the embodiment of an inescapable memory; a childhood experience imprinted on the adult.

An earlier work, *The People in the House* (16 mm, 22 minutes, 1994), is an experimental narrative that examines the dynamics of a 1950s Catholic household in crisis. Filmed in a highly-stylized and surreal style, the drama is played out within the confines of the house, its four walls becoming increasingly oppressive as the family members struggle to cope. The film breaks down idealized visions of family and religion, for in this house, they offer not consolation but despair.

Bourque's most recent film, *Jours en fleurs* (35 mm, 4.5 minutes, 2003), is quite possibly the first of her works that does not deal with family and memory. It's a beautiful work of abstract colour and texture, of contrasting dark and light. Here Bourque plays with the phrase *jours en fleurs*, which in Acadia refers to a woman's menstrual cycle. A truly process-based work, footage of flowers was soaked in menstrual blood for several months, which degraded the image and resulted in crystalline patterns and colours of gold, emerald, magenta and black. At a solo show at Cinematheque Ontario earlier in 2004, Bourque said "Disintegration is also transformation." Perhaps *Jours en fleurs* signals a new chapter for the artist, one in which despair has been transformed into something like hope.

PROP SHEETS for "The People In The House" by Louise Bourque

contact: DEBORAH STRATMAN, art director 312/73V-APOR
MARIA RAMIREZ, production manager 312/274-0960

Please let myself or maria know when/if you find items so we can okay them and make sure it hasn't already been found. THANKS. – deborah s.

KEEP IN MIND: PERIOD IS CIRCA 50's – 60's ... NOTHING POST 1969 PLEASE

★★★ BIG THINGS

1 Small formica Kitchen table
2 matching kitchen chairs
1 Large dining room table
5 Dining room chairs
1 Narrow shelves (approx 2' x 5')

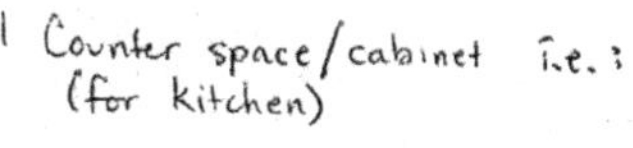

1 Counter space/cabinet i.e.:
(for kitchen)

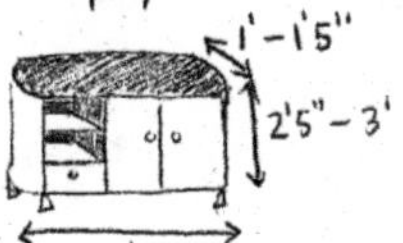

5 or 6 small tables (end tables, bed tables)
1 long coffee table
1 medicine cabinet
1 long carpet strip (approx 2' x 20') for stairway

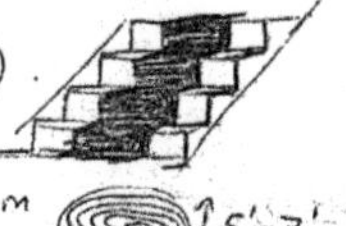

1 large floor rug for dining room

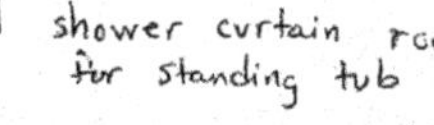

1 shower curtain rod for standing tub

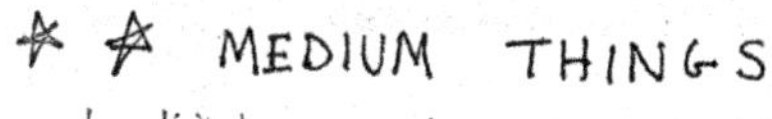

★★ MEDIUM THINGS

1 Kitchen garbage can w/ lid

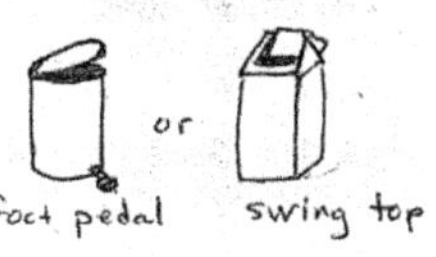

1 small trash can

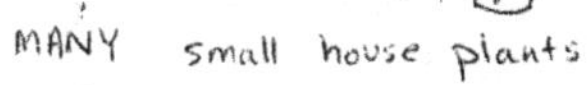

MANY small house plants
2 large plants i.e. RUBBER TREES
1 white rag rug (approx. 2' x 5')

continued →

** MEDIUM THINGS CONT. 2

white sheets for queen bed
2 pillows, white pillow cases
nice large table cloth for dining room table
bright bathmat
1 clothes hamper →
2 bright towels (diff. colors)
1 brightly flowered shower curtain
1 large towel rack (or 2 small)
Lots of Picture Frames ... all sizes
Wall paintings for rooms i.e. landscapes
7 or more white plates
5 sets of silverware
4 coffee cups
PLUS MANY NICE GLASSES, STEMWARE, DISHES etc. to fill a BUFFETT in Dining Room
Old 50's + 60's magazines
1 Magazine rack

* SMALL THINGS

1 Kitchen clock
refrigerator magnets →

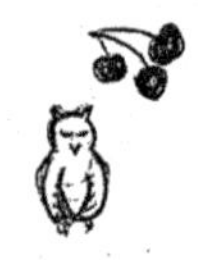

cream + sugar holders
farina + Quaker oatmeal boxes
LOTS of mason jars - any size
Food tins / tea tins
1 Bread box
Spices + spice rack
flour + sugar tins
nice coaster set
1 bright wash cloth
1 shower cap
1 hot roller set →

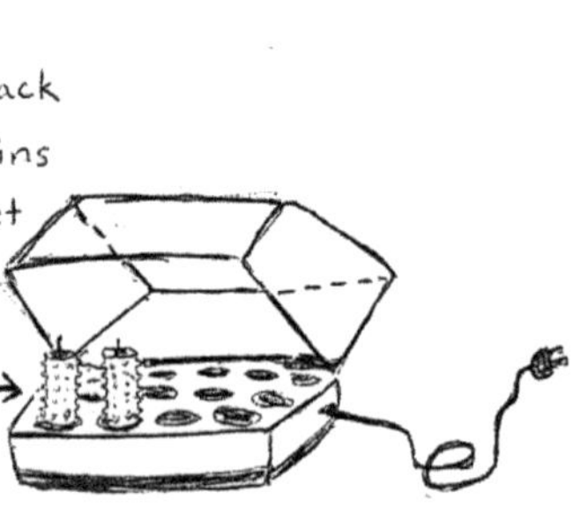

continued →

SMALL THINGS CONT. 3

1 nice hair brush + comb
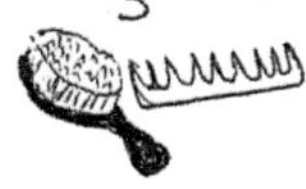
perfume bottles
1 jewelry box
wedding pics (wall size + small)
3 serving dishes
2-3 hot plates
LOTS of doilies or small lace cloths
(to put under lamps, small flower pots etc.)
6-10 Head + arm rest covers for Sofa + CHAIRS
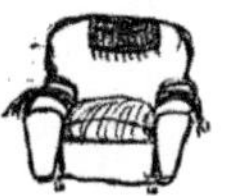

(CATHOLIC) RELIGIOUS ITEMS : NOT TACKY!

4 nice crucifixes (3 large, 1 small)
3 religious pictures / paintings
3 wooden rosaries
1 Holy water container (glass, crystal)
4 tall candle stands (3'-4' tall) →
flowered / religious condolence cards
1 religious calander

LIGHTS

2 long neon bulbs (2'- 3' long)
1 overhead circular neon bulb
1 chandelier w/ dimmer switch
5 table lamps
4 wall sconces → or
3 standing lamps
2 hanging lamps →

PLUS 6-10 colored bulbs
6-10 regular white bulbs
colored lamp shades

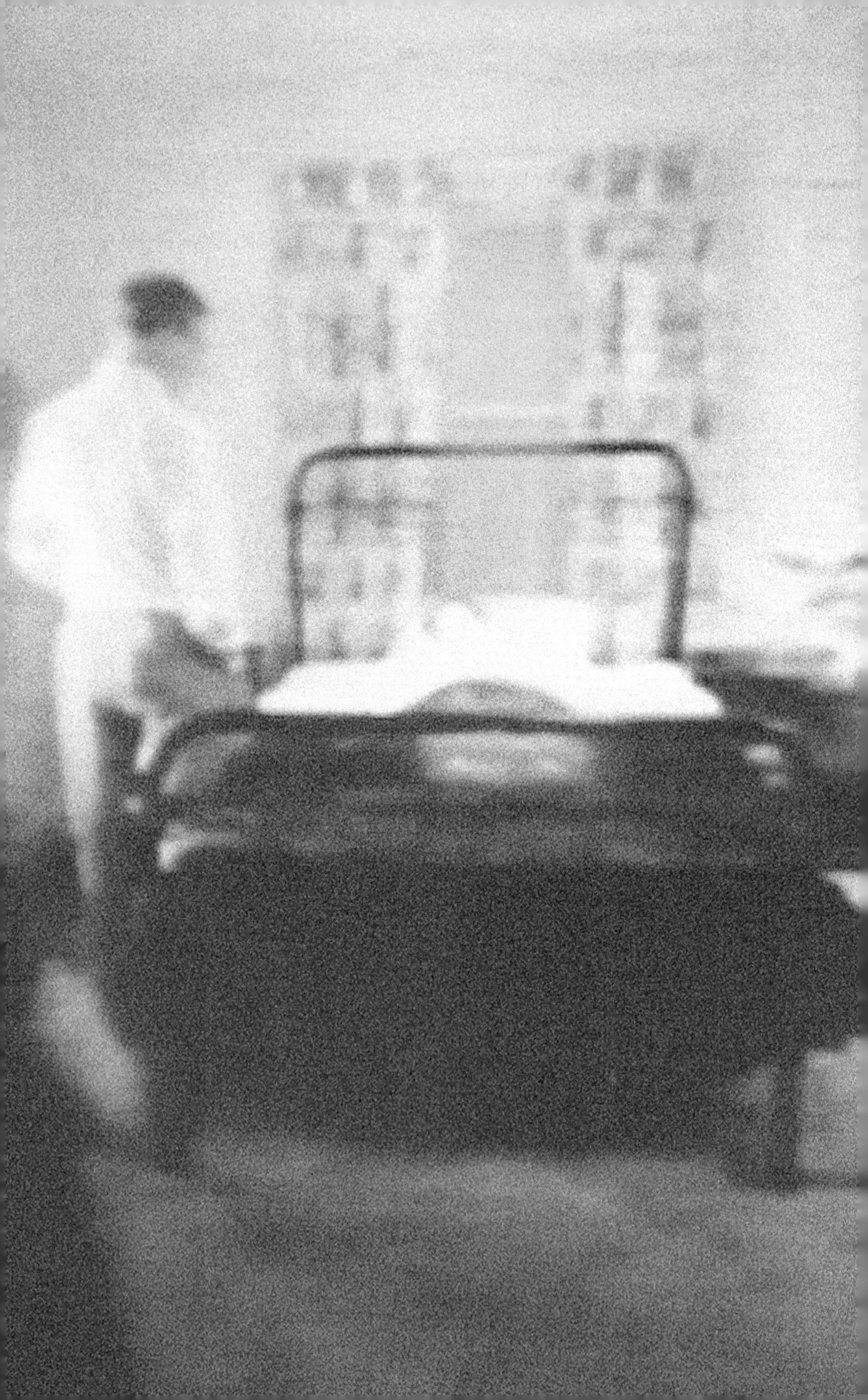

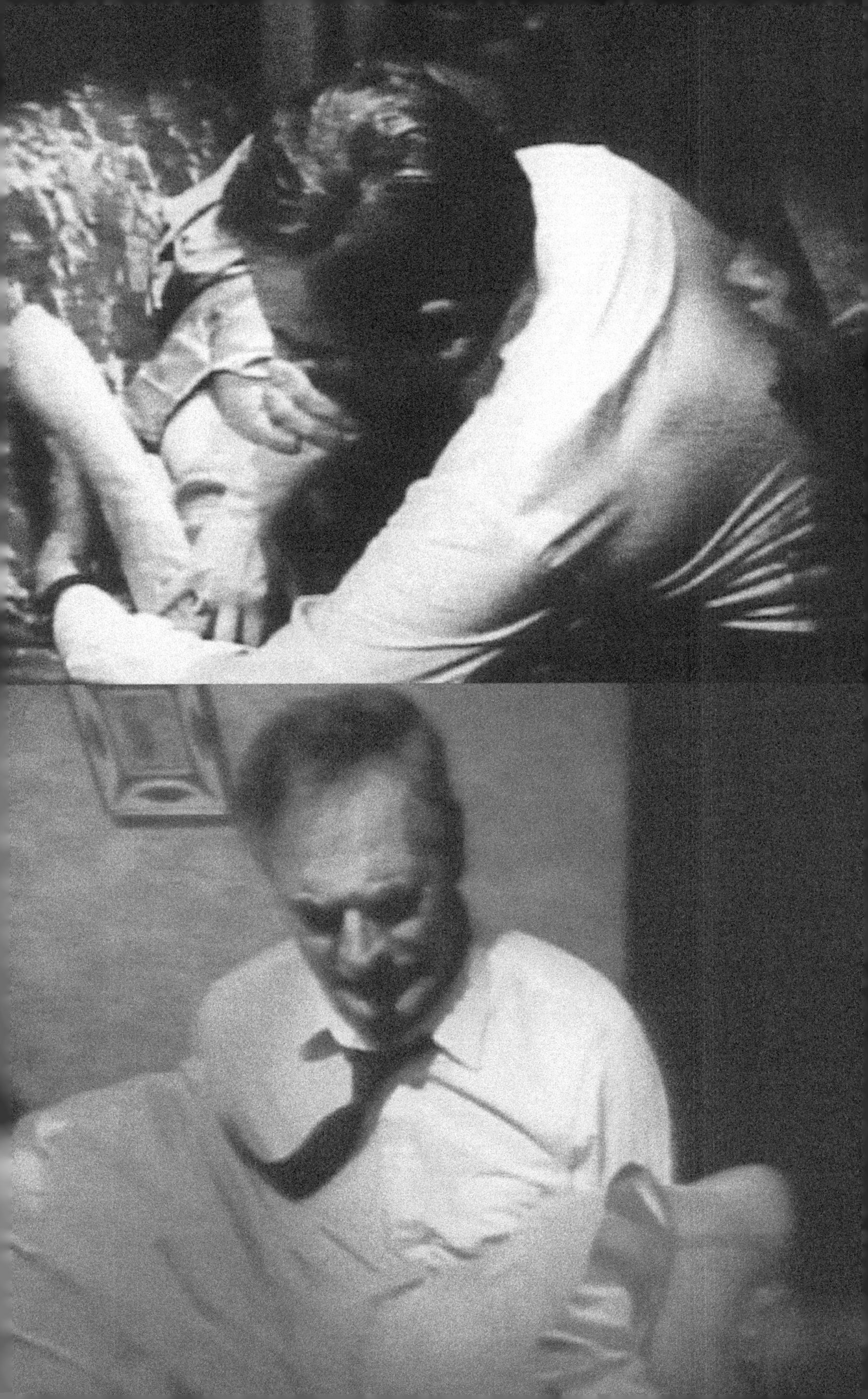

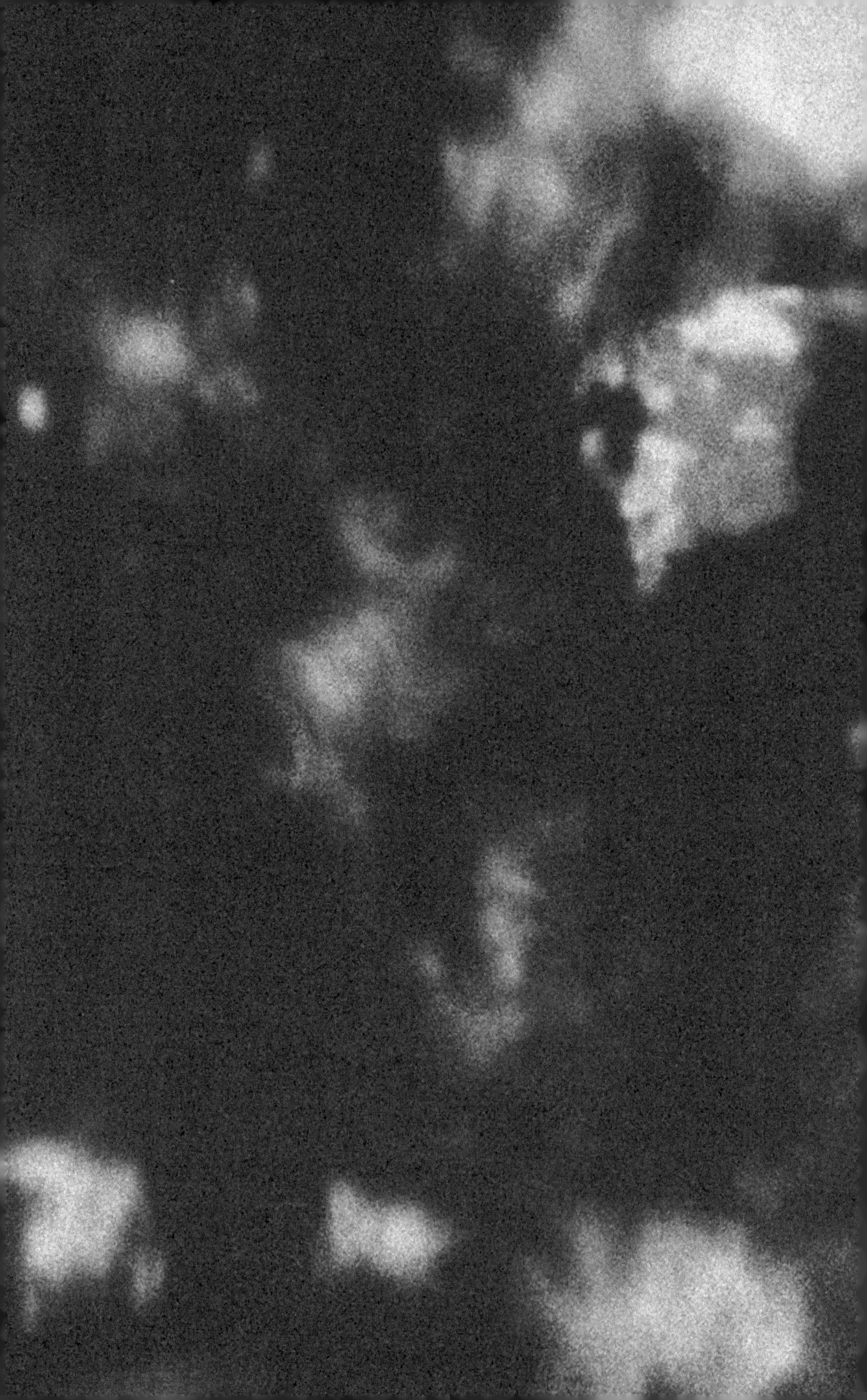

The Scene of the Crime

Gothic Poetics in L'éclat du mal / The Bleeding Heart of It

Scott Birdwise

Since the early 1990s, the fragmented or explosive house, and an attendant (sometimes only implied) subjectivity haunted by its images, has been a visual and thematic thread running throughout Louise Bourque's practice as a filmmaker. "Bourque's treatment of the house," as Michael Sicinski once observed, "as a site of drama, trauma, and a fragmentary struggle waged both on the personal (female) body and the social body, places her work in a unique position with respect to experimental film history in Canada."[1] While the emotional and psychological imagery in her films recalls the personal and lyrical dreamscapes of poetic filmmakers like Maya Deren and Stan Brakhage, her formal repetitions and loops intersect with the structuralist and medium-specific practices of artists like Michael Snow and David Rimmer. Bourque's approach is also redolent of feminist forebears like Joyce Wieland, particularly in the ways her process-oriented, handcrafted materialism engages with distinctive iconographic markers and currents, crossing thresholds between the national and the bodily, the public and the familial. Furthermore, in returning to and reusing home-movie footage—sometimes combined with voiceover (which can itself be a kind of found object)—her work also falls among both the decayed found-footage manipulations of artists like Bill Morrison and the diaristic assemblages of filmmakers like Philip Hoffman. When considered against the background of these various traditions of experimental film, the significance of Bourque's emphasis on the uncanny image-matter of the house becomes clearer.

In works ranging from *Just Words* (1991), *The People in the House* (1994), and *Imprint* (1997), through *Fissures* (1999), *L'éclat du mal / The Bleeding Heart*

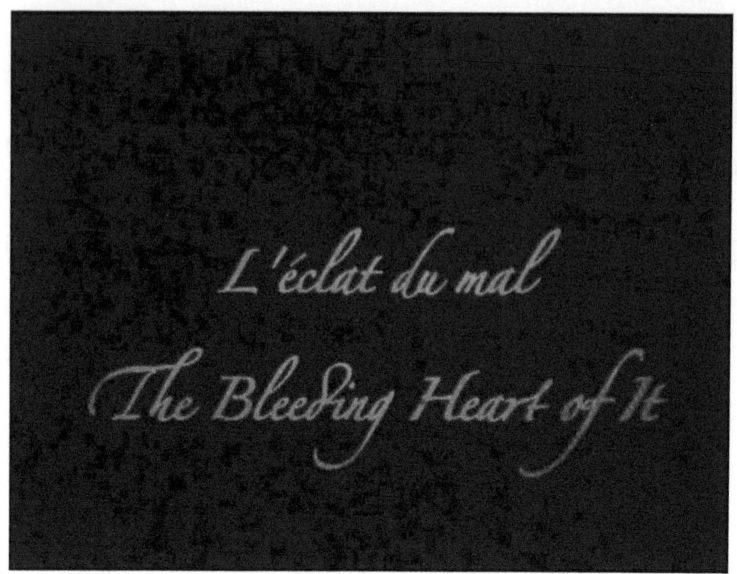

Figure 1

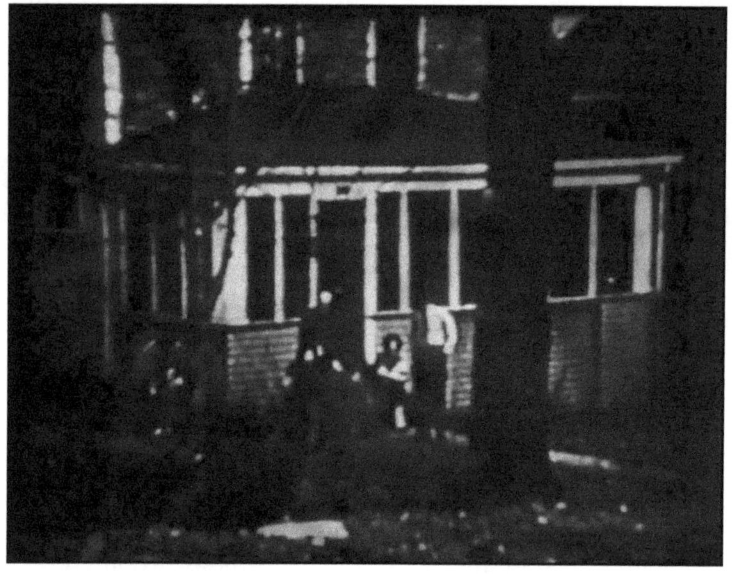

Figure 2

of It (2005) and beyond, Bourque, as Sicinski notes, "has moved through numerous strands of experimental film and video history, grounded herself in practices and traditions that once seemed incompatible, and is now pointing the way to something new."[2] Focusing on her film *L'éclat du mal*, I consider some of the ways Bourque's work illustrates how a feminist understanding of the intersection of the personal and the political with a Gothic vision of the "otherness" of home can reframe experimental film practice and image creation more generally.[3] Bringing together rigorous attention to the material properties of the medium with a critical and poetic understanding of their social and psychological effects, her films offer important insights into the relationship between memory, gender, and technical-representational media.[4] Through a Gothic reimagining of society's contradictions, no longer simply contained in homely structures or repressed in the systems of identification naturalized in home movies, Bourque participates in a feminist questioning of what count as significant social and historical phenomena, of what can be spoken about and who has the authority to speak of it. The eerie experience of home and the archetypal family drama that *L'éclat du mal* materially addresses, as if buried inside the unconscious of film, thus contribute to the imaginative and aesthetic conditions for transforming something—violence, abuse, repression, and so on—that has otherwise been limited to personal trauma in the domestic sphere into a shared, and thus social and political, experience.

"In my dream there's a war going on"

The first thing one encounters in *L'éclat du mal / The Bleeding Heart of It* is the haunting score, which begins as an unnerving drone over a black screen. The title soon announces itself in two lines of cursive handwriting—one in French, the other English. Its illuminated text burns red and orange for a few seconds before fading out and returning to the black (see Figure 1). Already the film unfolds as a theatre of fleeting apparitions, in which things shimmer and shift only to rapidly dissolve and disappear entirely. It is fitting, then, that the first half of the film's title, which can be translated as *The Radiance of Evil*, recalls Charles Baudelaire's mid-nineteenth-century menagerie of metamorphic visions, *Les Fleurs du mal* (*The Flowers of Evil*, 1857). Notwithstanding the profound differences between the two artists, both titles conjure images of fevered luminescence, a sickness that flowers—an illness-inducing force within the mortal world of appearance. Suggesting a process at once animating and draining, the English half of the film's title speaks to a similar malady. While *The Bleeding Heart of It* possesses overtones of Christian symbolism that resound with Bourque's Acadian-Québecois-Catholic origins, the bleeding heart can be further elucidated by remembering that it is also a type of flower symbolic of compassion and unconditional love, but is also highly toxic if eaten or even touched.

This duality is useful to bear in mind when considering Bourque's work upon the material of images, such as those which eventually emerge from the darkness following the opening title of the film: vintage home-movie footage of the family household (see Figure 2). Images of the front (and only the front) of the filmmaker's childhood home violently mutate and metamorphose into abstract shapes recalling bruises and dirt, blood and fire (see Figures 3 and 4). At the same time, a tape-recorded female voice—the filmmaker's own—recalls her childhood dreams. For example: "In my dream there's a war going on. It's Christmastime. I'm running and I'm carrying myself as a child. It's dark in the tunnel and I'm heading towards the light, the daylight." Her words hover over the decayed and chemically treated footage, disjunctively connecting with the images as their own representational qualities and the figures they carry become disfigured beyond recognition (see Figure 5). The voice conjures its own phantasmagoria of images before it too betrays itself as a lifeless artificial object and starts to repeat itself in sentence fragments.[5] The dream diary is thus at once the record of an epistemological inquiry into one's own identity and, in the widening gaps and fissures in the record as it deconstructs, an eerie failure of presence, a ruin.[6]

As exemplified by the use of tape-recorded dreams and images in home movies from a childhood long since passed, the uncanny power of *L'éclat du mal* lies in its working through of developmental structures, desires, and anxieties foundational to our very sense of ourselves. Along these lines, it is relevant to point out that Bourque's filmic corpus is populated by strange de/couplings of bodies and voices, images and words. More specifically, the use of the tape recorder as both an instrument of prosthetic memory and as a thematic device in *L'éclat du mal* recalls *Krapp's Last Tape* (1958) by Samuel Beckett, whose play *Not I* (1972) Bourque adapted for her earlier film *Just Words*. Both of these films engage with the fractured existence of the feminine voice by bringing it into dissociative relation with home-movie footage, the gap producing a sense of the voice as a malfunctioning machine that undermines the agency and memory of the speaker. Thus, when the voice fragments as a material effect of the age of the tape recording, the living subject and the mechanical object seem to exchange places.[7]

A Haunted House

Bourque has described her work as a way of approaching what she calls

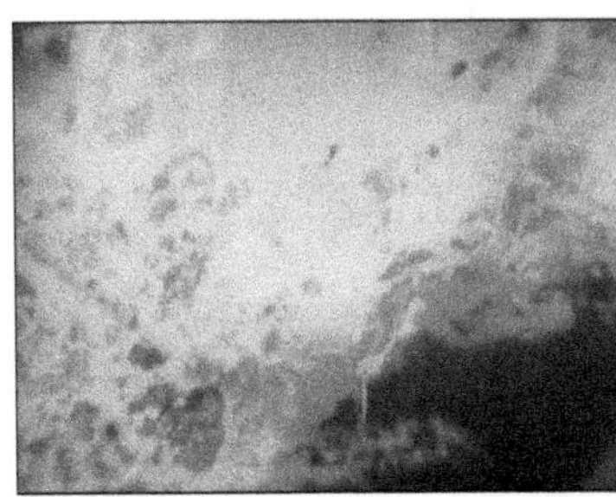

Figure 3

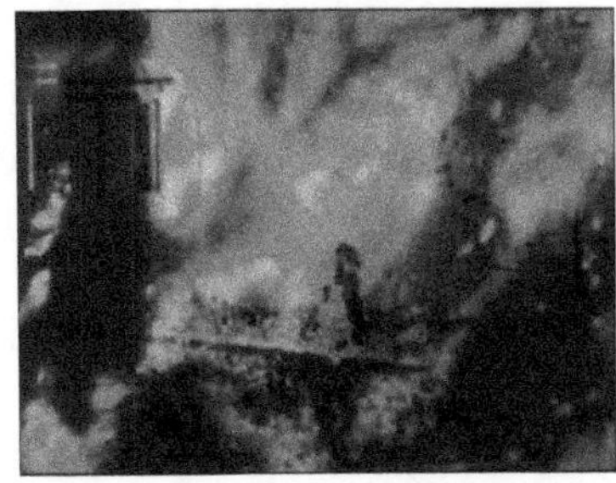

Figure 4

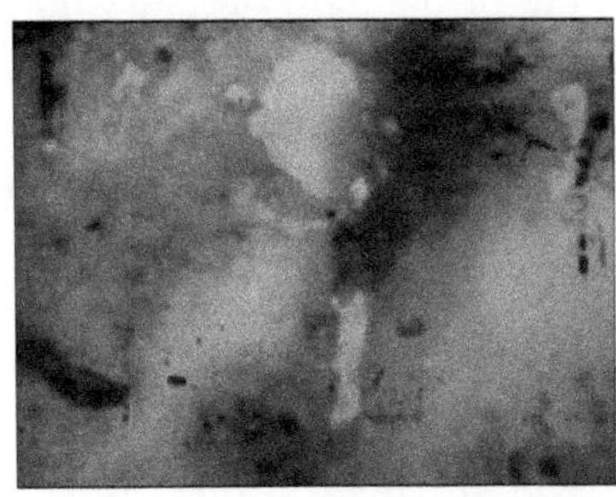

Figure 5

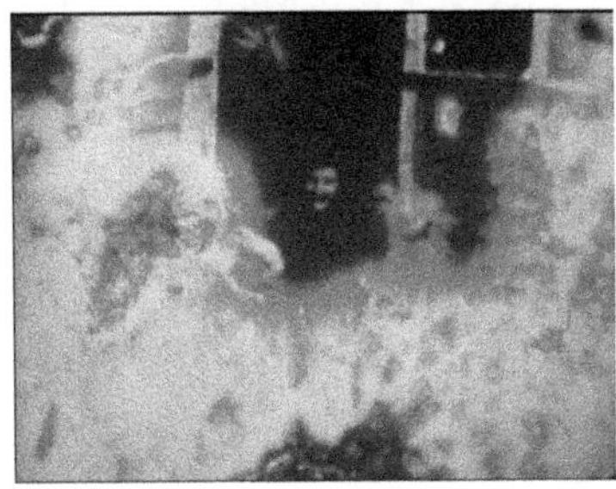

Figure 6

"things we struggle with and that we have a hard time to even begin to put in words."[8] She has also explained that she thinks of her films less in terms of the categories of experimental film and the avant-garde and more in regard to notions of the poetic.[9] In a famous definition of the poem, Paul Valéry succinctly defined it as "a prolonged hesitation between sound and meaning."[10] Valéry's definition also helps neatly capture the sense of suspended meaning in *L'éclat du mal*, certainly in the way the film opens a space between the dream journal (voiceover) and the home movie (image). In playing with the unfolded distances between these two referents, Bourque draws on and develops what I understand as a Gothic poetics—a self-conscious oscillation between composition and decomposition that thematizes the fraught relationship, the productive confusion, between subject and object, meaning and materiality.

More than merely a group of late-eighteenth- and early-nineteenth-century stories about ruined castles, aristocratic villains, deranged monks, and women locked inside towers, the Gothic is a hybrid tradition that offers artists from various periods imaginative means—including symbols, stock scenarios and scenes—for exploring the realms of repressed fantasy and desire, particularly as they play out in periods of social and historical uncertainty.[11] The Gothic deals with the unfinished nature of history, and its basic materials are things that have been considered over and complete, dead and buried, but that linger on in subterranean forms and unconscious traces; it also includes nameless things that suddenly explode from out of the most ordinary objects and places, notably the home. "The Gothic, too," as Kate Ferguson-Ellis writes, "is preoccupied with the home. But it is the failed home that appears on its pages, the place from which some (usually 'fallen' men) are locked out, and others (usually 'innocent' women) are locked in."[12] In Bourque's work, this "failed home" migrates from the page to the screen.

Understanding the house as a Gothic structure and symbol, consider Bourque's explanation of the "It" in the title for *The Bleeding Heart of It*, which indicates something traumatic at the "heart" of the home. "*It* is the House and all it stands for," as Bourque puts it,

> the House and the Family; it is the family dynamic within the house. It is the concept of the Home in our culture and what it is supposed to be, what it is and what it isn't … It has this loaded history going back generations—the Patriarchal Family, all the generations of the *It* at home; and it's the bleeding heart of It, because there's a lot of bloodshed (in metaphorical ways, and also in literal ways)—the house is like a wound.[13]

The image of the house, what Bourque describes metaphorically as both "a wound and a womb," is thus conflicted: repressing as it remembers, the house at once bleeds out and contains the family drama inside it. Like the scene of a crime, then, the house in question invokes off-screen activity, at once marking the place of systemic patriarchal power and obscuring it, hiding its secrets behind a homely edifice.[14] For this reason, Bourque repeatedly, perhaps compulsively, certainly obsessively, returns to the synecdoche of the house, its strange familiarity a problem of visibility connected to a problem of words, a question of symptoms and of knowledge imprinted upon and refused by the image. And so this return to "It" is at once an archaeological dig into the material and nonorganic signifiers of film, a phenomenological return to the past through a damaged family record, and a paranormal investigation into the image of the Gothic house in its disturbing manifestations—a flickering dream-symbol, an eerie apparition of "home."

The Gothic and feminist poetics of *L'éclat du mal* can be further elucidated when brought into the context of Canadian visual art. Gaile McGregor, for instance, has written about Canadian art in terms of a thematics of "boundary management," a dialectical tension between interior and exterior space constitutive of "the construction of place."[15] Representations of house and home, for example, respond to settler-colonial anxieties surrounding what McGregor refers to as "the integrity and meaning of these enclosures." Pattern-making and layering in the image, she further explains, can be interpreted as civilization's defence mechanism against what it perceives as the threat of the outside to its established hierarchies of gender, race, class, and so on. Policing the boundaries between inside and outside, these techniques are used to maintain distinctions between social and domestic space, collective and singular experience. From this perspective, Bourque's Gothic intervention in *L'éclat du mal* draws from images (home movies) that privilege the house as the site of security in order to materially decompose identification with its structuring presence and the attendant desire for the imaginary plenitude of "place." By evoking the uncanny *return* of what lies *within* it, Bourque reveals how the house itself, as a complex of material and meaning, is a source of anxiety and violence (see Figure 6). It is as if there were no choice, the film seems to fatally suggest, but for the house to collapse under the weight of its own destructive and decaying mythology.

NOTES

1. Michael Sicinski, "Impossible Trips Back Home: The Films of Louise Bourque," *Images Festival Catalogue* (Toronto: Images Festival, 2009), 42.
2. Ibid., 43.
3. Ejla Kovačević has identified a Gothic strain in *L'éclat du mal*, writing: "[Bourque's] highly sensual and elegant approach to the horrific is that key, additional layer that gives her films a certain ethereal aura, one that echoes the seductive beauty of 19th century gothic romanticism." Ejla Kovačević, "Women's Day: The War is Never Over—Transcendental Darklands of Lydia Lunch and Louise Bourque," *Ultra Dogme* (March 8, 2020), <https://ultradogme.com/2020/03/08/lydialouise/>
4. As Vicky Chainey Gagnon succinctly puts it, "Bourque's work evokes the heritage of second-wave feminism with its handcrafted quality and political explorations of the personal." Vicky Chainey Gagnon, "Behind These Walls: Contemporary Canadian Experimental Short Films," curatorial essay for film program shown in Sherbrooke in 2009. Available online at: <http://cbattle.com/wp-content/uploads/2015/01/Curatorial_essay_Espace_IM_média.pdf>.
5. Bourque explains the voiceover in an interview: "The voiceover is recounting actual dreams of mine taken from an audio dream journal I kept between 1990 and 1992. The narration starts off sort of calm; I think the first line in the voiceover, 'In my dream ...' is basically announcing, 'I'm going to tell you something. I'm going to tell you my dream.' But soon after, the deconstruction starts happening, the fragmentation. Things start falling apart, like 'all of the houses are falling apart,' as it later said in the film's narration." Micah J. Malone, "A Conversation with Louise Bourque," *Big Red & Shiny* (March 19, 2006), <https://bigredandshiny.org/4739/a-conversa-tion-with-louise-bourque/>.
6. As Mark Fisher writes, the eerie can be understood in terms of a *failure of absence* and/or a *failure of presence*: "The sensation of the eerie occurs either when there is something present where there should be nothing, or there is nothing present when there should be something." See Mark Fisher, *The Weird and the Eerie* (London: Repeater Books, 2016), 61.
7. This demonstrates how the present is paradoxically informed and interrupted by the coexistence of the object of inscription (record) that "mortally" decays and fragments (but is also for this reason animated), on the one hand, and the embalmed voice from the past whose once active, living presence now only remains as a "dead" object of playback, on the other.
8. Bourque in Malone, "A Conversation with Louise Bourque."
9. As Bourque puts it, "'Avant-garde' tends to be associated with the past, making the term lose its innovative connotation, while 'experimental' seems to imply an unfinished quality to the work." Bourque quoted in April Gardner, "Poetry in Motion," *NewEnglandFilm* (July 1, 2004), <https://newenglandfilm.com/ magazine/2004/07/poetry-in-motion>.
10. Paul Valéry, "Rhumbs," in *Œuvres II*, ed. Jean Hytier (Paris: Gallimard, 1960), 637. My translation.

11. Frederick S. Frank, for example, argues that the Gothic is characterized by "an attitude of discontent reflecting the subconscious fears and desires of an age grown too fond of reason and beginning to question its own empirical assumptions." Frederick S. Frank, "That Long Labyrinth of Darkness: *The Castle of Otranto*," in Horace Walpole, *The Castle of Otranto* and *The Mysterious Mother*, ed. Frederick S. Frank (Peterborough: Broadview Press, 2003), 13.
12. Kate Ferguson-Ellis, *The Contested Castle: Gothic Novels and the Subversion of Domestic Ideology* (Illinois: University of Illinois Press, 1989), ix. See also: Anne Williams, *Arts of Darkness: A Poetics of Gothic* (Chicago and London: University of Chicago Press, 1995): "the Gothic tradition as a whole, expresses the dangerous, the awe-full power of the 'female.' All Gothic trappings—ruins, graves, dark enclosures, madness, even the sublime—signify the presence of this 'other'" (xi).
13. Bourque in Malone, "A Conversation with Louise Bourque." Emphasis in original.
14. As Bourque has described the film: "The house that bursts; the scene of the crime; the nucleus. A universe collapses on itself: all hell breaks loose." See "*L'éclat du mal / The Bleeding Heart of It*," Canadian Filmmakers Distribution Centre (CFMDC), catalogue entry, <https://www.cfmdc.org/film/2826>.
15. Gaile McGregor, "A Case Study in the Construction of Place: Boundary Management as Theme and Strategy in Canadian Art and Life," *InVisible Culture: An Electronic Journal for Visual Culture* 5 "Visual Culture and National Identity" (2003), <https://www.rochester.edu/in_visible_culture/Issue_5/McGregor/McGregor.html>.

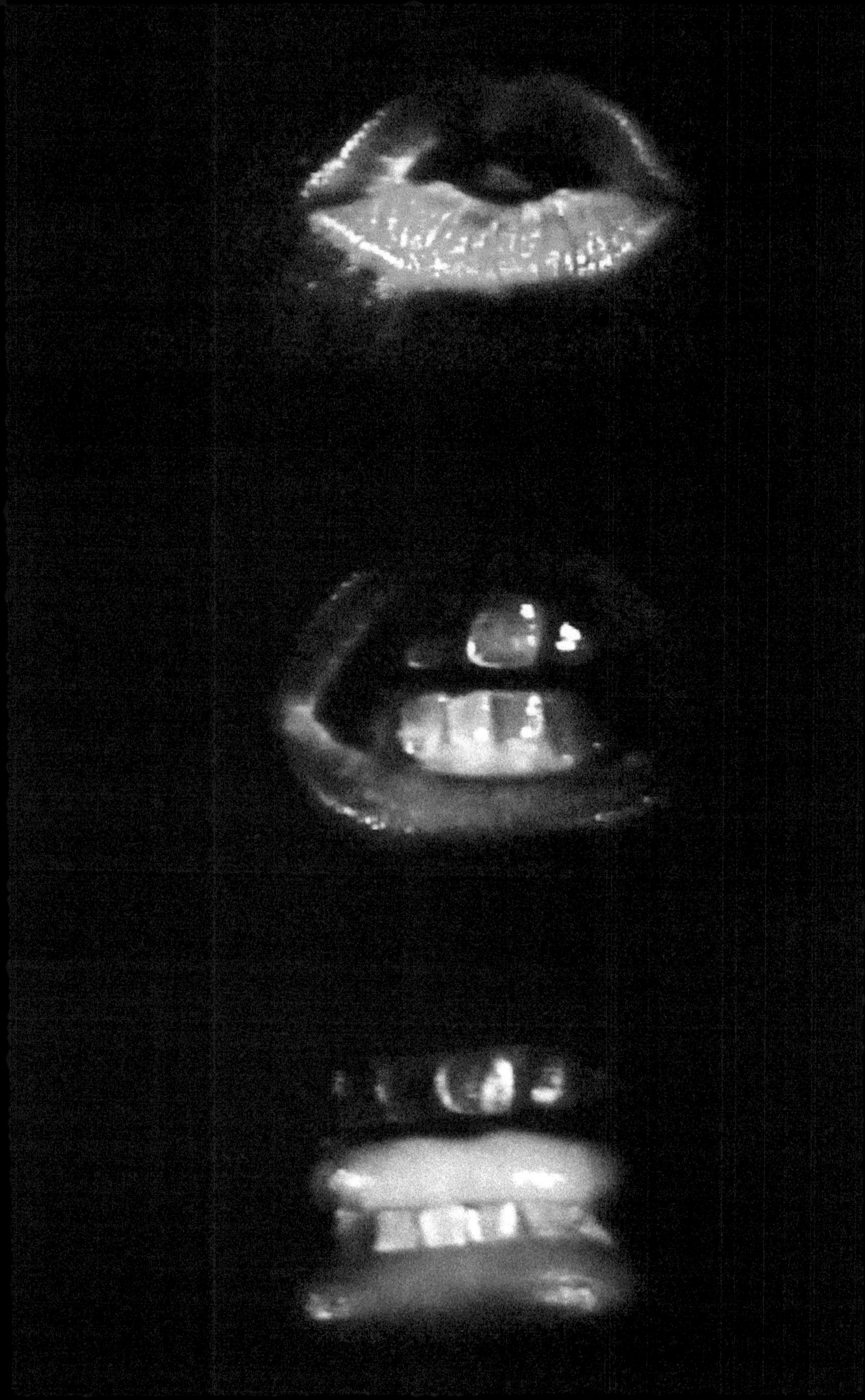

Une bouche, deux fois

Patricia MacGeachy

Updated from a text originally published as a French translation in *JEU Revue de théâtre* 64 (1992): 88–89.

I have performed Beckett's *Not I* (1972) in two different productions. The first for the stage, the second for the screen. The theatrical production was for Imago, a Montreal theatre company directed by Andrés Hausmann. The film production was for a 16mm short called *Just Words* (1991) by Louise Bourque.

My first experience allowed me to play the role of the Mouth in a way closest to Beckett's wishes.

Only my mouth was illuminated, smeared with lipstick and emerging from my blackened face. All in black, I was sitting in a box, my head bound and my body immobilized by a wooden bar affixed to my thighs. This bar, which I held on to with black-gloved hands, served as a support to counter any memory loss or distraction from the public and as a device to free my creativity when necessary.

It was quite a task to tackle this text the first time. The play is to be performed without emotion or feeling, which was quite challenging for me given my attachment to this character. The rendition was to be a verbal onslaught delivering a blow to the spectator. These were (are) Beckett's wishes. The play, which has 271 lines, was to be performed in less than sixteen minutes, and I don't believe I exceeded this duration! The text is very repetitive and, hence, difficult to learn. These repetitions reveal fragments of this woman's life. At the second or third "attack," I was able to better define the plot and structure of this text, which from then on became easy to learn. I grew attached to the character. Why? The language has a beautiful natural rhythm. I am attached to this woman who is part of me (of all women?). Or is it the fear of getting old? I have often cried for her (I still do cry).

She is a lonely old woman with little or no contact with the outside world. She's never been touched, embraced. No love. Banished from society. She talks to herself, rarely aware of doing so. She is also oblivious to her own body. Isolated. Beckett claimed that he'd heard of many such women in Ireland. We see some and we hear some here.

As with all the roles I have performed, I absorbed myself with that of the Mouth; whenever I had free time, I rehearsed it. Walking home from work, I must have looked like a crazy person as I would be then rehearsing my part. It became my evening prayers. I repeated the text before falling asleep. But I always work this way.

For my second experience, in the film *Just Words*, there was but one day of shooting. I did extensive polishing work. Once again, my mouth was at the heart of the action, but the film's director, Louise Bourque, took liberties with the text. I also read *Not I* slowly this time around, which pleased me very much. We only played a few passages in this way. It was as if I were savouring chocolates one at a time instead of gobbling them up.

My mother died in March 1990. I did work in the theatre around that time, with difficulty. I lost some of an earlier, easier verve. My mother's death? Who knows. My experience working in collaboration with Louise on *Just Words* was a cradling one for me. I retrieved lost confidence. Her manner, her sure direction, and perhaps the idea of the film, connected with me. Louise and I knew each other. We still do. I am going to stick my neck out here and say that such a subject worked because we were women. Ah! And we had both lost our mothers. I think the connection would have worked anyway, and if Louise asked me to work on another project I would not hesitate. These are the feelings I have today. Are we talking thirty years ago?

Beckett wrote this piece in twelve days! He was seeking "a vocal version of his artistic vision." It's a moving experience just to read the text and think about this woman.

JUST WORDS (Louise Bourque, 1991)
Written narration
Excerpts from Not I, a play by Samuel Beckett

Mouth (rapidly/in synch)*: VOICE OVER (SLOW):

*( ): *used where the two voices overlap; SLOW VOICE-OVER is given priority.*

....pick it up there...get on with it from there...another few-...what?..not that either?..nothing to do with that either?..all right...think something else again...try something else again...what?..not that either?..oh long after...sudden flash...something else again...think everything...keep on long enough...what?..not that either?..nothing to do with that?..nothing she could think...all right...nothing she could tell...nothing she could think...nothing she could...what?..who?..no!..she!..tiny little thing...before its time...what?..the buzzing?..yes...all the time the buzzing in the ear...dull roar in the skull...and the beam...moving around...but painless...so far...ha!..so far...then thinking...oh long after...sudden flash...can't go on...all this...all that...straining to hear...make something of it...her own thoughts...make something of them...what?..the buzzing?..yes...all the time the buzzing...out...into this world...this world...tiny little thing...before its time...:

Title of the film appears: ***Just Words***

...out...out...into this world...tiny little thing...before its time...in a godforsaken-...what?.. girl?..yes...tiny little girl...into this...into this...out...before her time...godforsaken hole called...called...no matter...parents unknown...unheard of...he having vanished...thin air...no sooner buttoned up his breeches...she similarly...eight months later...almost to the tick...so no love...spared that...no love such as normally vented on the...speechless infant...no...nor indeed for that matter any of any kind...no love of

Mouth (rapidly/in synch)*: VOICE OVER (SLOW):
*( ): *used where the two voices overlap; SLOW VOICE-OVER is given priority.*

any kind...any subsequent stage...so typical affair...nothing of note...coming up to sixty when she was what?.. seventy?..good God!..coming up to seventy...wandering in a field...looking aimlessly for cowslips...few steps...stop...stare into space...then on...a few more...stop and stare again...so on...drifting around...when suddenly... gradually...all went out...all that early April morning light...and she found herself in the- ...what?..

...what?..who?..no!..she!..found

(herself in the dark...) WORLD...

...and if not exactly...insentient... insentient...for she

(could still hear the buzzing...) THIS WORLD...

...so-called...in her ear...and this ray of light came and went...

(came and went...) OUT...

...such as the moon might cast...drifting in and out of cloud...but so dulled... feeling...

(so dulled...she did not know...) INTO THIS WORLD...

...what position she was in...imagine!..

THIS WORLD...

TINY LITTLE THING...

BEFORE ITS TIME...

IN A GODFOR-...

...what position she was in...whether standing...

(or sitting...) WHAT?..

...but the brain still...

(what?..) GIRL?..

...kneeling?..yes...

(whether standing...) YES...

...or sitting...or kneeling...

(but the brain still...) TINY LITTLE GIRL...

...what?..lying?..yes...whether standing...

(or sitting...) INTO THIS...

...or kneeling...or lying...but the brain still...

(still...in a way...)

OUT INTO THIS...

(...her first thought was...)

BEFORE HER TIME...

...oh long after...sudden flash...

(being brought up as she had been

GODFORSAKEN HOLE

to believe...)

CALLED...

...with the other waifs...in a merciful... (Brief laugh.)...

(God...)

CALLED...

(Good laugh.)...

NO MATTER...

...first though was...oh long after...she was being punished...for her sins...a number of which then...

SO NO LOVE...

flashed through her mind...one after the other...then dismissed as foolish...

(oh long after...)

SPARED THAT...

...this thought dismissed...as she suddenly realized...

(gradually realized...)

NO LOVE OF ANY KIND...

...she was not suffering...imagine!..not

(suffering!..indeed could not remember

AT ANY SUBSEQUENT

...when she had suffered less...)

STAGE...

...unless of course she was...*meant* to be suffering...

(just as the odd time...in her life...)

SO TYPICAL AFFAIR...

...when clearly intended to be having pleasure...she was in fact...having none...not in the least...not a twinge... this other thought

(then...oh long after...)

BUT SO DULLED...

sudden flash...thing she understood perfectly...

(first occurred to her...being)

SHE DID NOT KNOW...

brought up as she had been to believe... with the other waifs...in a

(merciful...(Brief laugh.)...)

WHAT POSITION SHE WAS IN...

...God...(Good laugh.)...

INDEED...COULD NOT

REMEMBER...WHEN SHE HAD SUFFERED LESS...

UNLESS OF COURSE SHE WAS...*MEANT* TO BE SUFFERING...HA!.. *THOUGHT* TO BE SUFFERING...JUST AS THE ODD TIME...IN HER LIFE...WHEN CLEARLY INTENDED TO BE HAVING PLEASURE... SHE WAS IN FACT... HAVING NONE...

...what?..

NOT THE SLIGHTEST... IN WHICH CASE OF COURSE...THAT NOTION OF PUNISHMENT...

THIS OTHER THOUGHT THEN...

(oh)

long after...very foolish really...she might do well to...groan...on and off...

OH LONG AFTER...

(writhe she could not...as if in actual) agony...could not bring herself...some flaw in her make-up...incapable of deceit...

SUDDEN FLASH

(or the machine...more likely the machine...)

...so disconnected...never got the message...powerless to respond...like numbed...

SHE MIGHT DO WELL...

(couldn't make a sound...)

...no sound of any kind...

TO GROAN...

(no screaming)

for help for example...scream... (Screams.)...then listen... (Silence.)...scream again... (Screams again.)...listen again...

(Silence.)...no...spared that...

BUT COULD NOT...

(all silent as the grave...no part-...what?..)

the buzzing?..yes...all silent

(but for the buzzing...)

COULD NOT BRING HERSELF...

...oh no!..

COULDN'T MAKE THE SOUND...

(no!..)

NOT ANY SOUND... NO SOUND OF ANY KIND...

...but the brain still...still sufficiently... oh very much so!..into control...under control... at this stage...to even question this...for on that April

TIME SHE CRIED...

(morning...so it reasoned...)

...that April morning...she having

ONE TIME SHE COULD REMEMBER...SINCE SHE WAS A BABY... MUST HAVE CRIED AS A BABY...THEN NO MORE TILL THIS... NO SOUND...JUST THE TEARS...SAT AND WATCHED THEM DRY...ALL OVER IN A SECOND...

(reasoned...)

...suddenly realized...words were coming...imagine!..words were coming...a voice she did not recognize... at first...so long since it had

AND NOW

(sounded...then)

finally had to admit...could be none other...than her

THIS STREAM...

(own...certain vowel)

sounds...she had never heard...

(elsewhere...so that people would stare...)

STEADY STREAM...

...rare occasions...once or

(twice a year...always winter...) SHE WHO HAD NEVER...

...some strange reason...

(stare at her) ON THE CONTRARY...

uncomprehending...she

(who had never...on the contrary...practically) PRACTICALLY SPEECHLESS...

speechless...all her days...speechless...
how she survived!..

ALL HER DAYS...
HOW SHE SURVIVED...
HOW SHE SURVIVED!..

...whole body like gone...just the
mouth...the lips...the

(cheeks...the jaws...never-...) AND NOW

...what?..tongue?..yes...

(the lips...the cheeks...the jaws...) THIS STREAM...

...the tongue...never still a second...mouth
on

(fire...steady stream...in her ear... practically in her ear...not catching the half of it...not the quarter...) NOT CATCHING THE HALF OF IT...NOT THE QUARTER...NO IDEA...

...no idea what

(she's saying...imagine!.. no idea what she's saying!..) WHAT SHE WAS SAYING...

...no idea...and the whole brain...

THEN THINKING...
OH LONG AFTER...
SUDDEN FLASH...
PERHAPS SOMETHING
SHE HAD TO TELL...

...she!..SHE!..what she was trying...what to
try...

(no matter...keep on...hit on it) TINY LITTLE THING...

in the end...then back...

(God is love...tender) BEFORE ITS TIME...

mercies.. new every

GODFORESAKEN
(morning...back in the field
HOLE...
... April)
morning...face in the grass...nothing
NO LOVE...
(but the larks...)
...pick it up from there...get on with it
SPARED THAT...
(from there...another)
few-...what?..not
SPEECHLESS ALL HER
(that?..nothing to do with
DAYS...
that?..try)
something else...think
PRACTICALLY
(something else...oh long after...)
SPEECHLESS...
...sudden flash...something else
again...then on...
HOW SHE SURVIVED!..
(no...the buzzing...what?..)
the buzzing?..yes...all the time the
buzzing...dull roar in the skull...and the ray
or beam...like moonbeam...but probably
not...certainly not...
SOMETHING THAT
(always the same spot...now
WOULD TELL...
bright..now shrouded...)
...but always the same spot...as no moon
could...no...no moon...just all part of the
same wish to...torment...
HOW IT WAS...

Talking Oneself into Being

Louise Bourque's Just Words

Dorottya Szalay

The exposure of the destructive narratives of North America's so-called containment culture seems to be a recurring topic in Louise Bourque's moving-image works. Her films re-examine and question traditionally reassuring concepts like home, family, and religion while illustrating their ability to serve as weapons in the (still ongoing) war against the liberation of women. Bourque fearlessly unveils the oppressive political power of these ideals that for many have always been regarded as safe havens. *Just Words* (1991) is her first work to communicate these unresolved issues and give voice to the internal struggle of domestically entrapped and socially suppressed women.

Using Samuel Beckett's short dramatic monologue *Not I* (1972), Bourque's *Just Words* works as a ten-minute-long mental purge, a suffocating confession of a woman of a certain age. The film partly incorporates Beckett's original instructions for staging the play as it focuses on the illuminated mouth of an actor (Patricia MacGeachy) in a pitch-black space. But by splicing in footage of her own family life, Bourque modifies the original piece and shifts the emphasis towards a more specific dilemma. Cuts to footage of Bourque's mother and sisters from old home-movie sequences, while the relentless ranting audio of the film continues, suggest a clear political and personal statement against the social silencing of women.

According to several sources, Beckett himself proposed that the intellectual content of the monologue of *Not I* was supposed to be secondary to the visceral impact of the play.[1] As Linda Ben-Zvi explains: "The words are barely audible, the image barely discernible but the power of the vision is unforgettable."[2] Yet there have been countless theories aiming to contextualize and conceptualize the text and its unique form, relying on ideas by modern thinkers including Carl Jung, Jacques Derrida, and Gilles Deleuze.

While these interpretations do offer a more complex understanding of the original piece, Bourque's method for recycling the play suggests that most of these theoretical reasonings should probably be considered with a degree of distance. Bourque, herself known to be "disinclined to be overly intellectual about her filmic pieces,"[3] in many ways consciously deviated from the original material and moved away from its canonical readings. Besides adding her own images to an already televised version of the play, she used two different audio tracks, one following the initial fast pace of the monologue, the other one inserting slow excerpts of Beckett's text, sometimes replacing and sometimes crossing the original ramble. By intercutting the two voices and highlighting certain parts, she blocks the authentic impact of the speech and repurposes it to support her argument. Nevertheless, Bourque's found-footage method is clearly connected to its primary material and references some of its more mainstream interpretations. Bourque's main approach to Beckett's work and its interpretations is not to change it completely but to narrow its scope by emphasizing a certain aspect: the exploration of the female experience and the societal construct labelled "Woman." Beckett himself was no stranger to such an approach.[4]

When asked about the women's parts Beckett has created, English actor Billie Whitelaw, who is considered one of the main interpreters of the playwright's works, named *Not I* the most dramatic example of feeling that a play was about her own life.

> I read it through—not understanding one word of it, may I say, intellectually. And when I got to the end, I could not stop crying … And yet if you were to say, why were you, I couldn't tell you other than I recognized—and I have said this before—the inner scream, I recognized a wound that's in there somewhere.[5]

Bourque's *Just Words* also gives a palpable context to this emotion and implicitly registers a set of weapons that might have caused that wound "that is in there somewhere." Even though Bourque uses her own mother and own family as illustrations, the range of those affected does not stop with her personal circles but refers to all women trying to speak themselves into being. Raising seven children in postwar North America, Bourque's always smiling mother recalls the beginning of an era defined by suburbia's domestic divas and the politics of domestic containment. Preying on the exhaustion of people at the time, this artificially created and government-supported social model exploited the ideal of the stable and secure family life and consolidated strict gender roles to serve the construction of a new national identity. One of the pillars of this

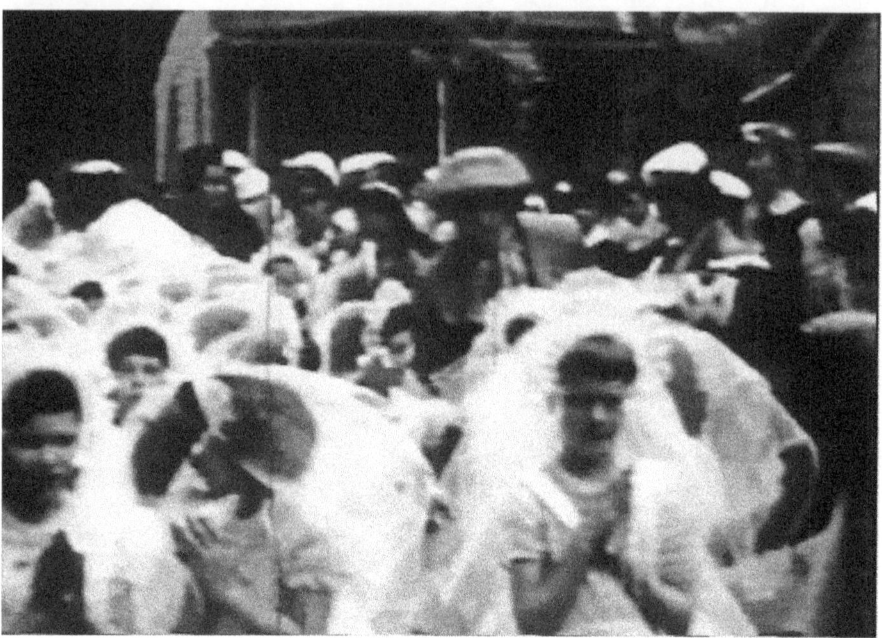

lifestyle was the obedient, morally pure housewife living in the outskirts of the city in almost complete isolation, with a sole purpose of raising children and passively awaiting the husband's arrival from work. "The problem that has no name,"[6] as Betty Friedan referred to it in her groundbreaking book, *The Feminine Mystique* (1963), was in fact the inner scream Whitelaw was talking about, the realization of a long-lost identity.

Bourque's *Just Words* opens with a completely black screen and a distant voice muttering indecipherable words. In a few moments a tiny, vague image appears in the background, slowly heading towards the viewer. The image of moving lips becomes clear just as it leaves the frame at the left corner of the screen. The voice falls silent and from the middle of the black screen the title of the film emerges. When the Mouth suddenly resurfaces in the following moment it dominates the whole image. The colours appear to be somewhat distorted: the lips are painted with bright red lipstick; the teeth are yellowish brown, and the tongue is bright pink. This time the centrally placed Mouth recites Beckett's monologue from the very beginning while taking up the whole frame. After a few fragmented sentences its hegemony ends with the debut of Bourque's mother smiling directly into the camera. The next minute of the film is defined by a rhythmic exchange between the two. Images showing the relentless chatter of the Mouth are replaced by scenes of the mother in different settings, wearing different outfits. By the time the second voice appears we have seen the mother in a shy white blouse, in a luxurious golden-brown fur, and in a discreetly sensual bathing costume—always pretty, always smiling.

It is important to recognize that when the second verbal stream appears, the new voice only quotes segments of the original text, peeling off all words and expressions that could divert the interpretation into other directions. This second voice sets a much calmer pace, helping the viewer decode its message. Even though the revised confession keeps the fragmented nature of Beckett's narration, the text gives a rather clear-cut report about a woman's realization of her identity crisis.

> world ... this world ... out … into this world … this world … tiny little thing … before its time … in a godfor– … what? … girl? … yes … tiny little girl … into this ... out into this ... before her time ... godforsaken hole called ... called ... no matter ... so no love … spared that … no love of any kind … at any subsequent stage … so typical affair … but so dulled … she did not know … what position she was in … indeed ... could not remember … when she had suffered less … unless of course she was … *meant* to be suffering … ha! … *thought* to be suffering … just as the odd time … in her life … when clearly intended to be having pleasure … she was in fact … having none … not the slightest … in which case of course … that notion of punishment ... this other thought than … oh long after ... sudden flash ... she might do well ... to groan ... but could not … could not bring herself … couldn't make the sound ... not any sound … no sound of any kind … time she cried … one time she could remember … since she was a baby … must have cried as a baby ... then no more till this … no sound … just the tears … sat and watched them dry … all over in a second … and now ... this stream … steady stream ... she who had never … on the contrary … practically speechless … all her days …how she survived! ... how she survived! ... and now this stream … not catching the half of it … not the quarter … no idea … what she was saying ... then thinking … oh long after … sudden flash … perhaps something she had to tell … tiny little thing … before its time … godforsaken hole … no love … spared that … speechless all her days … practically speechless … how she survived! … something that would tell … how it was …

In Beckett's play the Mouth shares the stage with the Auditor, a figure placed downstage left, fully illuminated and integrally covered by a black djellaba. The figure is staring almost motionless towards the stage, raising and lowering its arms "in a gesture of helpless compassion."[7] The Auditor stands as a visualization of the Mouth's negated wholeness, but the schematic movements of the former contrast the impulsive reactions the organ performs. Even though the dynamic between the Mouth and Bourque's mother in the film is undoubtedly different, the basic roles are familiar. The Mouth, "whose disconnected psychological state is related to a failure to achieve a coherent sense of an individual self,"[8] could find a more concrete manifestation of itself in Bourque's mother, but after a while it becomes clear that this woman's character is akin to the anonymous figure covered in black, crouching in the left corner of the stage. As suggested by the context of the film (and the cultural and political landscape of the mother's time), her movements of habit, her conscious and unconscious poses, reflect the schematic movements of the Auditor. The mother's smiles, her winks and blown kisses, are not reflections of her own personality but imitations of a predesigned role. The role of the Ideal Woman, an "image created by women's magazines, by advertisements, television, movies, novels, columns and books,"[9] constantly shaping women's identities, programming their dreams and determining their futures. Even though Bourque uses personal footage, home movies of her mother, her representation does not provide an image for the disembodied voice to find itself. Just like the figure concealed behind the Mouth, the woman in the footage seems unable to realize, accept, and affirm the totality of her experience and perception as belonging to her individuality.

According to Friedan, the feminine mystique permits, even encourages, women to ignore the question of their identity. The mystique says they can answer the question "Who am I?" by responding "Tom's wife ... Mary's mother."[10] By incorporating images of her sisters and her father, consciously or not, Bourque confirms this statement. Those few moments she allows us to see her mother unknowingly letting her guard down therefore become the catharsis of the film. After the sixth minute Bourque presents her mother in an ordinary white summer blouse, without makeup or a hairdo, looking down and slowly turning away from the camera. Her movements are emphasized by a slow-motion shot. For a brief moment, she forgets her role, stops posing, and quits smiling. This short episode is followed by a drawn-out sequence showing the Mouth, with the lips moving in slow motion but without producing any words. Instead the audio is dominated by the monotonous rings of a (church) bell, which rings eleven times, accompanying the writhing of the groaning Mouth. By the end of the scene the atmosphere changes back to normal: the mother has a broad grin on her face, birds chirp in the background, and the Mouth carries on rambling.

In Beckett's play both the isolated Mouth and the fully covered Auditor suffer from the burden of containment. Nonetheless the false freedom of the mother in Bourque's film still seems more tragic. One brief moment aside, she appears to be entirely unaware of, or in complete denial about, her social and psychological imprisonment. She absorbs the idea transmitted through various forms of images surrounding her and adopts their lies as her own reality. The mother never unites with the questing voice of the Mouth. The shocked awakening is not followed by any change. Neither the disembodied Mouth nor the silenced mother finally says, "I."

Besides their obvious role in the postwar North American family, the children in *Just Words* represent the cyclicality of gender roles in the nuclear family. The little girls parading around in their white dresses at the First Communion scene look like little white brides, while the images showing them with their dolls in their arms foreshadow their future roles as mothers and housewives. The implied inevitability of this outcome viewed from a contemporary perspective brings about a sobering conclusion and explains the timeless power of Bourque's piece. Today when extreme nationalistic ideas are spreading through Western culture, the image of the ideal family defined by strict gender roles once again becomes a useful political weapon in the propaganda arsenal of governments. *Just Words* serves as a compelling reminder of our regrettable past, which might just sneak in through the back door if we fail to pay attention.

NOTES

1. Brater Enoch, "The I in Beckett's *Not I.*" *Twentieth Century Literature*, no. 3 (July 1974): 200.
2. Linda Ben-Zvi, "*Not I*: Through a Tube Starkly," in *Women in Beckett: Performance and Critical Perspectives* (Chicago: University of Illinois Press, 1992), 243.
3. April Gardner, "Poetry in Motion," *NewEnglandFilm* (July 1, 2004), <https://newenglandfilm.com/magazine/2004/07/poetry-in-motion>.
4. See: Linda Ben-Zvi, ed., *Women in Beckett: Performance and Critical Perspectives* (Chicago: University of Illinois Press, 1992).
5. Billie Whitelaw quoted in Linda Ben-Zvi, "Billie Whitelaw Interviewed by Linda Ben-Zvi," in *Women in Beckett: Performance and Critical Perspectives* (Chicago: University of Illinois Press, 1992), 4.
6. Betty Friedan, *The Feminine Mystique*, Second Edition (New York: Dell Publishing, 1974), 11.
7. Samuel Beckett, "*Not I*," in *Collected Shorter Plays* (New York: Grove Press, 2010), 215.
8. James Knowlson, *Damned to Fame: The Life of Samuel Beckett* (London: Bloomsbury, 1992), 815n98.
9. Friedan, 27.
10. Ibid., 64.

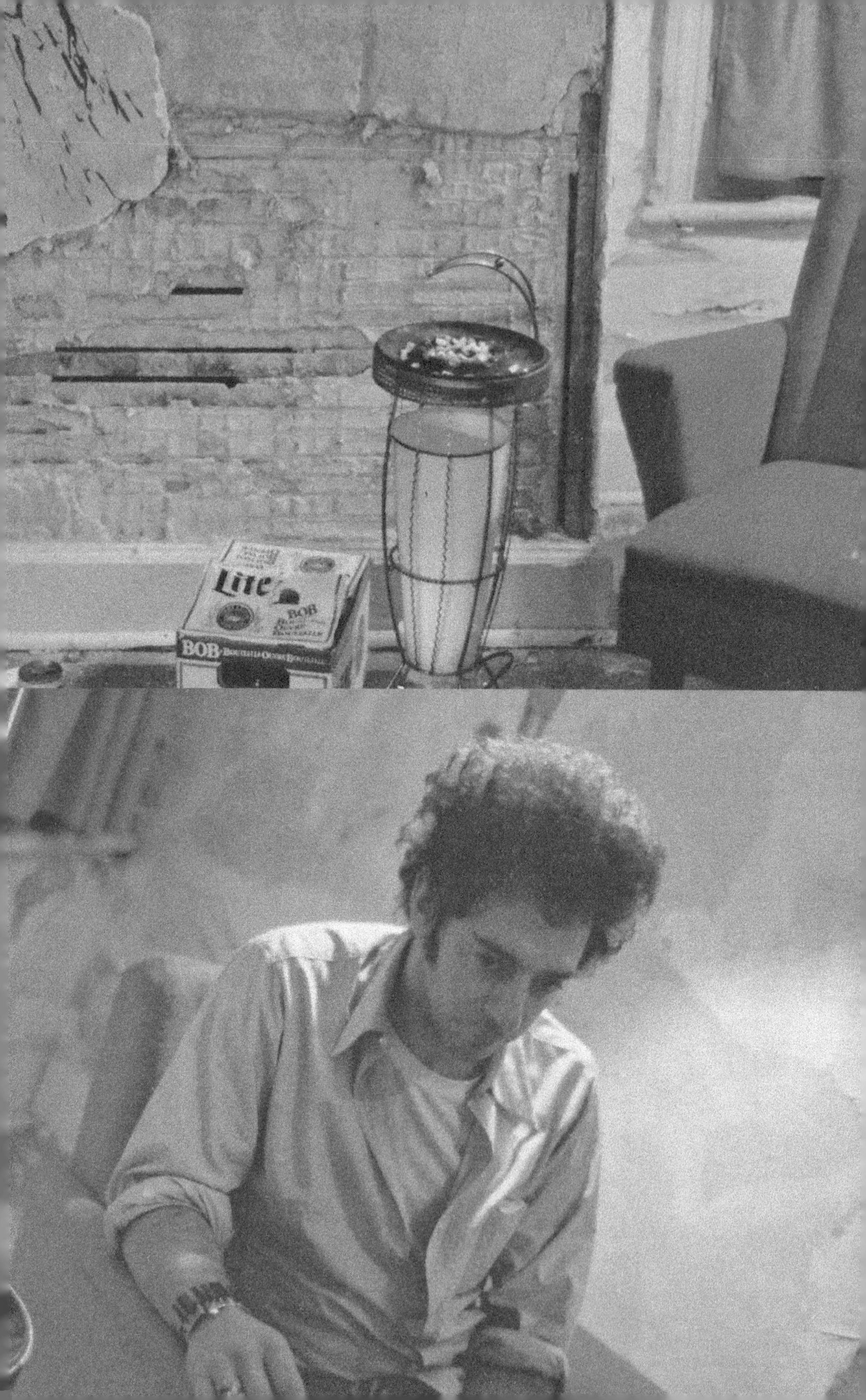
Lite
BOB
BOB

A Fractured Narrative

Notes on Jolicoeur Touriste

Brian Wilson

Jolicoeur Touriste, made in 1989 while Louise Bourque was a student at Concordia University, is an evocative portrait of internal struggle and isolation. The film was made with traditional production methods, using a script, storyboards, an actor, and a small crew. It begins with a shot of a red chair, sitting empty in the alcove of a room in a tourist inn. After a static establishing shot, the camera moves towards the chair, during which time a nearby lamp switches off and back on. We then see two successive shots of a man, dimly lit in red, reclined with his eyes nearly shut. A hard cut interrupts the scene and takes us to an image of a picturesque beachscape, before returning back to the dimly lit room and the man. Throughout the film, we see the man sitting and watching television, while he heavily drinks and chain-smokes cigarettes. Bourque intercuts these shots with imagery she shot on super 8 during a trip to Ireland. We see the ocean, a countryside, and small cottages with thatched roofs. Within the context of the film these images suggest the man's memories, his desire to return to a different place and time.

In the man's room, Bourque uses colour to striking effect, alternating between the red of the room's lamp, the green of a harsh fluorescent, and the blue of the television screen. As the film progresses, Bourque uses shifts in motion (achieved through step printing) and a chaotic soundtrack to emphasize the man's increasingly inebriated state. The film ends with a shot of the same corner we saw at the beginning, but now in darkness. Through the use of optical printing and masking, the outline of the man appears in the chair, but instead of seeing his features we see the imagery of the sea projected onto his body. He has effectively become his memories.

Bourque describes *Jolicoeur Touriste* as "an enclosed space, a struggle against the constraints of personal isolation explored through a fractured narrative. … A film about loss and absence." The film places a strong emphasis on travel. The character desires to travel to another space, another time. The film follows a circular structure, beginning and ending with the shot of the corner of the room. The alcove is strangely shaped, its sharp angles almost resembling those of a tilted rocket ship. The soundtrack underscores the film's emphasis on travel. It initially consisted of musical excerpts and natural sounds Bourque had recorded. But after deciding they didn't fit, Bourque collaborated with then-boyfriend Jean-Pierre Morin, who read from a 1950s children's book about space travel, called *Rocket Away!* (Frances Frost, 1953). His narration plays over a slowed-down version of XTC's "Procession Towards Learning Land." One almost gets the sense that it is the film's protagonist we hear narrating his own childhood memory.

Jolicoeur Touriste conveys aspects of the psychodrama, but Bourque says she was equally influenced by the work of European filmmakers like Cocteau, Fellini, and Antonioni. Bourque's background in poetry was also a defining factor in the film's shape, both formally and conceptually. Bourque says later in life, she recognized the film shared a common sensibility with Schlesinger's *Midnight Cowboy* (1969), although she was unconscious of such a connection at the time of the film's making. Like *Midnight Cowboy*, *Jolicoeur Touriste* is a film imbued with hope. Just as Joe Buck and Ratso Rizzo long to travel to the sunny beaches of Florida, the desire of *Jolicoeur Touriste*'s protagonist to transcend his physical and emotional state and return to the countryside, to a seemingly more idyllic space, implies that the possibility for better things still exists. The figure's desire to live beyond the room became a reality through Bourque's outtakes, which later took on a second life.

In the late 1990s, Bourque buried outtakes and behind-the-scenes shots from her early films in the backyard of her family's Edmundston home. She would unearth them five years later for use in a series of films that drew from the rot and decay that had occurred with the celluloid itself during the burial period. An image of her as a young woman, on the set of *Jolicoeur Touriste*, became the basis for *Self Portrait Post Mortem* (2002). Whereas Bourque's presence in *Jolicoeur Touriste* is only implied from her role behind the camera, in this film we see her, eternally young, as the relics of decay shift and unfold around her.

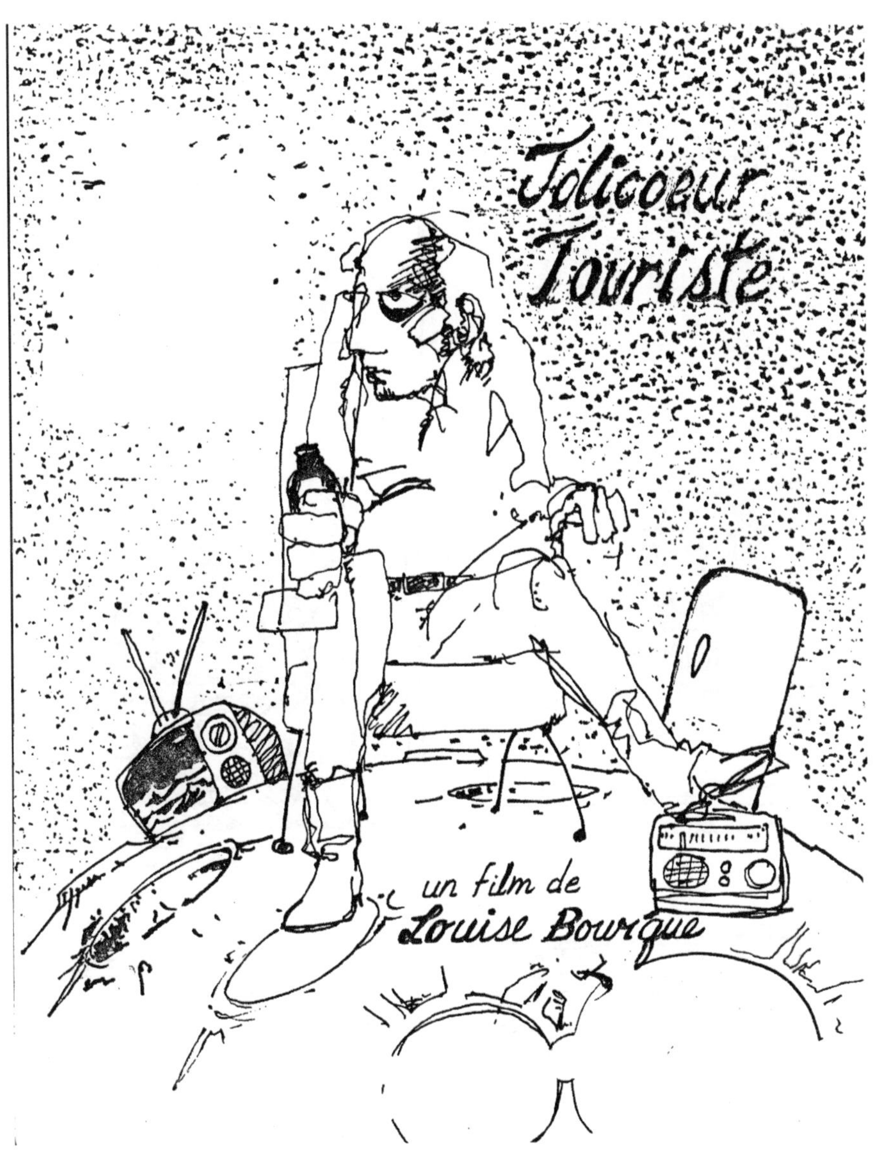
Jolicoeur
Touriste
un film de
Louise Bourque

Découpage technique

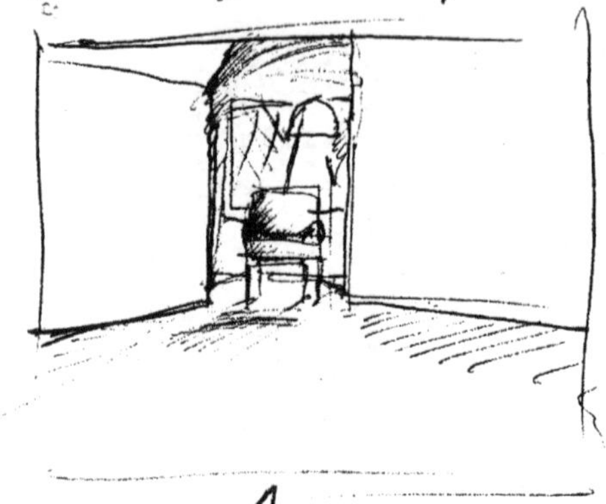

A

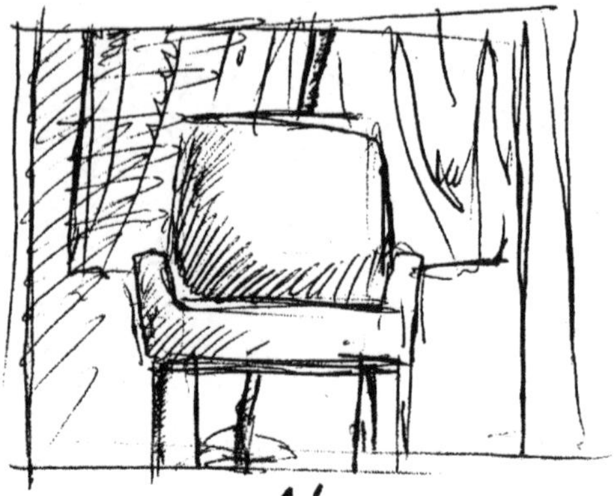

A'

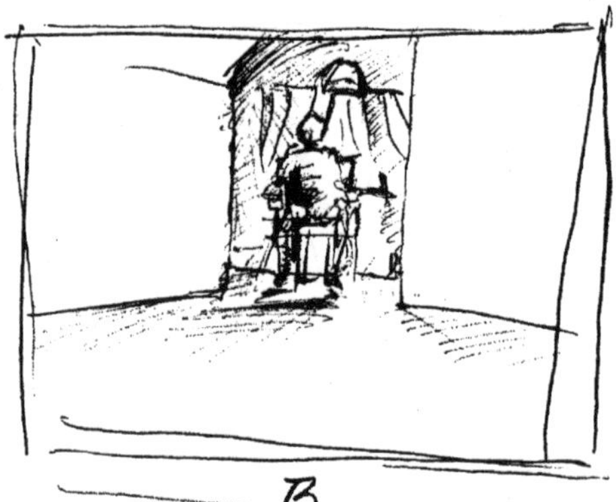

B

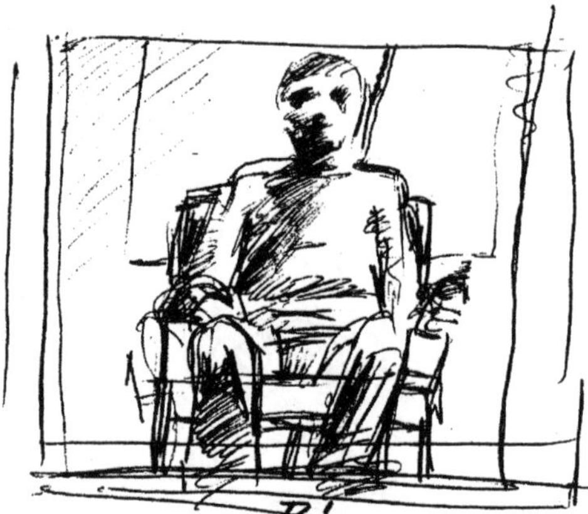

B'

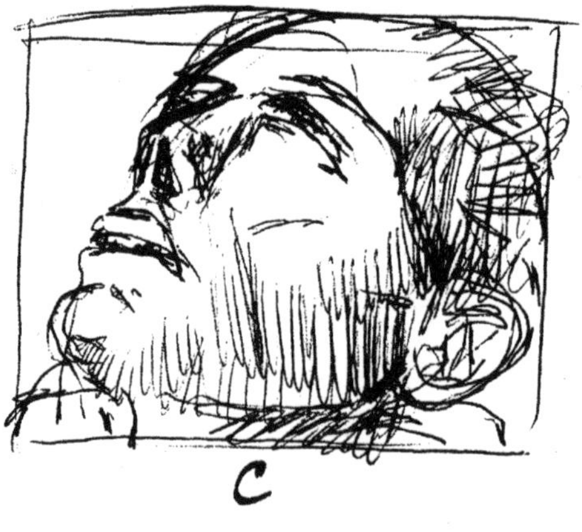

C

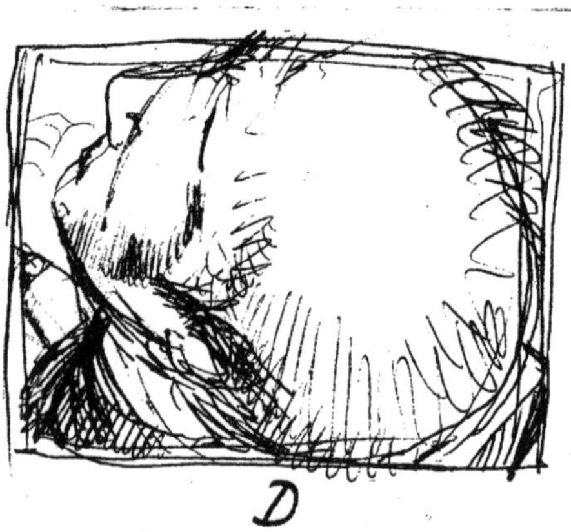

D

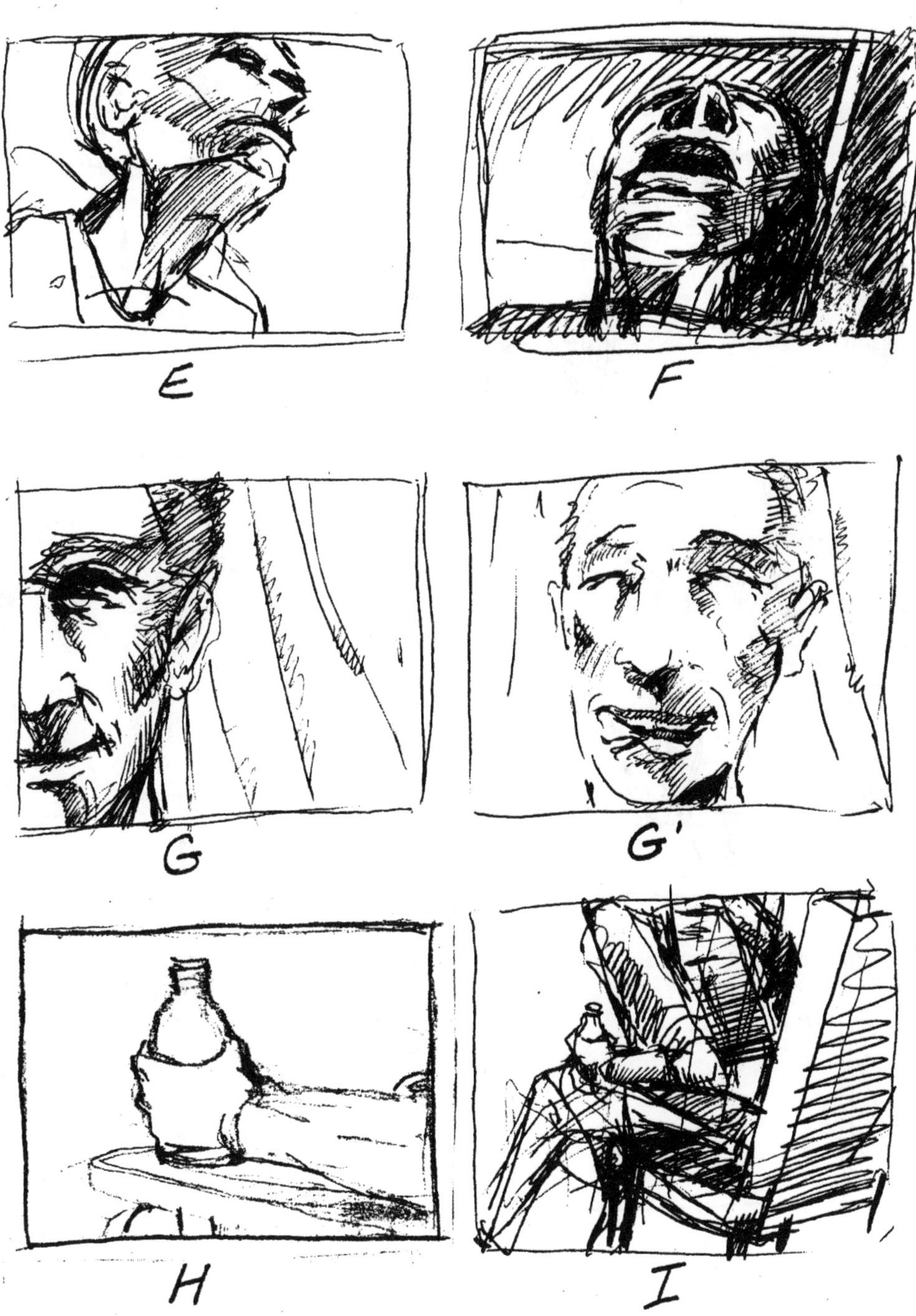
E
F
G
G'
H
I

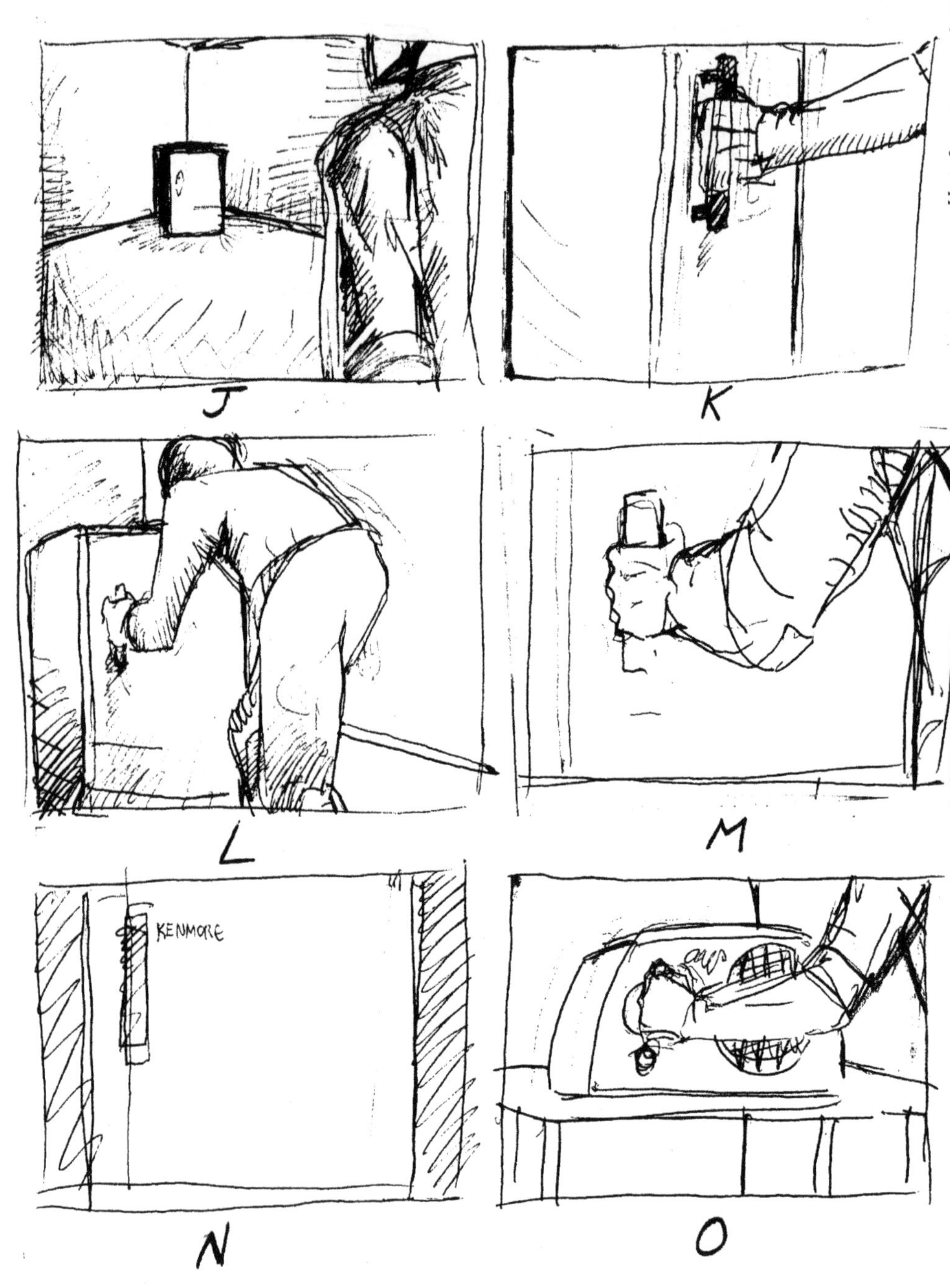
J
K
L
M
KENMORE
N
O

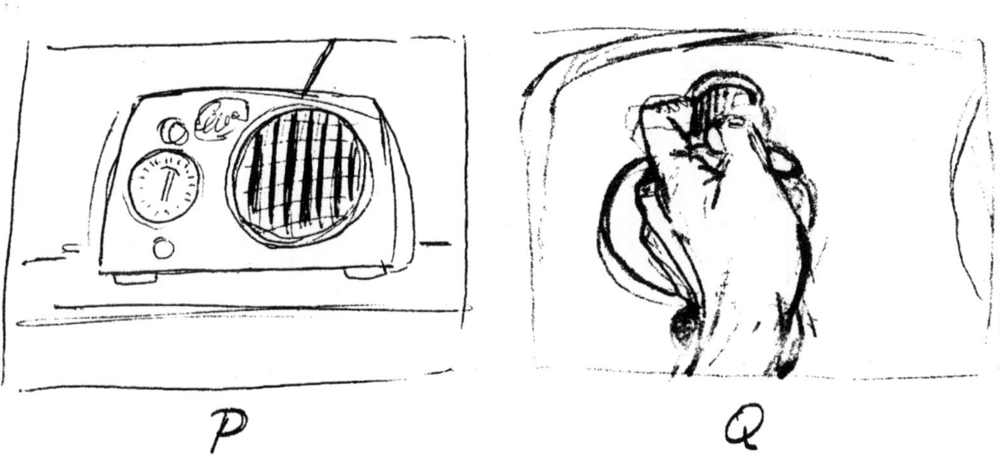
P
Q

Emplacement des principaux éléments du décor

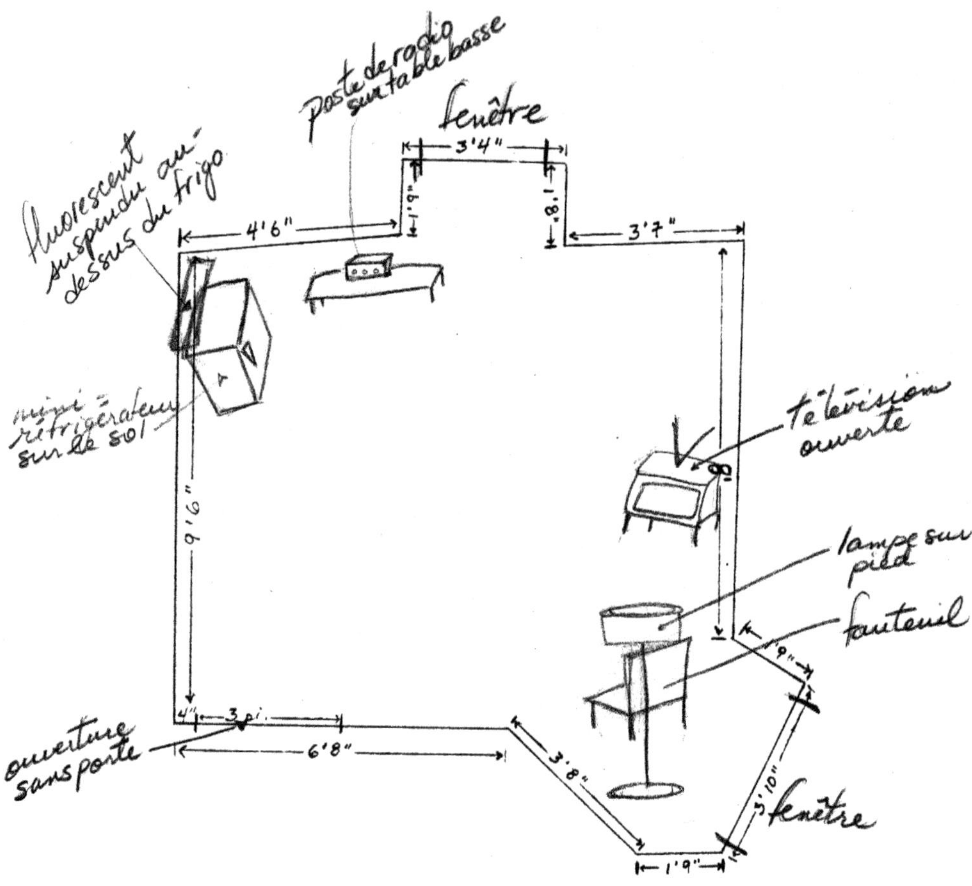

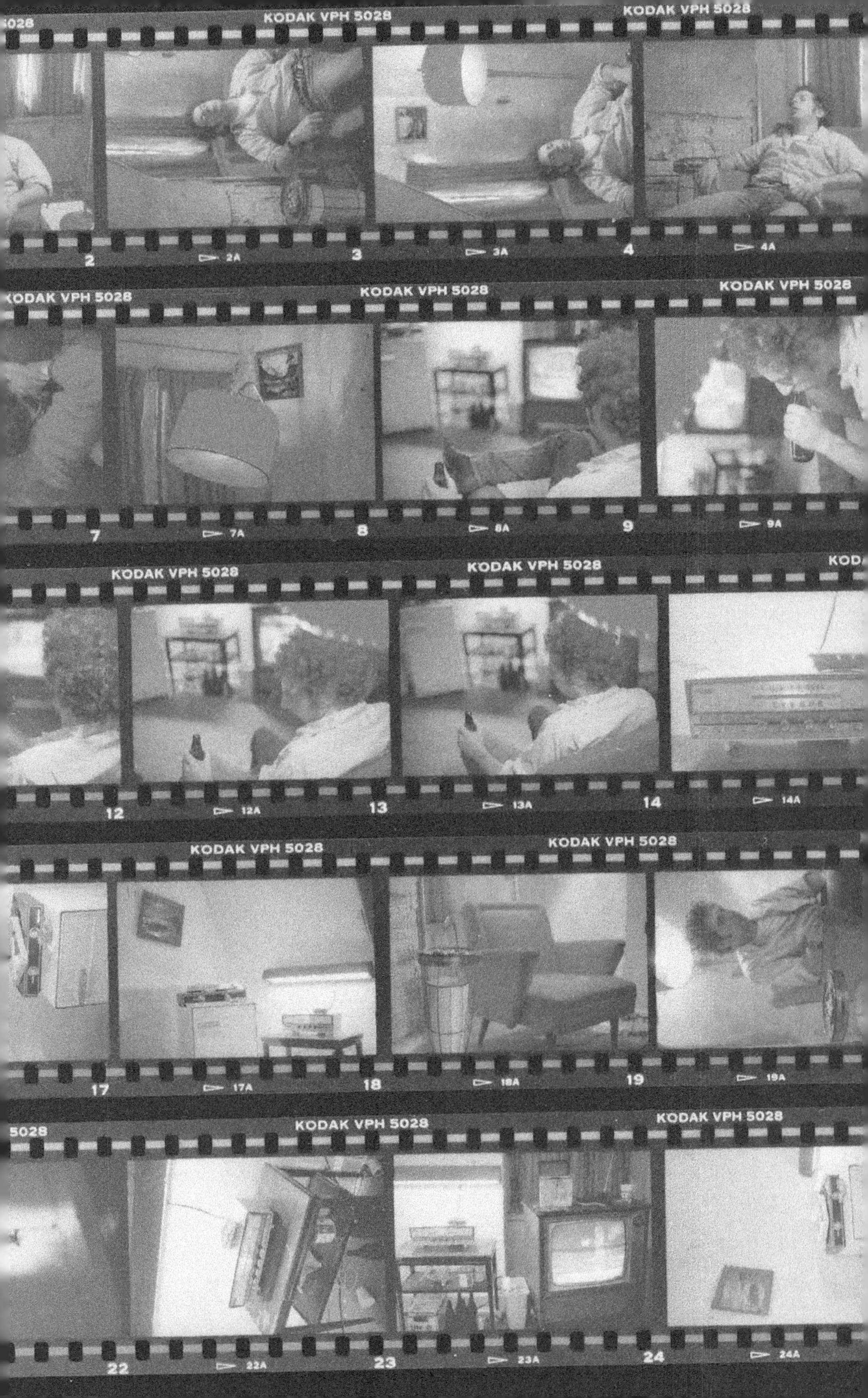

5028
KODAK VPH 5028
KODAK VPH 5028
2
2A
3
3A
4
4A
KODAK VPH 5028
KODAK VPH 5028
KODAK VPH 5028
7
7A
8
8A
9
9A
KODAK VPH 5028
KODAK VPH 5028
12
12A
13
13A
14
14A
KODAK VPH 5028
KODAK VPH 5028
17
17A
18
18A
19
19A
5028
KODAK VPH 5028
KODAK VPH 5028
22
22A
23
23A
24
24A

Notes sur The Visitation

Sébastien Ronceray

Ce qui étonne immédiatement dans *The Visitation* (2011) de Louise Bourque, c'est la relation sensuelle que tisse la cinéaste avec cette statue de la Vierge Marie. Elle y arrive de par la liaison instaurée entre la statue et la source de la lumière (une simple bougie), la caméra cherchant à saisir l'une et l'autre, l'une au profit de l'autre, en ayant comme trame sonore une voix murmurant des prières dans une luminosité dominée de vert mais toujours mystérieuse. Cette interaction entre ces éléments nous plonge dans une réflexion qui anime souvent les films de Louise Bourque, une pensée instable, vibrante. Ce que la cinéaste met en scène, c'est en fait la dégradation d'un motif très ancien (la Vierge Marie) subissant de nombreuses et inédites détériorations. Elle propose une nouvelle adoration, au sens ancien du terme (porter à la bouche, énoncer, baiser, aborder ; « je me prosterne à vos pieds » susurre la prière dans le film). Un voile de lumière participe à cette adoration, créant de l'incertitude dans notre appréhension de la statue qu'il recouvre. La Vierge se retrouve dissimulée, presque inatteignable, par le double jeu de la lumière vacillante et de la caméra qui se glisse entre les reflets du verre portant la bougie, et les ondulations liquides de la cire fondue dans ce verre. Les éclats, miroitements, brouillages, et autres perturbations visuelles dissimulent la Vierge devenue icône purement symbolique, masquée, cernée, ourlée par le cadre et la lumière. Une relation intense naît de cette mise en scène de l'évitement: toujours à distance de la statue, la caméra la visite, par irruption anxieuse, et tentant de percer un secret ; elle ne saisit l'image de la Vierge que par bribes, dessinant un portrait incomplet, la laissant ouverte à la projection des désirs. Ce film renvoie ainsi aux plus profondes envies d'attraction qui germent du cinéma des premiers temps: cette volonté de saisir le désir du spectateur dans une exhibition inachevée.

Dans *The Visitation*, Louise Bourque cherche à supprimer la séparation entre image et prototype comme caractéristique importante du culte des formes de représentation. Le visage statufié de la Vierge varie au gré des évolutions de l'image qui lui donnent une profondeur d'émotions. Ces variations font écho aux changements plastiques qui s'opèrent dans d'autres films de la cinéaste à travers les mutations dues au travail sur les émulsions chimiques. À la manière d'un rituel apotropaïque autour de la statue, la cinéaste fait subir à cet objet figé le même sort qu'aux images retravaillées dans d'autres films: elle lui donne une fonction iconographique proche des mystères moyenâgeux, théâtralisant matériellement une cérémonie qui se présente autrement à nous, qui littéralement se représente par le biais de sa mise en scène énigmatique (la statue, liée à son enfance, provient de la maison où elle a grandi). La magie cinématographique de Louise Bourque place ici le fond vert, propice aux trucages contemporains ou apparitions magiques, au devant de l'image, le rendant littéralement obscène (au-devant de la scène) et faisant de la couleur verte l'élément premier du masquage des images de son film: la magie et le mystère se fondent autrement dans la couleur qui les irrigue complètement. Sa bougie devant la statue est telle que la torche que l'abbé Jean l'anachorète plaçait dans sa grotte devant l'image de Marie et qui ne s'éteignait jamais (alors qu'il partait pour de longs voyages), la Vierge veillant elle-même sur la flamme. La prière de Louise Bourque devient une histoire miraculeuse; la superposition des mots, leur répétition, les scintillements de la lumière et les variations de cadres donnent une puissance magique à ce film.

Notes on The Visitation

Sébastien Ronceray

Translated by Kathryn Michalski

What is immediately striking about Louise Bourque's *The Visitation* (2011) is the sensual relationship that the filmmaker weaves between herself and the statue of the Virgin Mary. She achieves this by establishing a connection between the statue and the light source (a simple candle), through the camera shifting focus between the two, and with a voice whispering prayers, all lit by a mysterious green light. The interaction between these elements immerses the viewer in the thoughts that often inspire Bourque's films; unstable, vibrant thoughts. What the filmmaker is staging is, in fact, the deterioration of a very old motif (the Virgin Mary) undergoing numerous and new degradations. She proposes a new form of worship, in the old sense of the term (to put to speech, to enunciate, to kiss, to approach; "je me prosterne à vos pieds" ["I bow down to your feet"], whispers the prayer in the film). A veil of light participates in this adoration, creating a feeling of apprehension about the statue it covers. The Virgin finds itself obscured, almost unattainable, through the dual play between the flickering light and the camera as it sneaks between the reflections of the glass holding the candle and the liquid ripples of melted wax in it. Flashes, shimmers, blurring, and other visual disturbances conceal the Virgin, who has now become a purely symbolic icon, masked, surrounded, hemmed in by the frame and the light. An intense relationship is born from this staged avoidance: always at a distance from the statue, the camera visits it in nervous bursts, attempting to unravel a secret; it captures the image of the Virgin only in fragments, drawing an incomplete portrait, creating space for the projection of desires. This film harkens back to the deepest desire for attraction that germinates in the early days of cinema: the desire to enthrall the viewer, leaving them wanting more.

In *The Visitation*, Bourque seeks to eliminate the separation between image and concept, an important characteristic of the cult of representation. The sculpted face of the Virgin varies with the evolution of the image, adding a depth of emotion. These variations echo the physical changes that are present in Bourque's other films through the mutations resulting from her chemical manipulation of emulsion. In the manner of an apotropaic ritual around the statue, the filmmaker subjects this frozen object to the same fate as the images reworked in her previous films: she gives it an iconographic function, a Middle Age aura, materially dramatizing a ceremony that presents itself differently to us by her enigmatic staging (the statue is linked to her childhood, as it comes from the house where she grew up). Bourque's cinematographic magic draws the green background into the foreground. As opposed to contemporary use of green as a backdrop to stage magic or trickery, with this work, Bourque uses green as the primary element for masking the images of the film: magic and mystery merge differently as the colour floods the image completely. Her use of the candle in front of the statue is reminiscent of the torch that Father John the Hermit would place in his cave in front of an image of Mary, the flame never going out (even when he left on long journeys), as the Virgin herself watched over it. Bourque's prayer becomes a miraculous story; the superimposition of the words, their repetition, the shimmering of the light, and the variations of frames, all give this film a magical power.

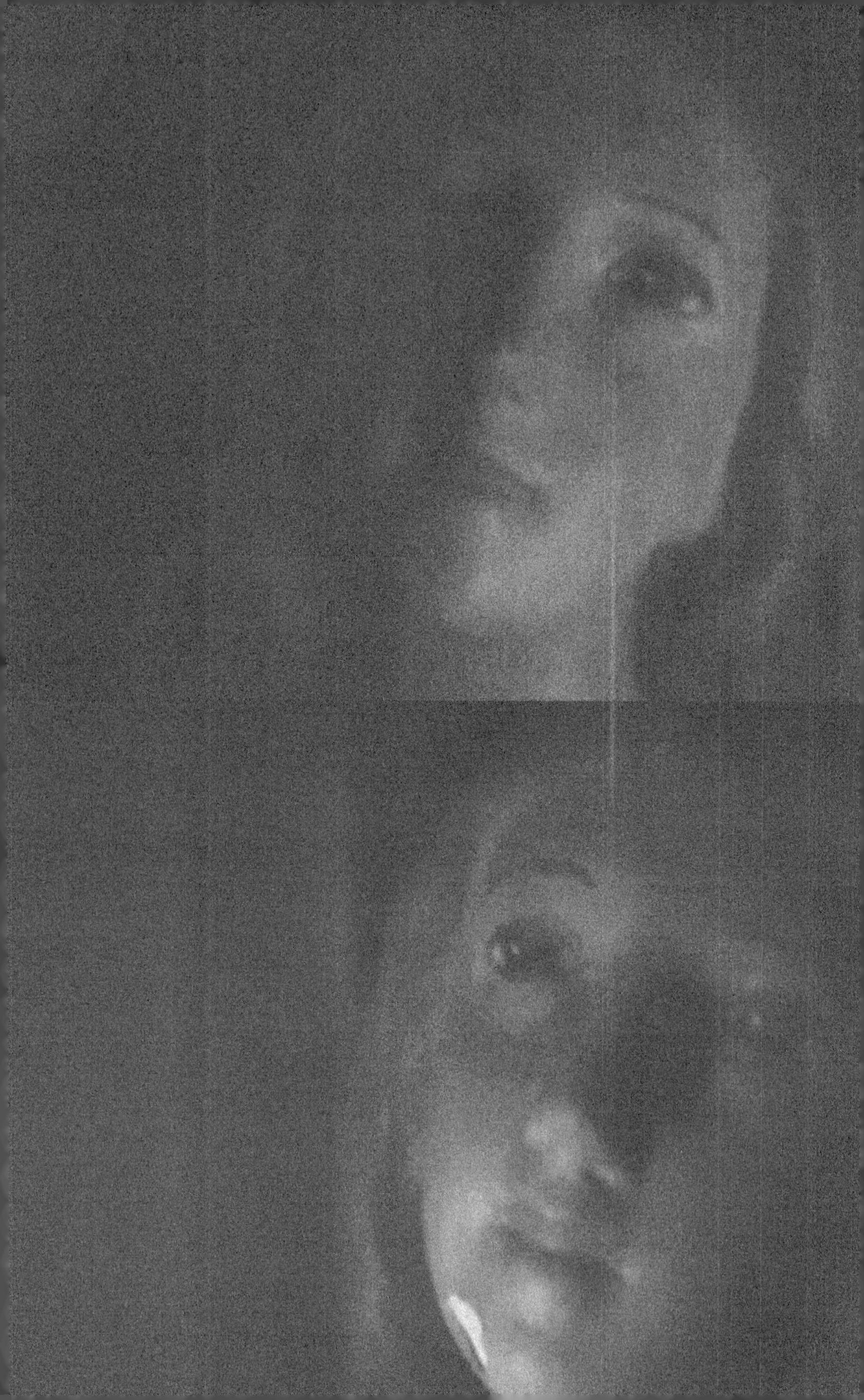

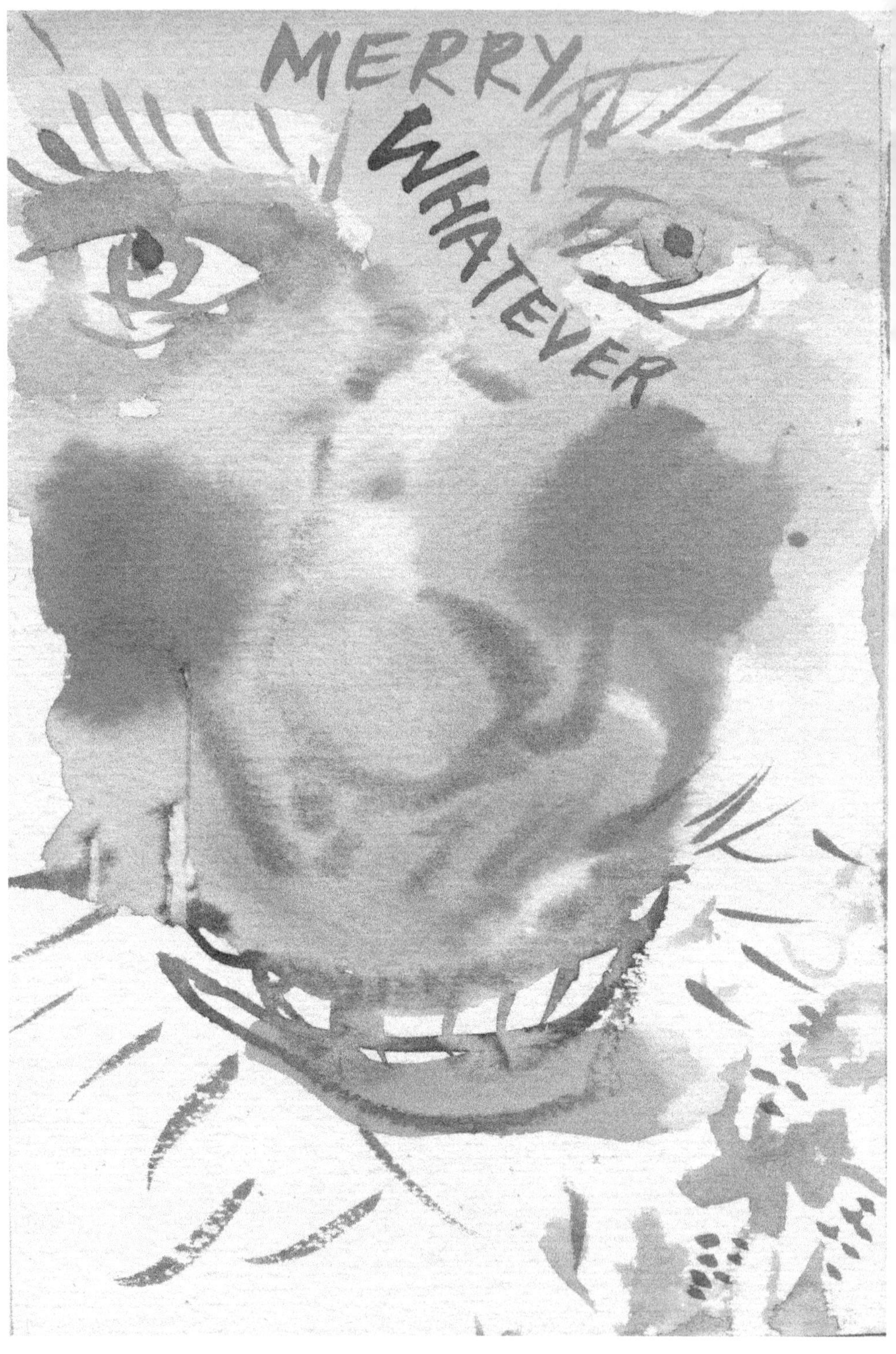
MERRY
WHATEVER

Merry —
This is late.
I ♡ your
Kitty. C-U-
Soon -
♡ Martha

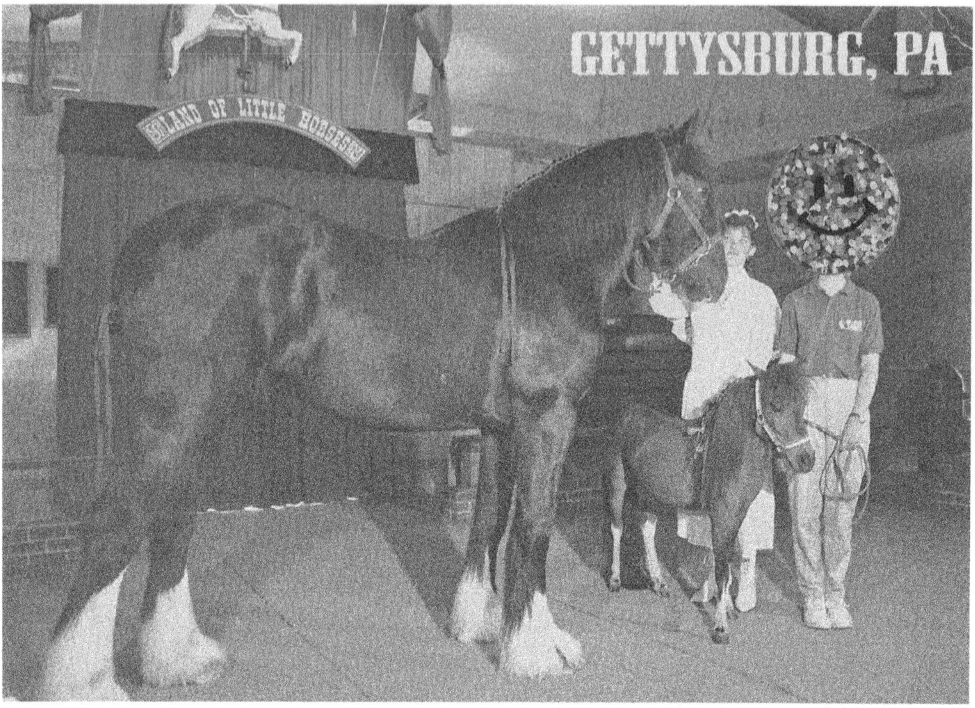

GETTYSBURG, PA

LAND OF LITTLE HORSES

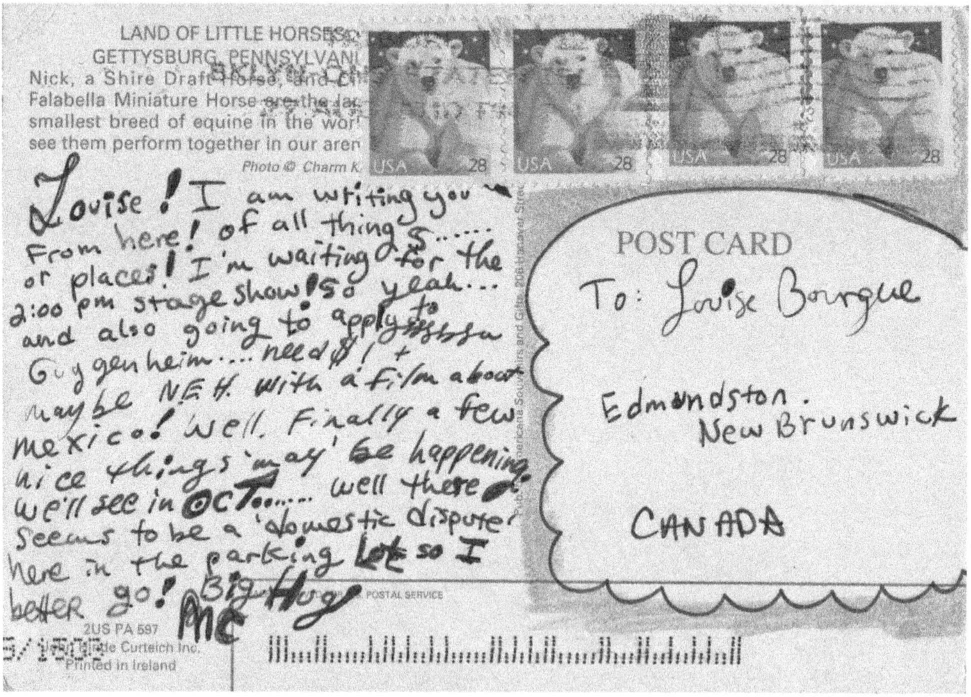

LAND OF LITTLE HORSES
GETTYSBURG, PENNSYLVANI
Nick, a Shire Draft Horse, and Ch
Falabella Miniature Horse are the la
smallest breed of equine in the worl
see them perform together in our aren
Photo © Charm K

Louise! I am writing you from here! of all things...... or places! I'm waiting for the 2:00 pm stage show! so yeah... and also going to apply to Guggenheim.... need $! + maybe N.E.H. with a film about mexico! Well. Finally a few nice things 'may' be happening. we'll see in OCT...... well there seems to be a 'domestic dispute' here in the parking lot so I better go! Big Hug me

POST CARD

To: Louise Bourque

Edmundston.
New Brunswick

CANADA

POSTAL SERVICE

2US PA 597
Curteich Inc.
Printed in Ireland

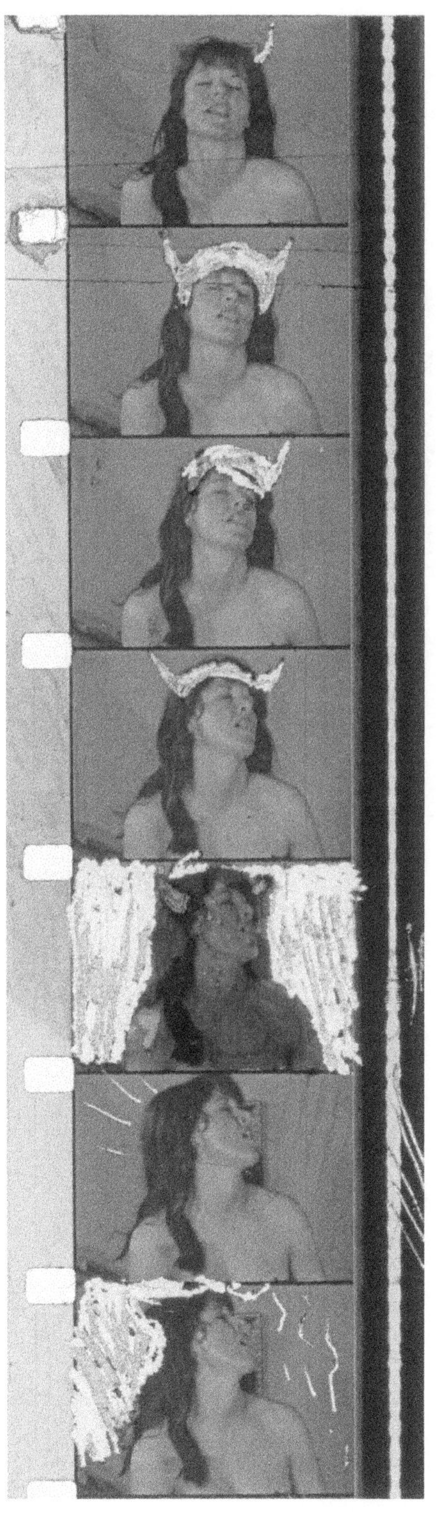

www.geocities.com/Hollywood/Theater/1809
photo, Elliot Caplan

DR. BISH REMEDIES —
for Commuters
Pat. Pend.
© 2000
Alternatives to Success

6/19/01

dearest Louise,

Finally sat down – lay down in fact – with your good films. Sorry so long a time – life's exigencies. Haven't seen the Jubilee Tourist yet. Your range is wonderful – so many, so much to say – see – from you to me! Favorite work on first viewing is your abstract (mostly blue). Real "videology." Anyway, thanks, & keep it up – unless the unavoidable suffering is too much. (I like what Thomas Merton had to say about art, loving & living —).

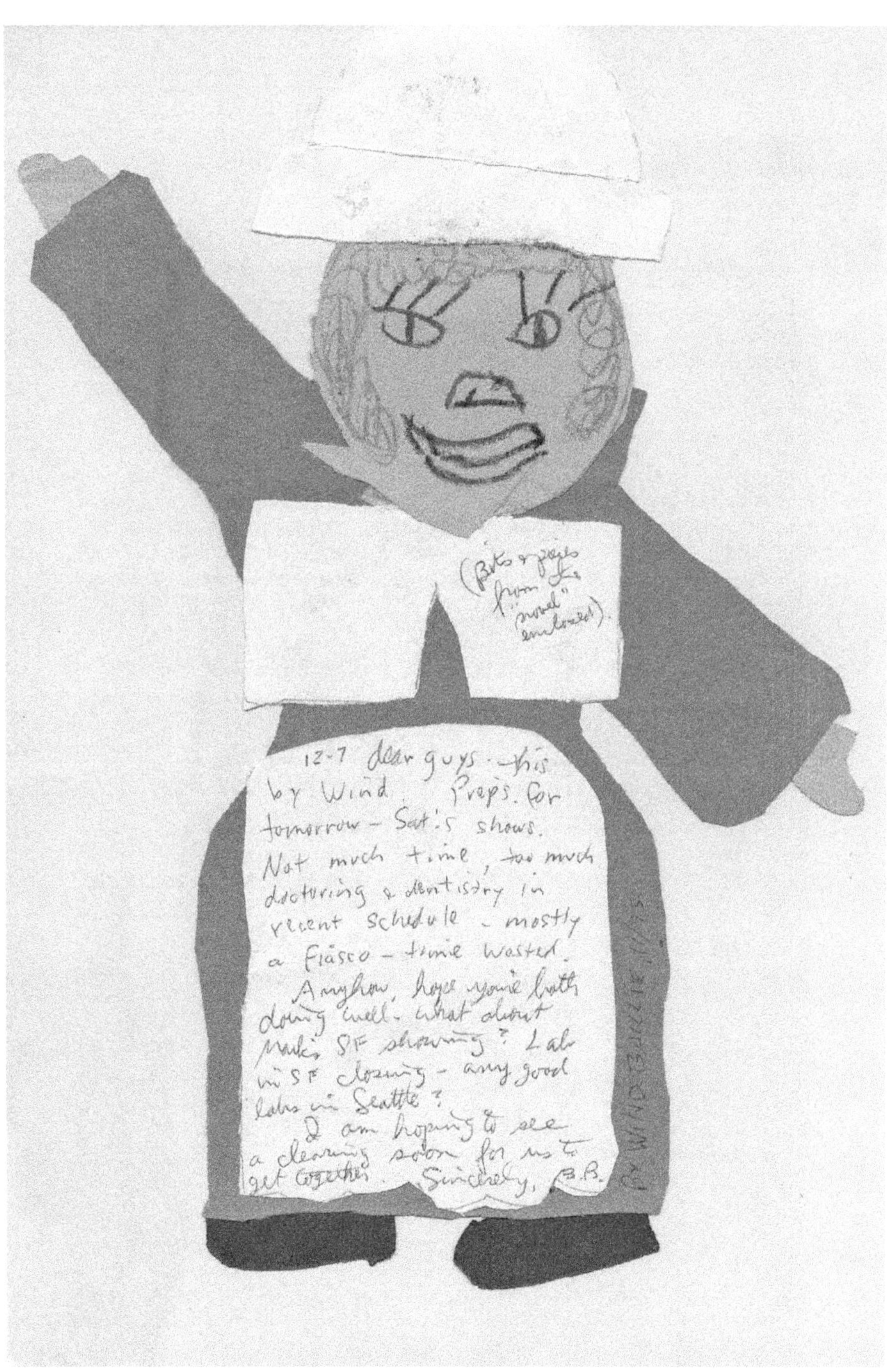
(Bits & pieces
from the
"novel"
enclosed).
12-7 dear guys - this
by Wind. Preps. for
tomorrow - Sat.'s shows.
Not much time, too much
doctoring & dentistry in
recent schedule - mostly
a fiasco - time wasted.
Anyhow, hope you're both
doing well. What about
Mark's SF showing? Lab
in SF closing - any good
labs in Seattle?
I am hoping to see
a clearing soon for us to
get together. Sincerely, B.B.

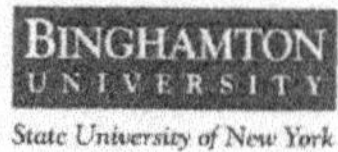

October 17, 2005

To Radcliffe Institute For Advanced Study:

I am familiar with Louise Bourque's entire output. I know her (as people know each other two cities apart) for almost as long as she's been making films, with a great quickening of interest after seeing THE PEOPLE IN THE HOUSE, which astonished me, and which I felt was a needed recapturing of the "haunted house" theme in American cinema (in avant garde film, examples are FALL OF THE HOUSE OF USHER and MESHES OF THE AFTERNOON), a recapturing and a further elaboration of that state of mind that cannot resolve unspeakable issues. No doubt Louise Bourque is haunted, stuck with some terrible event or terrible interpretation of an event, that finds objectification in the dynamics of the family in the one-family house she returns to repeatedly; that she haunts. And repeatedly destroys, in staged fire, or more usually in (accelerated) film-emulsion decay. I was aware of her sensitivity and invention (and her disciplined working habits) before THE PEOPLE, but was blown away by her spatial sense especially in this dramatization. Brilliant expressionist color and an expressionist feel for spatial volumes got to me. While I usually do all I can to escape narratives of suffering, and for all the stylized puppetry of her characters, of-a-piece with the decor, she succeeded in engaging me in her story and it was devastating.

As an artist she is blessedly stuck, I'd have to say (happily, she doesn't wear her affliction when one meets her and enjoys her company), and there's no doubt Louise will come through given the opportunity for a larger production. Reading of her ambitious plans for the new work fills me with both dread and anticipation. 35mm. and I suspect "full-length", perhaps this work could make it through to the many serious movie-goers that demand characters and story, but don't know what to make of absolute abstraction. An expressionist utterance from the realm of necessity would do them some good.

Thank you.

Ken Jacobs

Ken Jacobs
Distinguished Professor of Cinema Emeritus
Binghamton University
Department of Cinema
SUNY at Binghamton

1/12/99

Louise!

Obviously, here's your print back. please make sure to tell 'Cinema Libre' that you now have custody of it.

Also, please find enclosed some royalties— (we can only pay you 5¢/min.).

It ... to

g...

d... patrons per show).

P... I am also

encl... ped articles on my 'tribulation 99'. I hope that you can get Emerson to buy the videotape (from me personally would be best).

Well stay in touch!

— Craig

S.O.S. Log

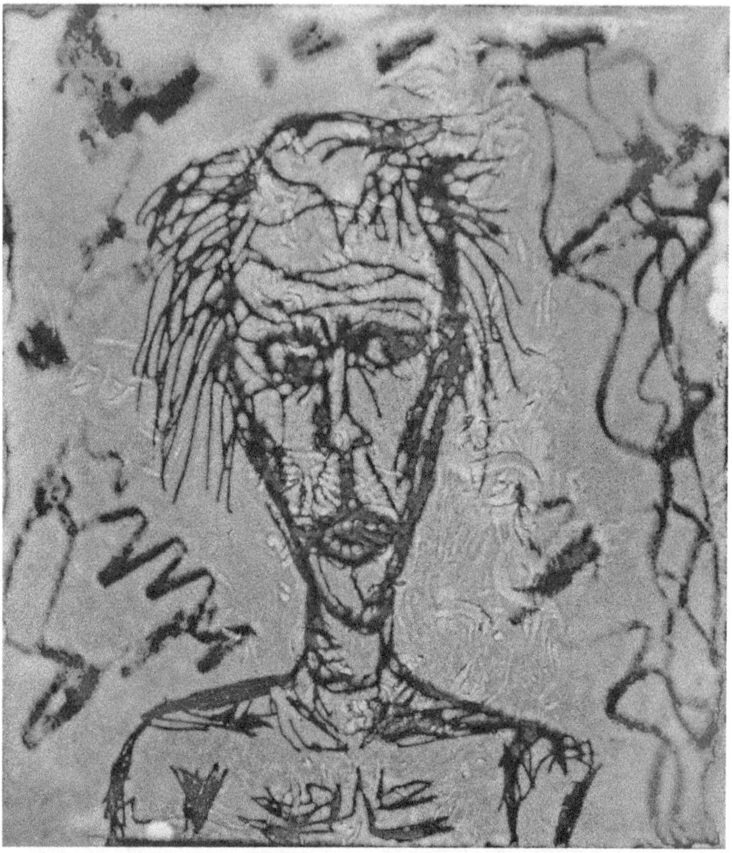

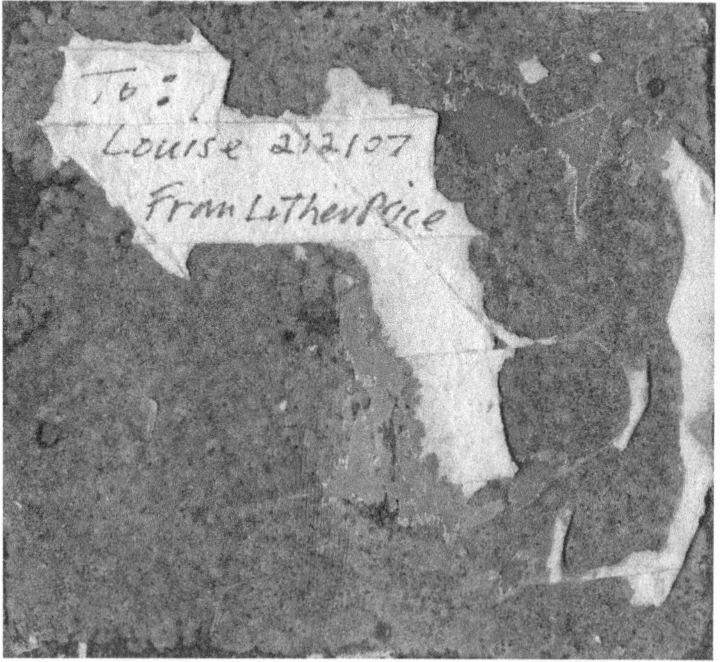
To:
Louise 2/2/07
From Luther Price

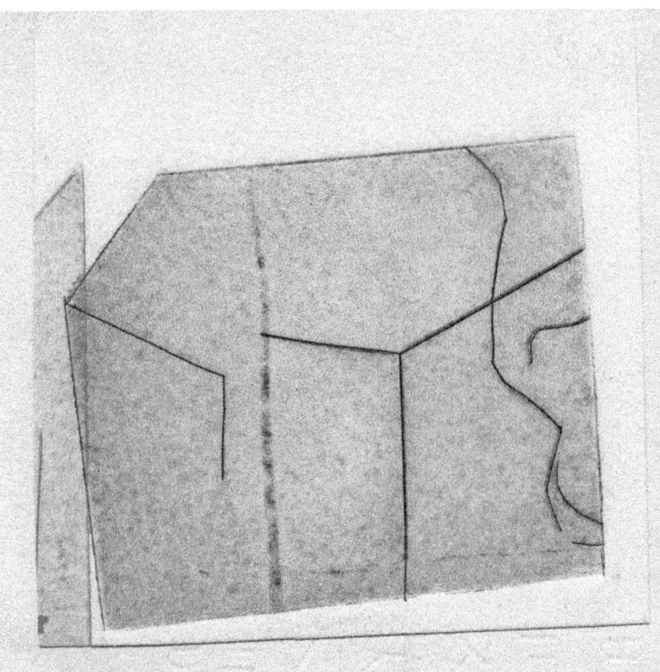

May 15, 1997

Louise - -

Thank you for not only nominating me for the scholarship, but also for simply being supportive, insightful, influential, and etc. as far as my film work goes. I always appreciate recognition!

I'm going to give you a little film show after some crucial splicing and dicing, and. . .

I also hope to have classes with you in the future. Thanks!

B.g.

11/18/03

Dear Louise

Herewith your tape and new project outline.

I wrote a recommendation as strong as I know how and really hope you get a Guggenheim!

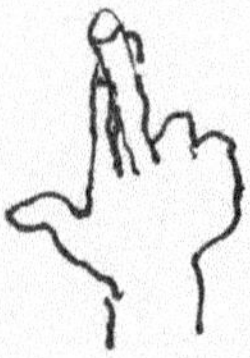

my (crossed fingers)

Bob

(feb. 1994)

For Louise;

-as soon as I opened this journal I thought of you and your poetic nature in filmmaking. Your films affect me in ways that cannot be explained with verbal language. a unique combination of conscious & unconscious emotional responce that I get only very rarely when I view great art. It is this responce that drives my own work and creations; and that is why, you my dear, are such a great influence in my life.

Happy Reading,

Love
Mark

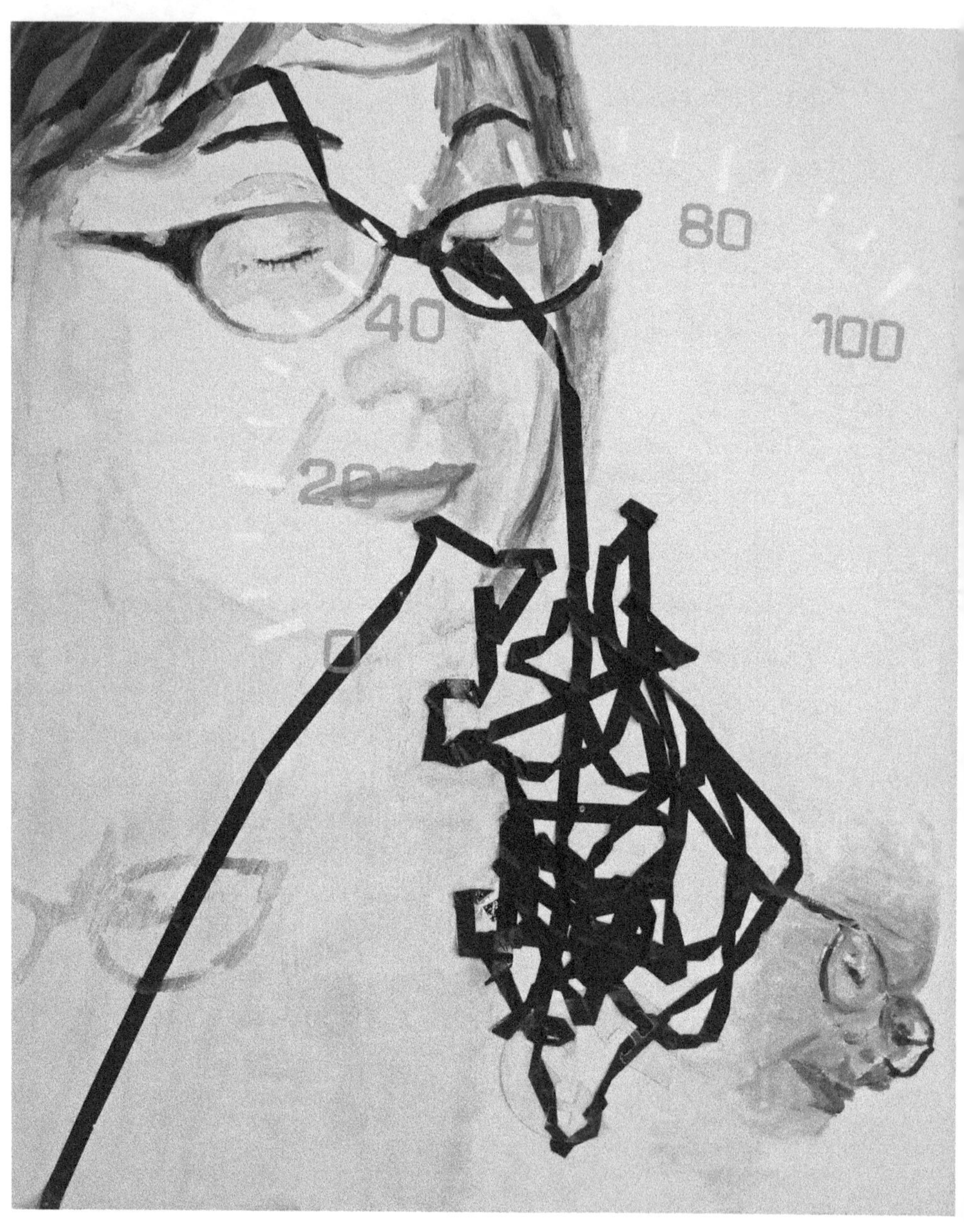
80
40
100
20
0

WILL YOU TAKE MY RING AND
MY HAND AN A

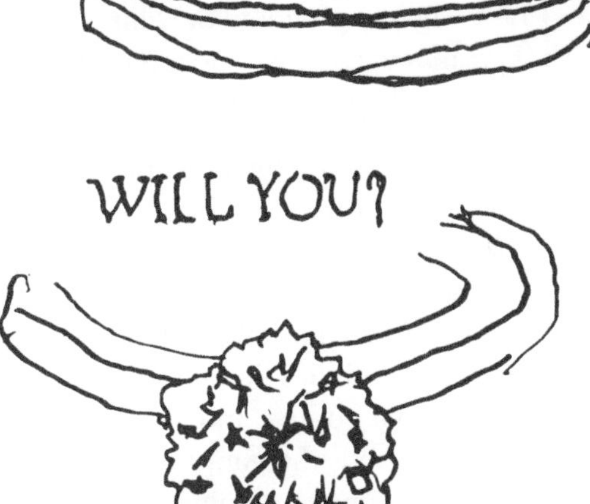

TIFFANY & CO

A Conversation with Louise Bourque

Micah J. Malone

Originally published in *Big Red & Shiny* (March 19, 2006).

MM: In looking at your films, I was thinking of the concept of "in-between" and how that particular space-time is rarely represented in film. For instance, your film *Fissures* (1999), where throughout the film you are literally in between the frames. I was linking that to memory and it is perhaps akin to the "frames" in between shots from a family photo album.

LB: When you think of a fissure it connotes this idea of the in-between. It suggests the idea of the gap, as what you are missing. But it's also space that's opened up, a place to explore, perhaps even something inviting. And this can bring up the idea that what we're missing can also be something that is rich as well. So you can think of it like a positive and negative space—there is a bit of a pun intended when I say this (it's literally what is going on in the image, a photographic shift between a positive and a negative through solarization). In the case of that film [*Fissures*], the gap, the memory, is represented very specifically by the home-movie images coming and going and the film material itself has the markings of fissures on it, actual fissures in the film's emulsion created by my hand manipulations in the printing and developing of the film image. So it's "missing" emulsion, it's "missing" information; the absence is literally inscribed on the material. But it's not necessarily an absence only, it's the suggestion of a presence in the absence, or it is what takes the place of the "missing" images of the home movies, for instance, the violent rhythm of the colour and the texture and what they suggest.

MM: Since you mentioned the material aspect of your films, can you talk just a bit about the technical aspect of your films and how they come to look so

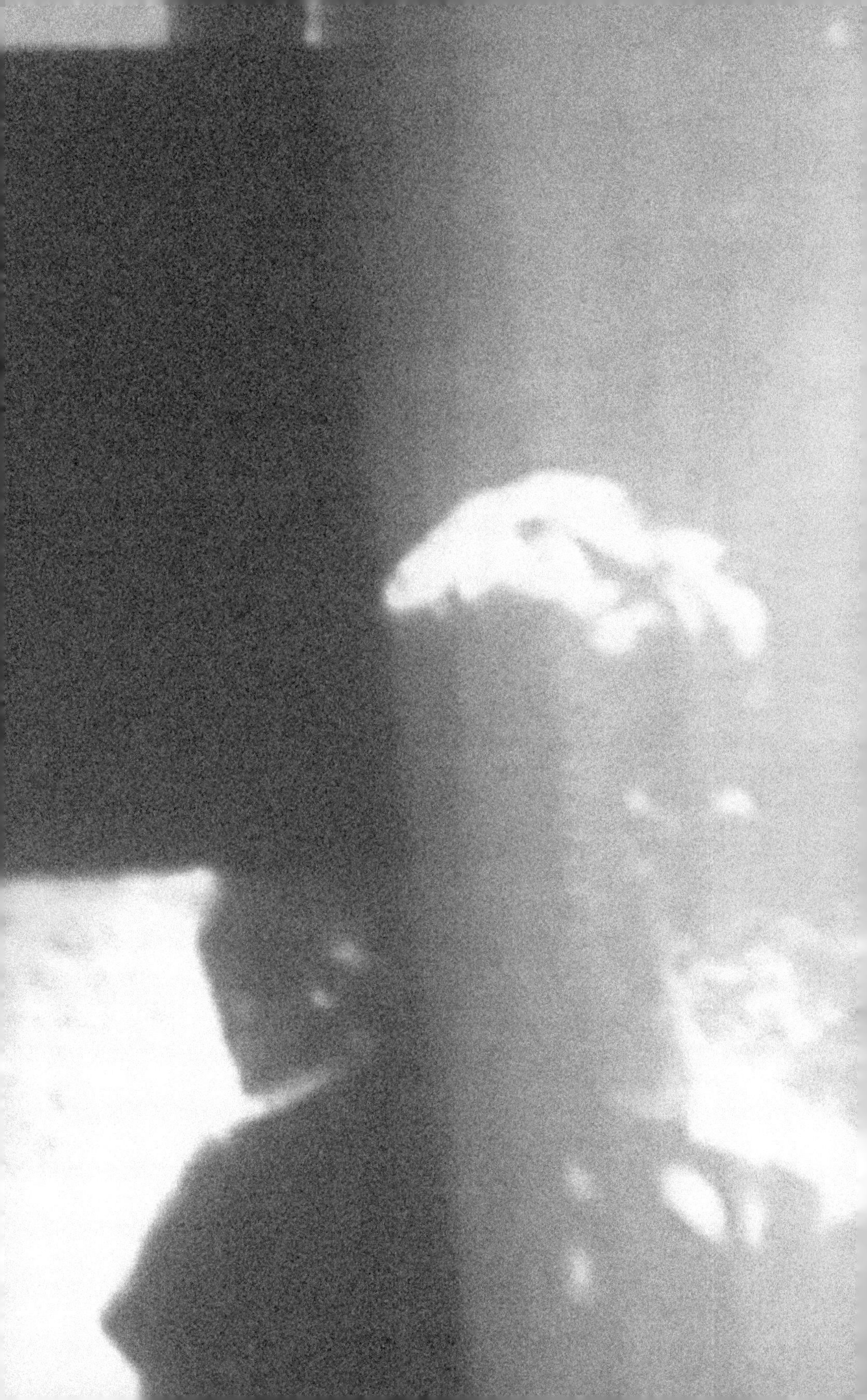

scratched, scorched, etc.?

LB: I've explored a lot of different ways of messing with the film image that could give me not just interesting results but results that I felt had meaning to them in the context of a specific film I was working on. In the case of *Fissures*, for instance, the fact that lost memory or—not just lost memory, actually; it has to do with loss in general and in this case, with longing and loss of a parental figure, or loss of ideals of home—all those types of things that have to do with nostalgia, or what could have been or what was. So it's not just what the image is, but how it's treated. In *Fissures* it becomes very symbolic of this opening up of this other space, like it's another dimension, you know?

MM: I was thinking of how the manipulation, and the general chemical treatment to the stock film, operates like a veil, concealing the home films and the imagery, not just in *Fissures* but in all of the films I watched, and how it creates a specific spatial relationship. You mentioned the symbolic aspects, but it's also very formal. It's almost like, from the viewer's position, if one were to walk through that space, they would have to start with the decay and manipulation and move through to a clearer image, but that clearer image isn't necessarily trustworthy, or you might say reliable.

LB: I like that. That's a good interpretation of it. I think you put your finger on it. Well as much as possible because, in a way, I guess it is about trying to put your finger on something and it's very slippery. But I do think you put your finger on the idea that it is slippery. This idea of trying to get to something and it's something that you're not always clear about. And it's all so complex. You might have many feelings attached to a memory. And I think that it's not just in the realm of the memory but also in the realm of the present and how we feel about past experiences. It's really complex. But also in the moment, like in the now of the viewing, I try to bring that to the experience of the viewing so that it's there, too, this slipperiness, and perhaps how we negotiate those things interiorly.

It has to do with our mortality as well. It's these things that are lost, things that are ephemeral, things that we try to hold on to that are just slipping by, and also the things that we let go of that we might be attached to, the things we are attached to that we let go of. And there's just this kind of movement as we try to navigate this whole human experience, I guess [chuckles]. I laugh a little when I say this because it's so big, but it's little too because it's so common. The things we struggle with and that we have a hard time to even begin to put in words. And in some ways that's why I make films. I used to write poetry but I felt frustrated with my inability to capture some of those issues I'm trying to explore in my films. I couldn't do it, at least in any way that was satisfying to me. And when I discovered film, I felt there was this possibility to give some kind of voice to those things that are so hard to put into words, and that have to do with experiencing different things through our senses.

I think for me there are three things that probably come out the most on that sensory level in trying to give shape to these things: the visual, the auditory, and the tactile. I usually try to use sound that has a very low frequency. Sounds you don't just hear but feel physically. And then the other tactile aspect, of course, is more like a representation of the tactile. With the idea of texture and the idea of the things that might evoke the tactile, the delicate, almost disappeared thing when you feel the world through this, or its sharp edge, for instance; those kinds of textures.

MM: You were mentioning sound. I'm interested in the sound or the voiceover, particularly in *L'éclat du mal / The Bleeding Heart of It* (2005), where, at the beginning of the film, it's like a narration and the voiceover is speaking directly to the viewer. As the film progresses, she (the female voice) changes, and she begins to become muffled and her voice echoes. She's almost in the house, perhaps metaphorically at least, and in that sense it changes the position of the viewer. The viewer is then distanced away from the images, certainly their position in relation to the girl narrating.

LB: I like this idea that it sounds like she's inside the house. In the description of my film *Going Back Home* (2000), I refer to the notion of the dwelling as self, this idea of the house, the home as a metaphor for the self. So when you say that it feels like the voice is "inside the house" to me it's a great metaphor for "inside the self." It's like there's a turning inward and perhaps that's where there is real shelter. At one point, the voice seems to start talking to itself and more and more trying to convince itself: "I'm okay; I'll be okay ..." Recently I came across this line from Beckett saying, "I can't go on. I go on." I love that line. In some ways I think the voice in that film is saying that. "It's dark in the tunnel and I'm heading towards the light, the daylight. It's dark in the tunnel and I'm heading towards the light." It almost becomes a mantra like, "I can get through this." But then I think that it is perhaps at that point in the film where there might be a shift for the viewer in terms of possible identification with this disembodied voice. Hopefully it's inviting an engagement so that the viewers might bring their own subjectivity to the experience.

The voiceover is recounting actual dreams of mine taken from an audio dream journal I kept between 1990 and 1992. The narration starts off sort of calm; I think the first line in the voiceover, "In my dream ...," is basically announcing, "I'm going to tell you something. I'm going to tell you my dream." But soon after, the deconstruction starts happening, the fragmentation. Things start falling apart, like "all of the houses are falling apart," as it later says in the film's narration. Things are falling apart and I think that's what happens to the narrative. It's a piecing together of fragmentation, because the narration is literally a piecing together of excerpts from different dreams. The key, what is important to each part, is sort of like the story and it becomes what is essential. What is the essential part of this one dream? What is the strong image of that one? And the idea is to piece it all together while maintaining some kind of tension or contradiction from the association of sometimes conflicting emotions, attached to key moments from these dreams.

MM: In talking about the essence, it's interesting how the bits and pieces she gives in the dreams are very familiar. For instance, she talks about carrying herself as a little girl or running towards the light …

LB: They're like archetypes in a way; in any case it's trying to get to some kind of archetypal references.

And with the dreams, I think that ties in there, as well. Even the image of the house, I have so many home movies, but this is the third time that I used these particular images of the house in which I grew up. I have a lot of personal history with that house. Five generations of my family lived there at different times so it's very loaded personally in terms of family history. But it's more than that. That particular image of that house, as opposed to other footage I might have of it, presents it more like an archetype of the family home with the church steeple in the background and especially with the people in front. It's in *Imprint* (1997), it's in *Fissures*, and it's in *L'éclat du mal / The Bleeding Heart of It*—it's a haunting image!

MM: So *The Bleeding Heart of It* would be the house. And in that sense, it's interesting how formal the house is. It really holds the structure of the film.

LB: Yes, exactly. That's a big part of *The Bleeding Heart of It*. It's the "It." *It* is the House and all it stands for, the House and the Family; it is the family dynamic within the house. It is the concept of the Home in our culture and what it is supposed to be, what it is and what it isn't. So you're right, that is the *It*. Actually you're one of the few persons to bring up the *It*. It has this loaded history going back generations—the Patriarchal Family, all the generations of the *It* at home; and it's the bleeding heart of *It*, because there's a lot of bloodshed (in metaphorical ways, and also in literal ways)—the house is like a wound.

MM: Wound? Or womb?

LB: A womb and a wound. It's a complicated thing.

MM: There was a part towards the end of the film where the house actually starts to bow, and I was impressed that it still stood. It was/is such a buoyant, rubber structure, and metaphorically the house seems to bend but never break.

LB: Yes … but in *Imprint* there is a total obliteration of it. This film is about, in so many ways, my intervention, what I am doing to this film image of the house, what has imprinted me and how I'm in turn putting my mark on it through hand manipulations and chemical decay processes. In the last segment, where the decay has almost totally obliterated any trace of the house and all that's left is abstracted, coloured emulsion, there is still one frame left with a window from the house on it. If you look for it, you can see it, the one frame in a flash. The house is almost obliterated, but still there. And I chose to end with that segment because that is so strong. It's heart-wrenching in a way, makes you feel kind of sorry for the house: "Oh please don't forget about me! Don't abandon me!" I never put it in that way before, but it's a little bit like that. This idea that you can't completely get away from it, you know?

MM: I wanted to ask about titles. They seem to operate both formally and conceptually and their placement in the films seems particularly important.

LB: The titles are integral. In *Going Back Home* it's important that it's read at the beginning because it sets an expectation. How the titles work formally and conceptually affect how the films might get read. *Going Back Home* sets the tone, especially with the music that accompanies the film: very sweet and innocent, however what follows is chaos and destruction. On the other hand, there is beauty. The idea of longing is very strong: one can't go back home, but you keep on trying. The film is very sad to me. With the sweet or naïve music, you can't help but think of lost innocence. The note that is off-key on the toy piano gives it away. There is something in that little note … Also the images are beautifully rich with colours of gold, like something precious, full of light and warmth and in contradiction with what is going on in the images—found footage of homes being ravaged by disasters.

MM: I'm also curious about the title of one of the films in the Biennial: *Jours en fleurs* (2003), where the film is saturated in menstrual blood. We were talking earlier that the title is very difficult to translate.

LB: It is important that the title is in my original language because it alludes to the expression "être dans ses fleurs," which in the area where I grew up (New Brunswick, Canada) refers to girls having their period.

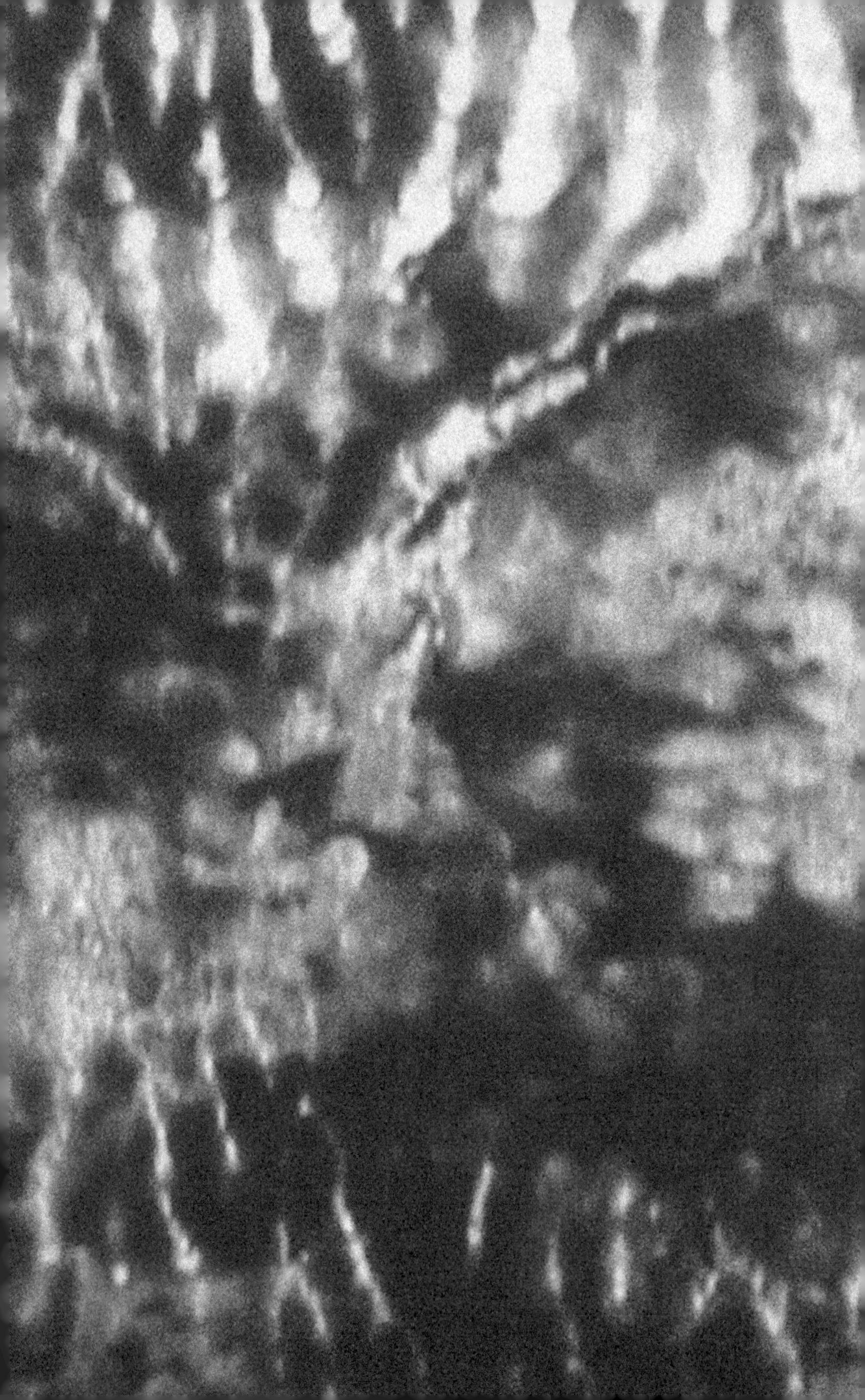

The expression translates loosely as "being in your flowers." It has a certain loveliness to it but also a certain violence, the idea that you can't say you have your period, because of the taboo. There is violence in omission, something we can't talk about and which denies women's experience. It is such a big taboo to represent it. Just look at the ads for tampons where blue liquid is used to simulate blood.

But I really wanted to keep the poetry of the expression in the title and its reference. The film captures both the beauty of nature and its destructive force. It's probably my most abstract film, but there are still recognizable images. You can still see traces of images of trees in springtime bloom even after the images' transformation resulting from their incubation in the menstrual blood. I think of the film as a collaboration with nature.

It's really essential to how I approached this, putting the background details in the [Biennial] program notes like that. But if someone doesn't have access to the backstory (i.e., the title and how the film was made), they can still get the references to nature and its various aspects: the materials and textures and colours of nature. It is dark and light; you have the tweeting of birds, but you also have the stressing quality, a rumbling sound underneath, and strange things emerging from the trees. The title refers to growth; the cataclysm speaks to the cycle of life.

MM: The manipulation of the film itself creates a pulse, the pulse of nature.

LB: It also sounds like a pulse, same as in *The Bleeding Heart of It*: this idea of a heartbeat. I want to translate that blood flow, that flow of life in my films. I remember when my partner Joe saw *Imprint*—he said it looks like someone bled all over the film! Blood is a complicated issue—life and death. But mostly life.

MM: Blood is mostly life until you see it.

LB: Exactly … but then again there's always blood at birth.

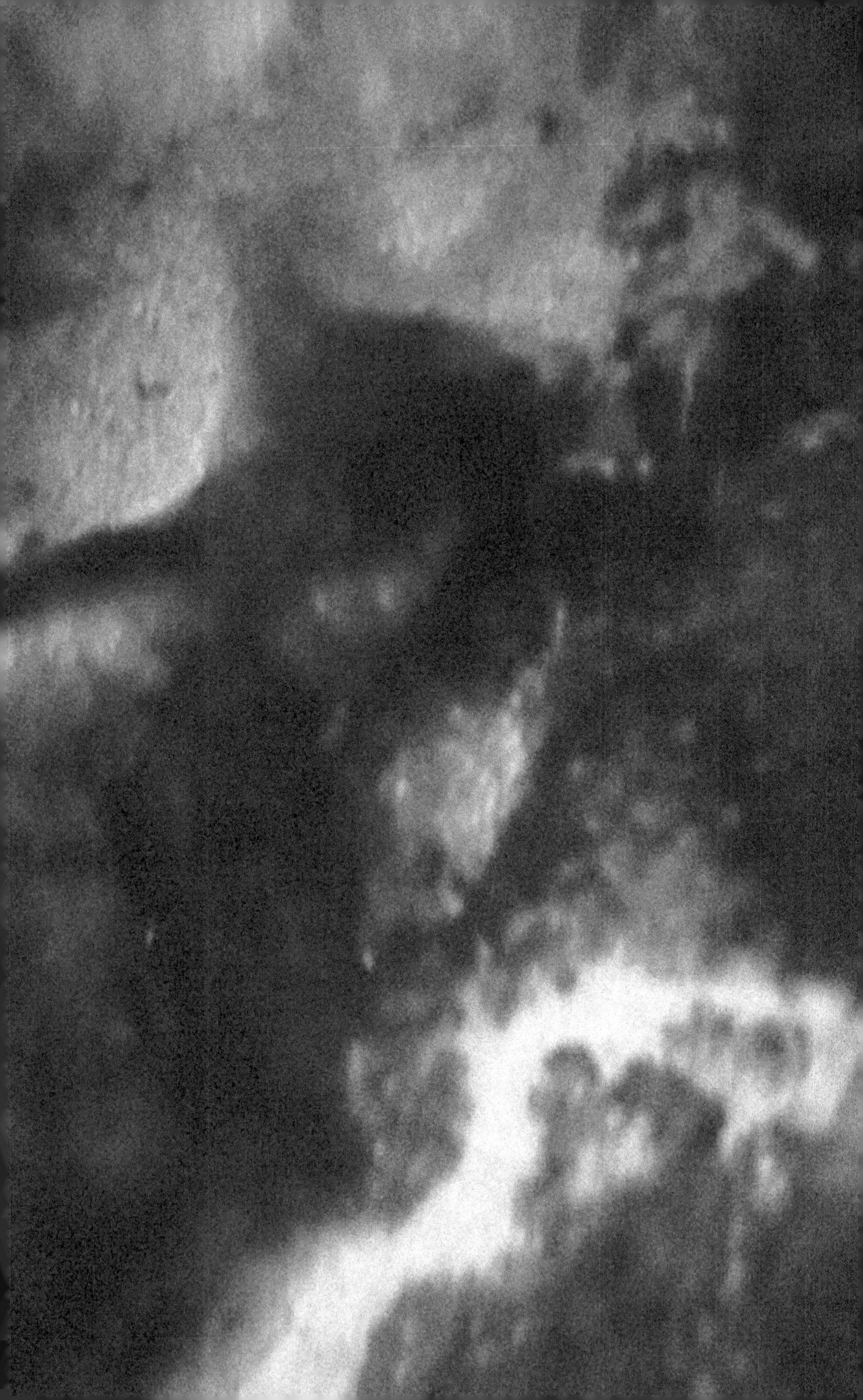

Past // Images :: Future // Remains

An Interview with Louise Bourque

Todd Fraser and Clint Enns

This interview is a collaboration between Louise Bourque, Todd Fraser, and Clint Enns. The initial set of questions, contributed by Fraser and Enns, were posed to Bourque over Skype and have been edited into their current conversational form by Enns and Bourque.

TFCE: Tell us about where your film education started and when you began using alternative approaches to moving-image production.

LB: In the 80s, while studying journalism at Université de Moncton, I took a course on silent cinema that introduced me to avant-garde and European arthouse cinema. The course was taught by Père Maurice Chamard, a passionate Catholic priest with the soul of a poet.

Before I went to Concordia University in 1987, I had never even used a 35mm still camera. In my second year, while studying under the guidance of Marielle Nitoslawka, I made *Jolicoeur Touriste* (1989). It was at that time I began to use experimental techniques and to develop technical skills. Not only did Nitoslawka introduce me to a wide range of experimental films and video art, she encouraged a hands-on approach to learning and helped me to develop my own voice. By my third year, I had started to teach the optical printing workshops.

In 1990, I moved to the United States to study at the Art Institute of Chicago. My thesis film was *Just Words* (1991), which I had started while studying at Concordia; however, most of the time was spent working on *The People in the House* (1994), which used fairly traditional production methods and involved a large crew that included many experimental filmmakers, like Deborah Stratman (art direction), Allen Ross (cinematography), and Zack

Stiglicz (narrator reading from *The Catechism of the Catholic Church*).

TFCE: *The People in the House* has a short companion film, a behind-the-scenes look at the shooting of the film. Is this where some of your source material was taken from for *Remains* (2011)?

LB: I have only recently released this companion piece. It is a short, 16mm film shot behind the scenes on the last day of our shoot. Since we didn't have much film left in the camera, we simply shot off the roll. I labelled the roll "People Shoot 'Home Movies,'" which eventually became the title of the film. I recently returned to this roll searching for images of Allen Ross, who was murdered after this film was made. Allen was an amazing cinematographer.

Remains was made using outtakes from *The People in the House*, not this footage.

TFCE: It seems inconceivable that you weren't introduced to moving-image cameras earlier, given the presence of home movies in your work. One gets the impression that your father was a shutterbug. Can you talk about your use of home movies?

LB: My father's home-moviemaking period was from 1955 until 1966 (I was born in 1963). My dad turned to photography later in life. He was also an accomplished painter with his own distinctive style and had a unique way of seeing the world. For example, my dad didn't believe children should learn to read and write before kindergarten, as he saw this as a time to develop their senses and to engage with nature. He encouraged us to see the world through our own eyes. Though he was a psychiatrist, he was always artistically inclined and it made sense that he made art later in his life.

I did not just inherit home movies, I inherited *beautiful* home movies. My father shot on regular 8mm Kodachrome film. In spite of my dad being self-taught, most of the images were in focus, and well exposed (despite the camera not having an internal light metre). His footage included closeups, sophisticated camera movement, and even impressive establishing shots. In the early 90s, I had a lot of this footage transferred to 16mm.

My first formal use of this archive was in *Just Words*. I had seen Patricia MacGeachy perform Beckett's *Not I* (1972) on stage, and was inspired to combine images from the play with images of my mother (who had recently passed away). The play features a disembodied Mouth delivering the internal monologue of a third-person self: She, a self as other. Before her death, my mother lost her sight and then fell silent.

TFCE: What was the influence of Anthony Page's *Not I* (1977) on *Just Words*? How does your work differ from the play?

LB: When I made *Just Words*, I was unaware of this film. I am now aware of it, but I have never seen it and have intentionally avoided it. I thought that filming the Mouth in closeup was transgressive given Beckett's stage direction. We also applied makeup to the teeth of the Mouth, making them look decayed; as if they were coming from the grave. By incorporating images of my mother, I transformed Beckett's text into something more personal. The She, the I. Beckett was meticulous by nature and given that he passed away while we were filming *Just Words*, I am unsure if he would be turning in his grave or granting his permission.

After working with images of the Mouth and images of my mother, I wanted to add an extra dimension to the work by including another voice. Beckett's text makes use of the ellipsis with sentences interrupted and returned to later, lending itself to the use of two voices. The sync-sound text was delivered with a quick tempo (although slowed down once my mother turns away from the camera) and the voiceover text was delivered slowly, making it sombre.

TFCE: Your work is personal yet deals with themes that are universal. Can you talk about how you navigate this line?

LB: In order to make my work universal, I make a point of avoiding anecdotal details specific to my personal circumstances. Although my home movies are personal, I treat them as "images" when selecting them. For example, while the house in *Imprint* (1997) is my family home, it is treated as a "house," which takes on further meaning given the traditional "patriarchal family" standing in front of it. In general, I select images for their visceral a/effect. When working within more traditional production methods my work disregards plot and character development in favour of oneiric tableaus acted out by archetypal figures. For instance, *The People in the House* uses family members as archetypes.

Images and sound can have an emotional impact without the audience necessarily being able to identify their exact source. Emotional complexity is conveyed through the juxtaposition of contrasting elements.

TFCE: Can you discuss the chemical treatments in *Imprint*? It seems like there are different kinds of tinting, toning, transfers, bleaching, emulsion lifting, hole punching—what was the genesis of this project and your exploration of the different techniques? The film seems to exist in the space between memory, nightmare, and nostalgia. What are the connections between these processes and these emotions?

LB: The project started out as an exploration of different forms of celluloid manipulation. I had received an Exploration Grant from the Canada Council for the Arts to experiment with different techniques, and *Imprint* came out of these experiments. The source footage was a short sequence of home movies copied multiple times. The film is about transformation, not necessarily about disintegration or distress. Imprints that form memories and imprints marking the surface of the film. Literally, moving beyond the emulsion as a way of moving past, or behind, the surface of the image.

Through my manipulations, I make the home-movie images my own, reclaiming them. I see the images as beautiful, although I am destroying them. For instance, at one point I rip the image apart before re-assembling it. At another, I add tissue paper to the surface of the image. I am using three types of processes: additive, subtractive, and chemical. Some are organic, others are photochemical. I tried to think about ideas these material processes can convey. For example, I intentionally scratched out the windows of the house as a way to look inside. This had a secondary effect that was unexpected: it made the house look like it was on fire. I was not just exploring the technical aspects, but their meaning and evocative power when applied to select images; that is, how the form and graphical elements created the content.

On a side note, while I was working on *Imprint*, I had the chance to visit Craig Baldwin in San Francisco. I asked him if he had any found footage of houses in distress in his collection—as source material for *Imprint*. I didn't end up using Craig's footage because the content of the images already conveyed distress and hence manipulating them would be redundant. However, these images became the foundation for *Going Back Home* (2000). Thanks, Craig.

TFCE: *Fissures* (1999), by comparison, is quite technically focused—perhaps because it was done with limited resources: a flashlight contact-printing system and short lengths of film. What is the original footage? How much of your films are shaped/determined by your access to materials, tools, and resources?

LB: For *Imprint*, no lab would handle my original since it was on the verge of falling apart. I was teaching at the School of the Museum of Fine Arts [SMFA] in Boston, which had its own 16mm contact printer. I did the contact printing with Joachim Knill, who introduced me to toning and other photochemical processes. In an effort to explore various toning techniques, I made black and white prints of some of my home-movie collection (which became the source material for *Fissures*) and of the footage Craig gave me for *Going Back Home*.

I was teaching at SMFA and had access to equipment, facilities, and other resources. It wasn't about limited resources, but an economy of means. Throughout my practice, I have taken advantage of the resources available to

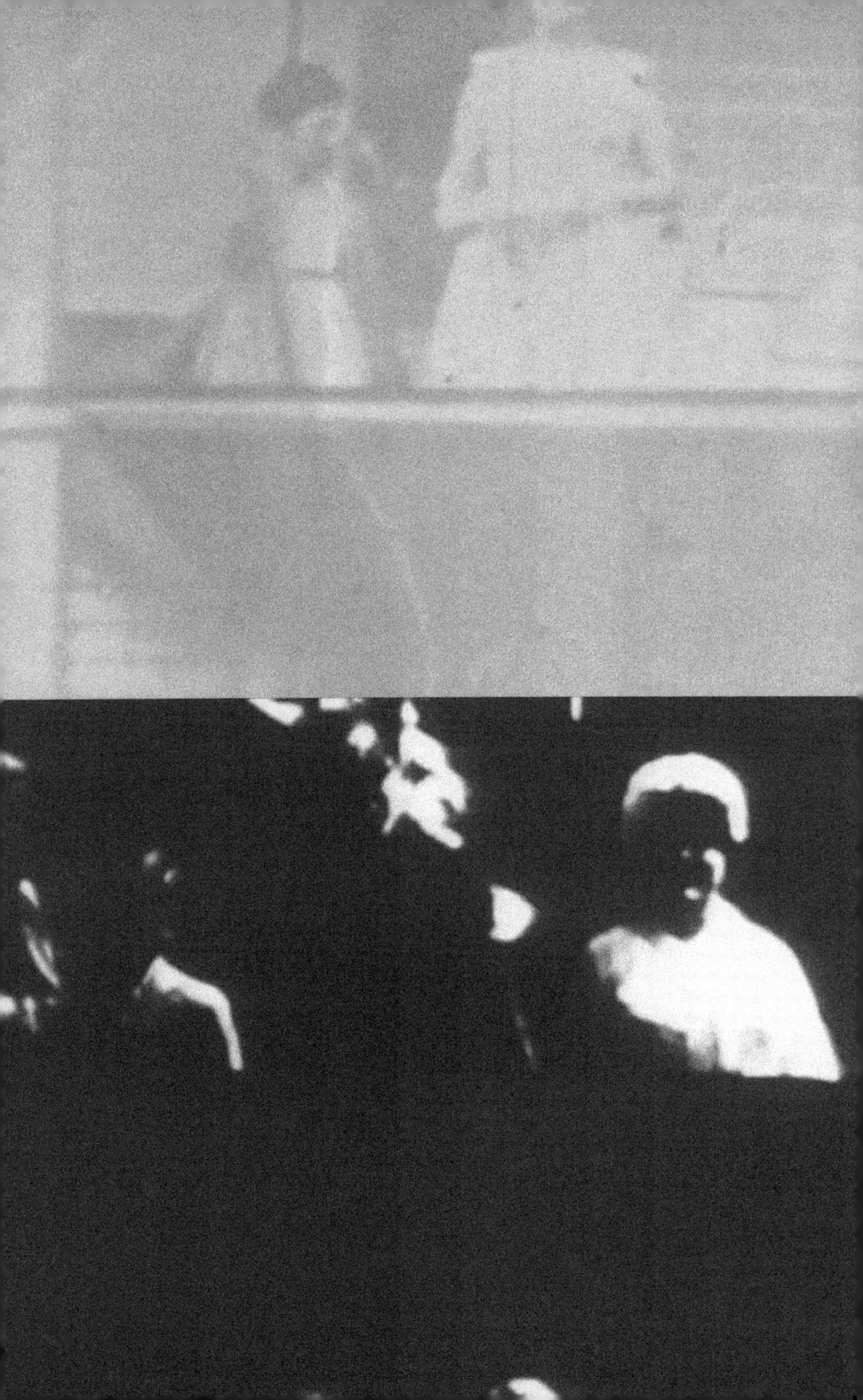

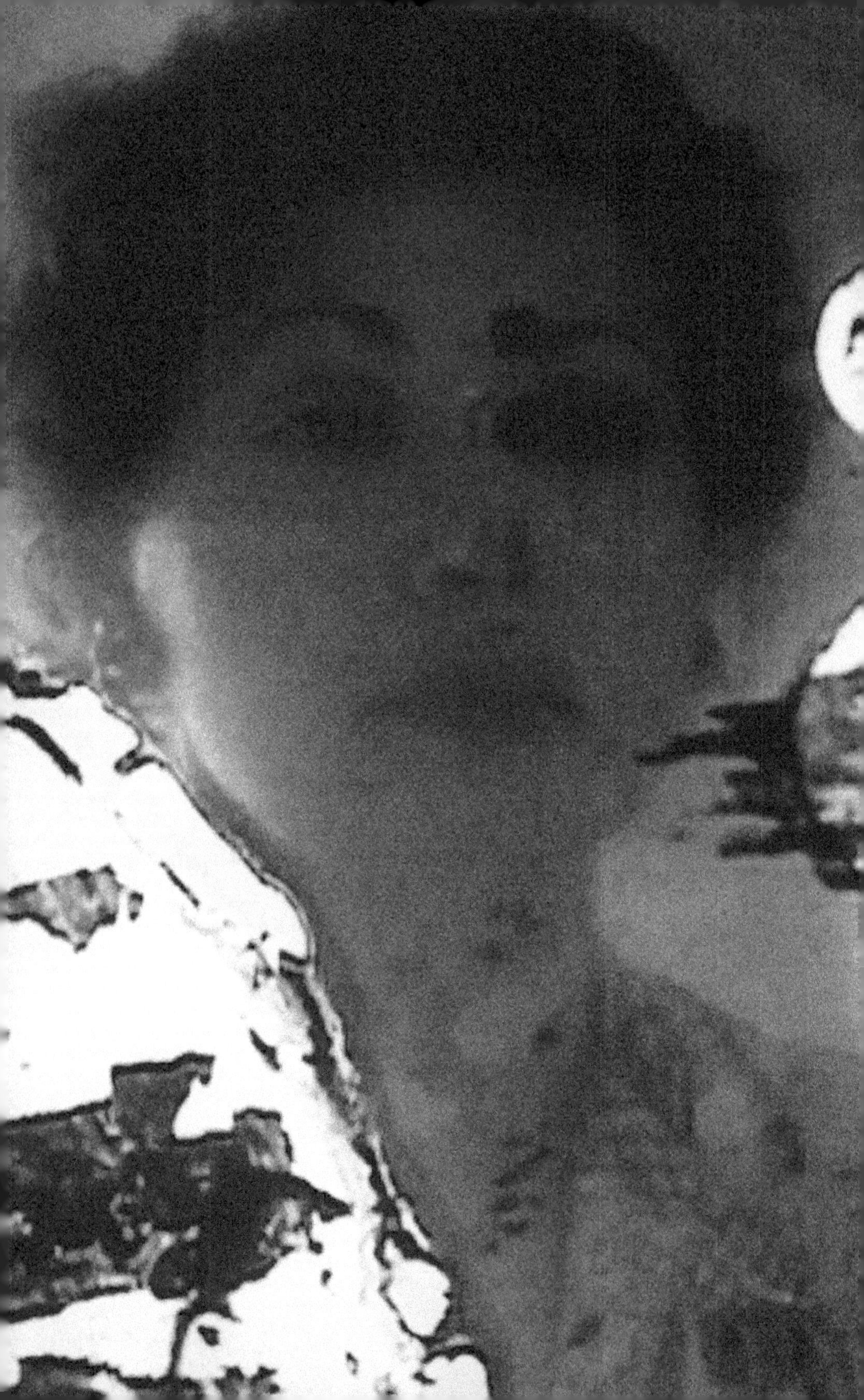

me and have not hesitated to seek out equipment when required to capture a certain vision.

TFCE: To what degree are *Remains* and *Self Portrait Post Mortem* (2002) determined by chance operations?

LB: There are chance operations throughout my work, but it is about finding the balance between control and "disorder." While I take meticulous notes in order to reproduce specific results, I am always seeking beautiful accidents. You get better results when you only leave one or two elements to chance while the other variables involved are restrained. You set up conditions for the element of chance to yield interesting results. It is a process of searching with some idea of what you are looking for.

Once you choose to include an image in your work, it is no longer random; it is a deliberate decision. However, it is also important to trust in process, to follow your intuition, and to be attentive to what is happening. While making work, I try to put my ego aside and to be totally in the moment.

My two buried films, *Remains* and *Self Portrait Post Mortem*, along with *Jours en fleurs* (2003), are collaborations with nature.

TFCE: Why was it important to have these burials occur at your childhood home in Edmundston?

LB: I buried outtakes from *Jolicoeur Touriste*, *Just Words*, and *The People in the House*—my first three films. I had heard Michele Fleming talk about burying films and wanted to try it. Logistically speaking, it was the only yard I had access to. Beyond that, the yard adjoining ours was previously a cemetery, so I felt that this was conceptually playful. Moreover, all of these films dealt with family, so I thought that burying them in my ancestral home was also compelling.

Since I was relocating to the United States, I felt the need to leave something behind. To let something take root. Also, I was attached to the outtakes and didn't want to simply discard them. They became my buried treasure. Five years later, I had to dig up my entire yard since the rock I used as a marker had been unknowingly moved by my father. Although they didn't help with the digging, my whole family was involved in helping me to find these images. To my surprise, in the first roll I found, there was an image of me that I didn't know existed. This was the source material for *Self Portrait Post Mortem*.

TFCE: Do you feel a strong connection or an affinity to the arts community in Atlantic Canada? Have you had many encounters with other arts and filmmaking groups in the Maritimes? For instance, have you worked with

Struts Gallery & Faucet Media Arts Centre, Festival international du cinéma francophone en Acadie [FICFA], the Atlantic Filmmakers Cooperative, or Galerie Sans Nom?

LB: When I was in high school, I took a poetry workshop with Acadian poet Gérald Leblanc. I remember the title of one of the poems I wrote, "Le fumeur de haschich" ["The Hash Smoker"]. He invited me to join the Association des écrivains acadiens [the Association of Acadian Writers]. It was there that I first met other poets, including Herménégilde Chiasson, Rose Després, Raymond LeBlanc, and Guy Arsenault. More than twenty-five years later I collaborated with Herménégilde on a work for a group exhibition of contemporary art at the Acadian Worldwide Congress, a project initiated by Galerie Colline (a contemporary art gallery in Edmundston).

After high school I moved to Montreal to attend Cégep du Vieux Montréal. Later, I moved to Moncton and quickly became involved in the visual art scene. At the time, Moncton was a hotbed for poetry and contemporary art. I wrote for *Le Front* [Université de Moncton's student newspaper], and I worked for Radio Canada Atlantique and Galerie Sans Nom. It was also in Moncton that I met Jean-Pierre Morin, who worked with me on *Jolicoeur Touriste*. He was the lead singer of Syntax Error, a seminal Moncton punk band that would project super 8 during their shows. He also introduced me to experimental film. Jean-Pierre and I met artist and poet Daniel Dugas and we later collaborated with him on a video poem based on writing by Gérald Leblanc.

My first retrospective was in Halifax at Mount Saint Vincent University Art Gallery in 2002, organized by Gerda Cammaer. After returning to Edmundston in 2012, I had a major retrospective organized by Huguette Desjardins (my visual arts teacher in high school) through the Association culturelle du Haut-Saint-Jean. My work was shown over the course of five days at various locations throughout Vallée du Haut-Saint-Jean. It included installations at libraries and churches, an artist talk, in addition to a screening at Cinéma V where the films were shown in 35mm. During the event, *Just Words* was shown at a literary club in Saint-Léonard where I was pleasantly surprised that people recognized my family from the home movies (my family briefly lived there). One of the women shared that my father was the doctor who delivered her.

In the summer of 2012, I took part in Ok.Quoi?! Contemporary Arts Festival put on by Struts Gallery, where I showed *Going Back Home Again* (2005), a 16mm installation version of *Going Back Home* at the Sackville Music Hall. The installation was the film shown looped and projected onto a postcard-size screen. Later that year, I had a retrospective at FICFA in Moncton. Amanda

Dawn Christie, who was the director at Galerie Sans Nom, organized a retrospective of my work after being approached by Images Festival in Toronto. Amanda went out of her way to transport a portable 35mm projector from the Atlantic Filmmakers Cooperative in Halifax. I was extremely grateful for this, as it is always my preference to show my work on film whenever possible.

TFCE: How do you decide the titles of your works?

LB: Sometimes I have a title before the film is made. Other times, it depends on the processes involved. For instance, for *Bye Bye Now* (2021) I knew the concept and title before I started the film. For *Auto Portrait / Self Portrait Post Partum* (2013), the title came early on. Once I knew I was going to film myself and knew I was going to explore the concept of separation, I chose a title that referenced *Self Portrait Post Mortem*, the only other work in which I appear.

For *Jours en fleurs*, I knew I wanted to explore the concept of fertility. At the time, I felt my biological clock ticking. The title is related to the Acadian expression equivalent to "visit from Aunt Flo," namely "être dans ses fleurs [to be in your flowers]." The Acadian expression is poetic; however, it avoids explicitly mentioning blood. This subject matter is still taboo. The source footage was of springtime blooms. These images were incubated in my blood for nine months.

TFCE: Who does your sound design?

LB: I do my own sound design, but often collaborate with others. The sound for *Jolicoeur Touriste* was done in collaboration with filmmaker Jean-Pierre Morin, who did the narration (he read a text from Frances Frost's children's book from 1953, *Rocket Away!*). He suggested a composition by XTC as the underlying soundtrack, which we slowed down to fit the duration of the film.

I worked with Mark Bain on a few films; most notably I used excerpts from Mark's composition "StartEndTime" in *L'éclat du mal / The Bleeding Heart of It* (2005). Mark's piece uses sound of the ground vibrations produced by the collapse of the World Trade Center in 2001. The first line of the voiceover says, "there's a war going on."

I often re-purpose and manipulate sound. For instance, in *L'éclat du mal / The Bleeding Heart of It* I use the sound of a flag blowing in the wind, which, in combination with the sounds of birds, sonically resembles the flapping of wings. In building the sound design, sometimes there are only one or two tracks. For instance, *Fissures* and *Imprint* only use one track. In *Fissures*, I manipulated the sound of a machine sourced from the BBC sound effects library. In *Imprint*, I used Enrico Caruso's "A Dream" played on a portable, hand-cranked gramophone. While editing the film, I was listening to the record and was so absorbed that when the record came to an end, it just kept skipping. I knew I had to use this sound.

In contrast, *Jours en fleurs* has sixteen tracks of sound. For that film, I wanted to assign a sound to each of the visual micro-events as they occur in the film. For instance, when a sprocket hole is shown on screen, there is an accompanying sound. When other visual elements occur, they have their own sounds.

For the underlying soundtrack of *Auto Portrait / Self Portrait Post Partum*, I worked with Joshua Bonnetta to record, once again, a gramophone. He used a contact mic to record the gramophone, which I was manipulating. The record playing was Doris Day's "Would I Love You." An un-manipulated, instrumental version is played at the end of the film over the credits. The film also incorporates excerpts from other sentimental pop songs in an attempt to deconstruct conventional representations of love.

TFCE: Can you talk about your collaborations with Joe Gibbons and Tony Conrad? Namely, *The Producer* (2005), *Rooftop Song* (2005), and *Down and Out in Buffalo* (2005). *The Producer* was shown at the 2006 Whitney Biennial. Are the other films considered finished? Have they been shown?

LB: Joe and Tony were really close friends and collaborators. In 2005, Joe and I spent some time in Buffalo at the Lenox Hotel, where we shot several films including *The Producer*, *Rooftop Song*, and *Down and Out in Buffalo*. *Down and Out in Buffalo* has been shown in Boston. *Rooftop Song* has never been presented. The soundtrack is the same one that I used for *Remains*; my vocalizations with Joe's effects. *Rooftop Song* was shot by Joe. I act in it and Tony is in the background performing as a lurker. *Down and Out in Buffalo* was also shot by Joe, and features Tony and me at an empty bar. The work explores the aesthetics of boredom and unspecified malaise. As an aside, Tony, Joe, and I had gone to record sound under Niagara Falls, which was a great experience. This sound was supposed to be for *a little prayer (H-E-L-P)* (2011); however, it was lost.

Joe and I helped each other on many works over the years, whether it was on their concepts, grant proposals, or more technical aspects like camera, editing, and sound. For instance, Joe was the co-editor of *Auto Portrait / Self Portrait Post Partum* and I helped with his film *Confessions of a Sociopath* (2001). Also, we both worked with editor Dan Van Roekel who co-edited *Jours en fleurs* and *Confessions*.

TFCE: Your co-editor, Guillaume Vallée, mentioned a "film puzzle" while discussing *Bye Bye Now*. What is it? Is *Bye Bye Now* considered a finished film?

LB: The "film puzzle" consists of my rejects, material that was too dark to use in *Fissures*. When I did a Banff Centre residency in 2014, I used toner to reveal the latent images and, at the time, the film was so brittle it broke into tiny little pieces. I decided to re-build the film using tape. It took me about six months to complete. Once it was re-assembled I shot the film at different speeds off a Steenbeck, similar to the way I shot *Self Portrait Post Mortem* and *Jours en fleurs*. I used some of this footage for the prologue to *Bye Bye Now*.

Bye Bye Now is a nearly finished work, and was presented at Montréal International Festival of Films on Art [FIFA] in 2019. At this point, I am not totally satisfied with it and think that the sound design needs some work. This became especially apparent after seeing/hearing it at FIFA.

TFCE: Are you currently working on any new artworks?

LB: I have a lot of material that I have generated over the years, mainly for specific projects that have been put on hold for one reason or another. This material will become the basis of future projects. I also have a longer piece that I have been working on since 2004, tentatively titled *A Secret Place to Hide (entre chien et loup or the incredible true life story of Jeanette l'invisible)*. The work blends autobiographical elements with fiction and is about the inner life of a woman who is coming to terms with childhood trauma. The film proceeds with the associative logic of memories and dreams, and uses a spiral-like narrative structure. In other words, it doesn't use a traditional narrative structure and incorporates many experimental techniques.

When my father was dying, I collected his gauze bandages. I wanted to hold on to something that was so close, so intimately connected to him. I want to use the texture of the gauze as layers, and the blood that was on the bandages to transform images. I am making the film for my dad and as an homage to his legacy.

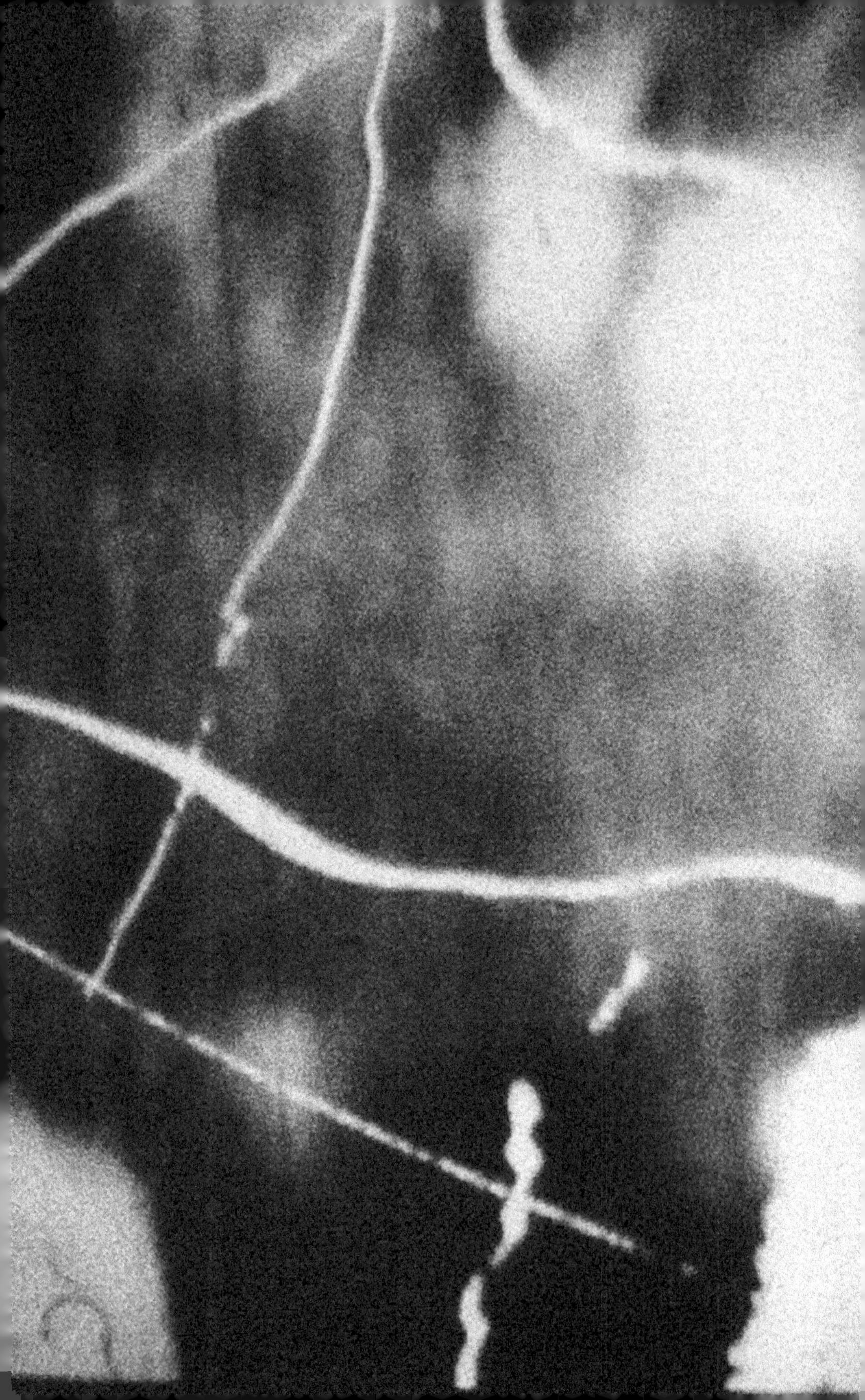

Letters from Hell

Mike Hoolboom

Why not begin with an admission? Like too many others, I once believed in progress. I was sent to the usual schools, where grades were counted in a steady addition, one could begin only with the first grade before passing on to the second, which was only a preparation for the third, which inevitably made way for the fourth. Each subject was presented like the old colonial maps, as half-finished continents that should be drawn and conquered in a steady campaign of attrition. The entire project reeked of progress, an incremental accretion of understanding, even of virtue.

But after school, the dutifully copied diagrams praised by my wise instructors were not able to contend with my playground bullies, the cruel hands that taught me the oldest and unwanted joys of submission. Capital had disciplined us well after all. It was difficult to find pictures for this new state, where every hope of order was crushed by a riot of compulsion. I searched for years, until arriving at last at the brief, hardly-there movies of the Acadian anti-princess Louise Bourque.

It feels strange to write about her picture ruins, as if I were calling out the most retiring person in the room. These are films that refuse notice. They rush past quickly, and are invariably short, as if concerned about overstaying their welcome. They are tangential somehow, they offer not a look but a glance, a glimpse even, a brief interval of openings. Perhaps the fantasy of speaking directly, or illustrating a point, is not where the rub lies, where the urgency calls. Does it seem strange that a projection vehicle like a movie, which is a machine for conserving time and memory, would shrink from the task of presentation? Perhaps these movies offer a different kind of picture, an alternating current even. Locked together, like conjoined twins, is the need to show and to keep a secret.

When I had reached the end of myself and became resigned to film school, I was met there with a population that had been failed by language. They couldn't talk at all. Sounds would come from their mouths but they were unrecognizable, even to the speakers. But there still burned within each one the desire to express themselves, and so we had arrived at this discount suburban hideaway, hoping the new tools of sound and pictures would allow us to say what words could never manage. I can imagine Louise as one of their number. She's spent a lot of time standing at the front of classrooms as it turns out, trying to make her rent, talking the film talk, even though she doesn't believe that explanations are helpful, or even necessary.

Perhaps in place of an interpretation, one could write about Louise's films as if words no longer mattered, or at least with the certainty that they will never manage to reveal anything of importance. Words can only point to some distant place where meaning and desire might be located. What a relief!

The artist began to work in 1989, and slowly produced a suite of miniatures drawn from her endless Catholic family. She was the youngest of seven children, the pope lived in the master bedroom encouraging reproduction even as the artist-in-waiting shrank from her expected roles and duties. Where are the bad boys, the ones who don't fit in? How can I become an escape artist and slip the knot of unwanted attentions? Speaking of knots: I only want what I don't want. I can only say yes to what refuses me, erases me, negates every hope and action.

In her work she begins with a ground, with first principles, and her ground is always the material. It's the feeling in her hands. She touches every frame, she runs them through her fingers, which are filled with what she hopes is loving indifference. The materials are the golden brick road of escape, she works the silvery tissues, processing her footage herself, introducing salts and baths and forbidden chemistries so that these stolen moments, clipped from someone else's hopes, can live again, resurrected, torn away from their former settings (some critics like to name this "the parent footage," as if every movie were a family scene). How else to speak about yourself, if you don't exist, than to work on an endless autobiography made of footage that others have created? These stolen pictures have roots in the artist's life, they might as well be flickering from picture frames on her desktop, in place of family albums or Instagram avatars. And they are likewise coping machines trying to accommodate the family banishments of religious-state capitalism. It is this passage, from the nameless dread of experience to the film materials, that creates her process and methods.

Let's look at a test case, chosen at random from the artist's modest body of practice.

a little prayer (H-E-L-P) (2011) is the artist's twelfth film, made twenty-two years after she set to work. It begins with a quotation from Dante's *Inferno*. Standing at the bottom three rings of hell, the pilgrim-poet remarks on the sunrise. "Such joy attends your rising that I feel / as grateful to the dark as to the light." Why this equal gratitude, this infernal equation of light and darkness? Perhaps there are things that can be seen only when they are not visible. Louise begins her own journey with a thanksgiving prayer sent into the darkness, which is her proper home and the subject of this interlude.

The *Inferno*'s rhyming scheme draws together "the light" and "troubled sight," reminding us that sight may be troubled in light or darkness. Surely the poet, having undertaken this infernal journey, is afflicted with "troubled sight." How to unsee, undo, erase? How to remove the unwanted experiences that live inside this body? How to stop the endless return to these wounds, the compulsive repetitions that are the hallmark of trauma?

The artist opens her movie with thanks. Thank you for this darkness, thank you for hell, and especially for the bottom of hell, for the very worst of all. How could I feel the sweetness in my life, if I hadn't been able to taste this, live this, become this too?

There are just a few pictures in the movie, and they circulate in a round dance. The first shows a man hanging, though his image is flipped, so he appears upside down. This strange reversal of perspective un-hangs him. He might be un-falling from his death, perhaps back into his life. He could be defying gravity, overturning every natural law, because only then would his life become possible. Hell of course is the place where everything is "upside down," inversion is the rule.

The second picture shows the same man pinned against a target. It's Harry Houdini, the famous American escape artist and showman. These pictures have been stolen from a newsreel, and flicker into view, offered only in brief glimpses. Houdini's arms are outstretched, his face slightly raised, as if he were receiving messages from his mother in the clouds. It's a high-contrast picture, so in place of eyes there are dark holes that bleed together to produce a ghoulish face, already dead. His hands are bound to a great wooden wheel that stands behind him. The unseen crowd can only wonder: how can he escape his latest trial?

The third image offers us Houdini drowning, his smeared face a mask of regret and unconsciousness. If only I could remember what I had done. All that is left is the smell of the bodies, the taste of him in my mouth.

The fourth shows the escape artist in chains. Here is the freedom one can achieve only in restraint. I can't help but admire his need to be tightly bound, to admit the caress of leather and steel in a return to the womb, before

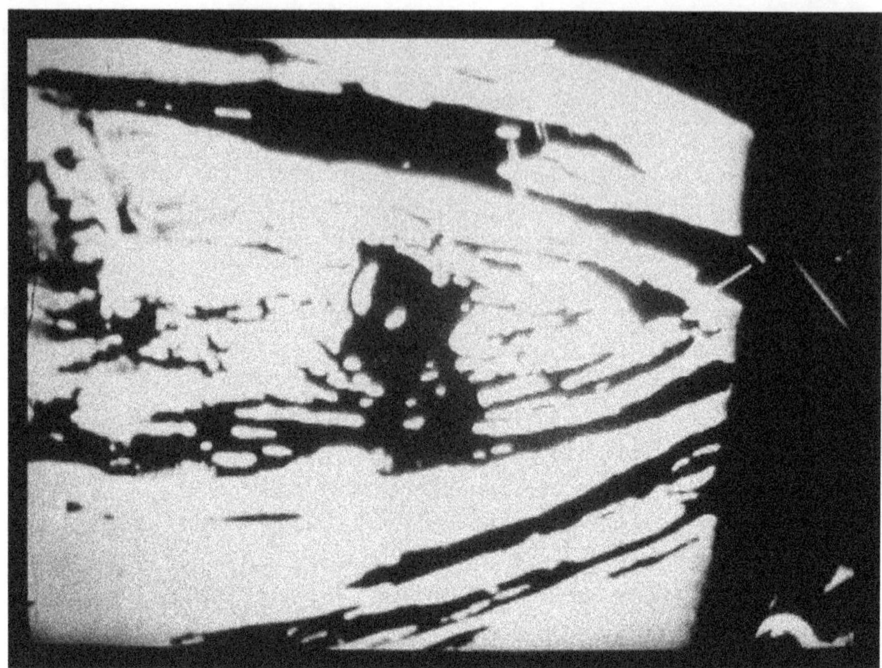

wriggling free of that obligation too. He offers a grim outlook, the eyes like holes poked into the doughy haze of a face.

Let's begin again with this admission: these words are a lie. The Houdini instants are not what the viewer encounters at all. This quartet of pictures appears in single-frame flashes, often as afterburns, they are sensed rather than seen impressions. Mostly what we witness are the marks of film processing, which is another way of saying: nothing. I guess this is the darkness that makes the sun possible, the midnights for which the artist is grateful. The emptiness, the abyss, the dark places it is necessary to go to in order to find a picture.

Is it possible to imagine again that one needs to make a journey in order to find a picture? That they are not already here, in profusion, hurtling across my apartment universe in a flood of biblical proportions, threatening to drown our lives, our politics, our social relationships, our attempts at culture? This artist is creating an image of a search, and perhaps it's no accident that she does so using "old-fashioned" methods, artisanal and handmade. She kneads the emulsion, applying developer before careful washings. Like all acts of love, her handling leaves its mark, and it is these scars that make her search possible. She names them little prayers. The man who is the object of this search cannot be shown directly. If you met him face to face, he would turn you to stone. So the artist enters into this silver labyrinth armed with metaphor and allegory, she finds his likeness somewhere else, and only then is able to move towards the dangerous and forbidden. In other words: she finds a way to face her unbearable truth.

This quest narrative is not resolved in triumphant discovery, there are no homecomings or arrivals. Instead, the film is an image of the quest itself, the artist's yields offer only glimpses of a man who cannot help seeking out his own bondage and subjugation. I am a prisoner of myself. And I need you to look at me. I need to make a show of this subaltern abjection. This is how we come together, this is what we might call love.

> Houdini, Buster Keaton, Charlie Chaplin and Harold Lloyd. All of them are embodied thinkers of the Capitalocene: their movements and gestures pose the question of the end of sovereignty of the living (human) body in relation to technological systems of production and measurement, from the clock to the Cloud. From Houdini to Yongning, the question remains: what does it mean to be free within capitalism? How can the individual body gain agency in relation to the processes of mechanical production and abstraction?[1]

Like Houdini, the couple in this film are refugees from the capitalist-machine body regime, hence Louise's truck with a medium—film—whose serial sprockets/pictures resemble nothing less than an assembly line of images. She takes this machinic art by the hand, trying to turn it. Fleeing modernity in their broken techno-bodies, stunned by the tidal wave of screen-culture prosthetics, the artist's soft machine cinemas are temporary shelters and arrangements for a fugitive reinvention whose tools can only point the way out of the old world dilemmas, without enabling the journey itself. Or as the film's title puts it: H-E-L-P.

The man is in chains, he can't help who he has become, he can't undo his life, nor can she unlock her criminal fascination. They are trying to create new forms of reproduction, new kinds of coupling outside the codes of what is acceptable, moral, reasonable. They want to make new pictures but these are not yet possible, so they have to live on garbage, on the refused and forgotten, and recycle the needs of others in order to find a language for resistance. It's only by telling someone else's story that I can arrive at my own. The escape artist is falling and I am falling with him. Enclosed together in a bio-techno-capitalist bondage.

The epigraph places the escape artist in the dark underworld of hell. In Dante's imagination hell appears as a series of circles that bottoms out in a great icy lake where Judas is forever frozen, a giant mirror reflecting hell back on itself. When the pilgrim-poet meets men running a race, or plunged in fire, he catches a glimpse of what they are condemned to do for all eternity. Eno once opined that repetition is a form of change, but here, the fundamental character of hell, the quality that makes hell hellish, is repetition.

Houdini in chains looks over at someone. If his body is trussed and frozen, his eyes are restless, opening to an unseen witness to his struggles. How can you help me if I can't help myself?

NOTES

1. Paul B. Preciado, "Voguing on the Roof of Corporate Architecture: RIP Wu Yongning," *Work, Body, Leisure*, Dutch contribution to the 16th International Architecture Exhibition of La Biennale di Venezia in 2018, <https://work-body-leisure.hetnieuweinstituut.nl/publication/voguing-roof-corporate-architecture-rip-wu-yongning>.

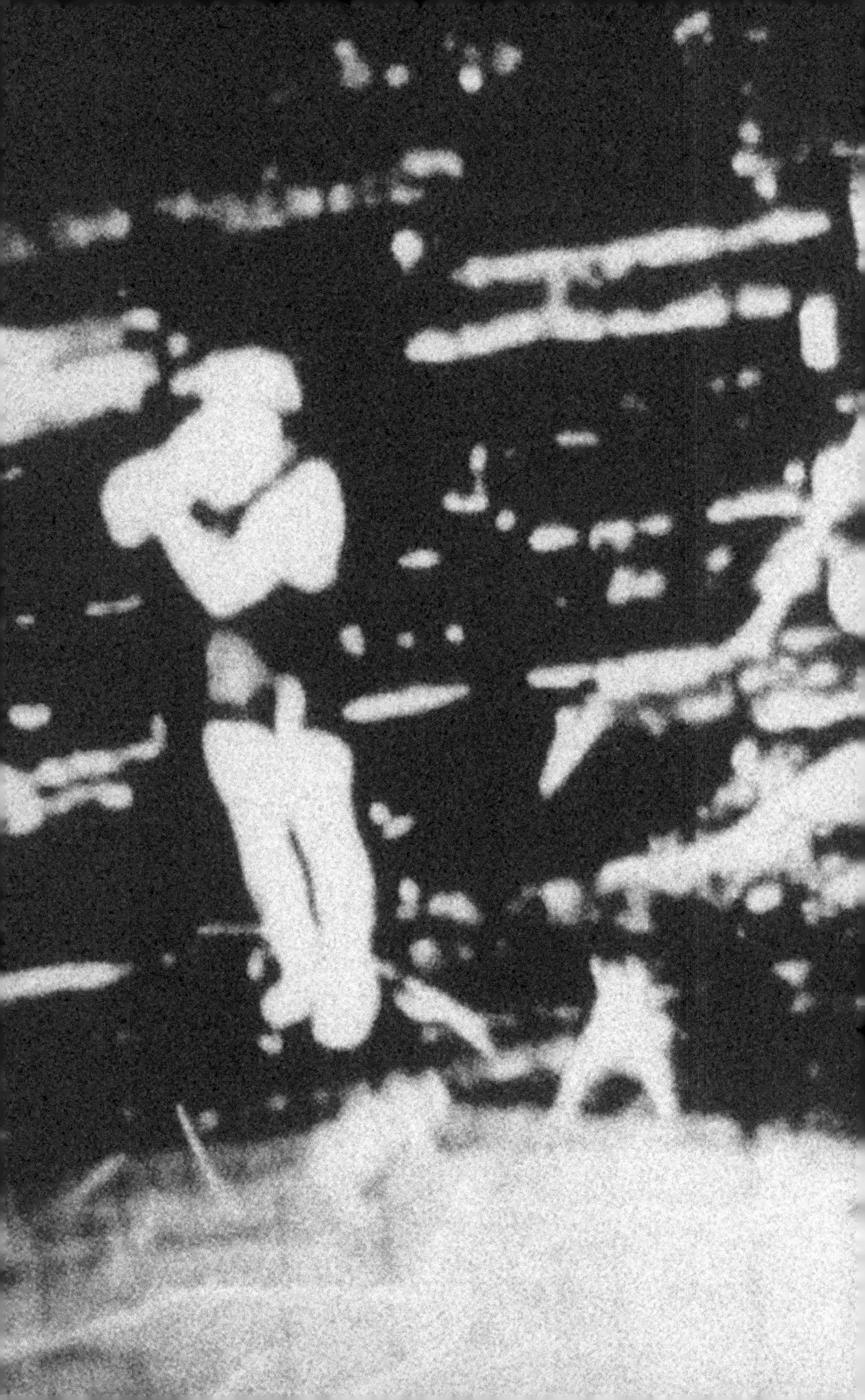

Le père derrière la caméra

Un voyage à travers l'archive familiale des Bourque

Guillaume Vallée

En 2018–19, j'ai eu la chance de faire le montage avec Louise Bourque pour son dernier opus, *Bye Bye Now* (2021). Voici quelques fragments de souvenirs de cette expérience.

J'ai rencontré Louise Bourque pour la première fois en 2014 lors d'un symposium sur le cinéma expérimental à DAÏMÔN, un centre d'artistes de Gatineau, au Québec. Ce fut une rencontre mémorable d'où est née une amitié qui, encore à ce jour, m'inspire. Nous devions nous retrouver quelque temps après à Main Film, à Montréal, pour une projection de *Auto Portrait / Self Portrait Post Partum* (2013), sa dernière œuvre à l'époque. En discutant de ce film avec elle, Louise me parla d'un projet en développement, un film qui consistait en une série d'images en boucle, d'enfants saluant la caméra, issue de ses films de famille.

Son père filmait régulièrement avec sa caméra 8mm le quotidien des Bourque, dont Louise possède toutes les archives familiales sur pellicule. À ce moment, je ne me doutais pas que j'allais plonger dans ce matériel quatre ans plus tard, et que j'y serais intimement lié. Ma première rencontre avec ces images a eu lieu, lors de notre première séance collaborative de développement à la main chez Main Film. Les images imparfaites et subtilement stroboscopiques, en noir et blanc, étaient celles de deux enfants assis sur un perron et saluant la caméra. Elles ont agi comme un vortex qui m'aspira et me fit découvrir l'univers familial de la famille Bourque. Bien avant le début du processus de montage, j'ai eu le privilège de voir d'autres images non-coupées de *Bye Bye Now* sur mon projecteur 16mm. C'est à ce moment où j'ai eu l'impression que quelque chose d'incroyable allait ressortir de ce projet.

Le premier film que j'ai vu de Louise est *Self Portrait Post Mortem* (2002).[1] C'était en 2007 ou 2008, si ma mémoire est bonne. Durant cette période, je portais un intérêt obsessif au *structural filmaking* et entre autres, au travail de Jürgen Reble et de l'ensemble Schmelzdahin dont il a fait partie. En intégrant la décomposition de l'émulsion au sein du processus créatif et en optant pour une approche matérialiste du médium filmique, le contenu se voyait renforcé et l'artifice esthétique devenait alors beaucoup plus profond. Le film de Louise m'a prouvé que l'on pouvait obtenir une symbiose idéale entre le concept d'une œuvre et le travail sur la matérialité. Cette approche apparait dans *Bye Bye Now* de par l'utilisation judicieuse de la répétition et de la réinterprétation de Louise par la rephotographie et le traitement chimique des images.

C'est en 2018 que la postproduction du film commença. Les problèmes de santé de Louise limitaient fortement son utilisation d'un ordinateur, alors elle m'a demandé d'être assistant monteur.[2] Notre amitié a créé un environnement propice à la patience et à la compréhension permettant facilement l'adaptation à ses besoins. *Bye Bye Now* est une œuvre très subjective qui revisite la passé familial de Louise ce qui rend délicat le processus de montage par quelqu'un qui ne la connait pas.

Les premières minutes du *Bye Bye Now* proviennent d'un film mystérieux que Louise appelle « *the film puzzle* »: un mythique objet cinématographique sur 16mm, dont Louise m'a souvent parlé. Je n'ai jamais eu la chance de la

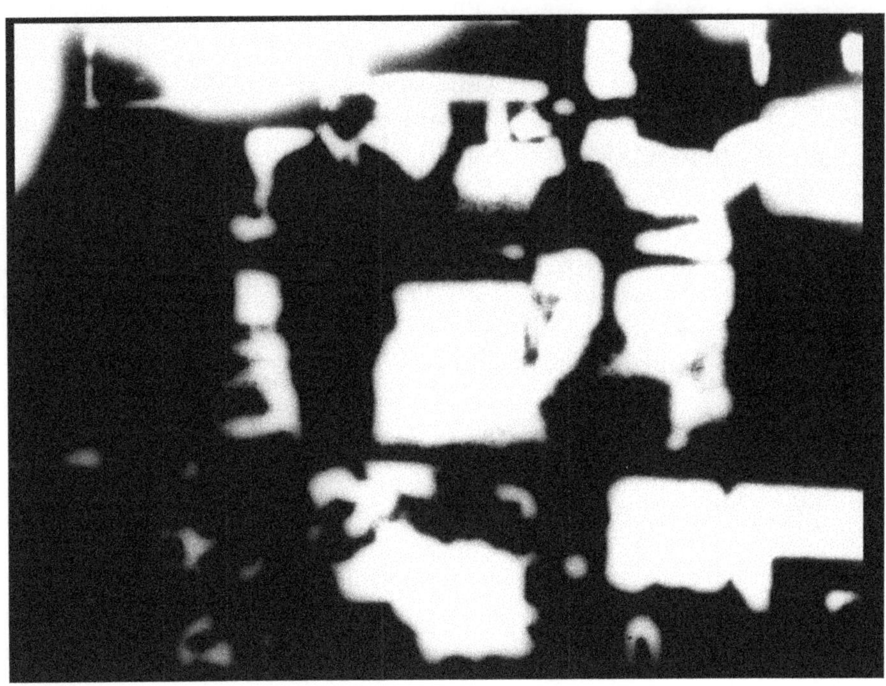

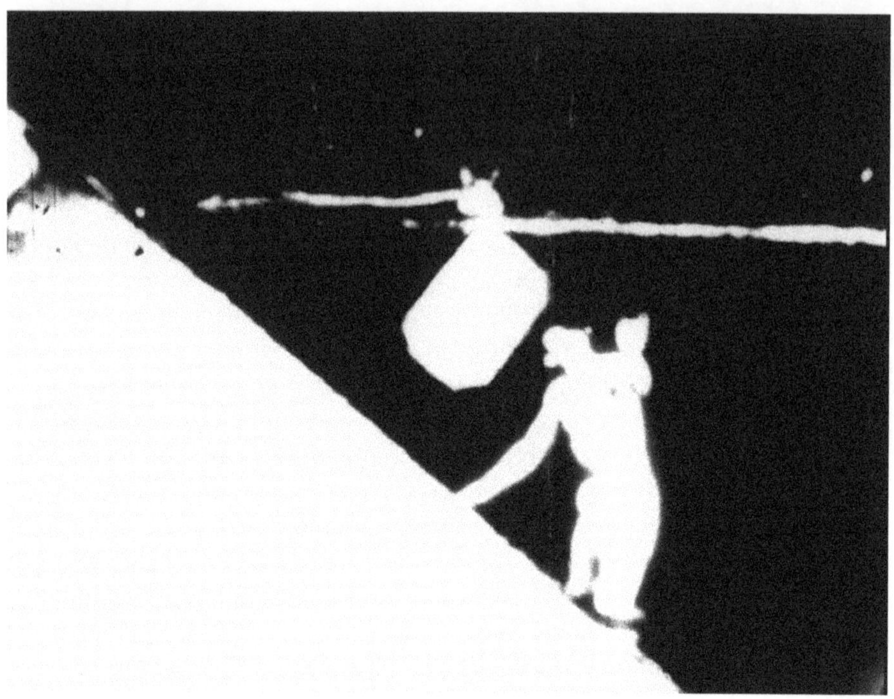

voir en entier mais il s'agit d'une bobine 16mm que Louise a confectionnée photogramme par photogramme. Elle a refilmé une Steenbeck avec sa Bolex en alternant la vitesse de visionnement. On retrouve cette même technique dans *Remains* (2011) — une poésie visuelle faite de lumière. Nous n'avons utilisé qu'une petite partie de ce matériel. À travers cette danse entre l'abstraction, le mouvement de la pellicule et les brefs aperçus de figuration, on y retrouve un voyage à travers la mémoire, les souvenirs de Louise; une recontextualisation des archives familiales. En réutilisant ce matériel, Louise se permet de préserver ses souvenirs, ou sa propre interprétation de cette mémoire d'antan. Comme pour son père, il s'agit pour Louise d'immortaliser des moments que l'on ne veut pas, ou qu'on ne peut pas, oublier et à travers ces images, on retrouve le coeur même de ses souvenirs.

Une grande partie du travail consistait à classer les images numérisées des ses manipulations en 16mm des films familiaux en 8mm de son père. Beaucoup d'images montrent les membres de sa famille saluant de la main la caméra. Nous avons finalement terminé avec quatre catégories: *Absolument*, *Pas Absolument*, *Possiblement*, et *Non*.[3]

Je vois le film comme un hommage à Jean-Clarence Bourque, le père de Louise; une forme d'éloge funèbre. La postproduction fut assez émouvante et en tant qu'élément extérieur à ces memento mori j'ai dû m'imprégner de ces souvenirs. Par ma posture plus objective, j'ai tenté d'amener à Louise une nouvelle perception de ces images et lui faciliter les coupures nécessaires au montage. À travers la banalisation de ce geste universel — la vague — et par la répétition des images, on retrouve le sen de l'au revoir : nous nous reverrons bientôt, soit physiquement ou virtuellement. L'expertise et la complexité de la rephotographie par tirage contact, avec une Bolex, en usant par la suite de toning et différents traitements chimiques nous montrent l'importance de ces images pour Louise. Dans cette accumulation volontaire de matériel, il y a une panoplie de réinterprétations plastiques qui forment une cohérence qui nous a grandement aidés durant l'assemblage. À travers cette réappropriation de ces films de famille, on y voit toute la puissance de l'amour pour son père et que les images doivent rendre hommage à tous ces doux moments captés sur 8mm.[4]

Nous avons donc nommé le matériel découpé par thèmes principaux, pour les reconnaître et les utiliser facilement. Ces dossiers étaient comme une archive méticuleusement mise en place de manière conviviale. *Jacques_ tricycle*, *papa_escalier*, *enfants_perron*, ou bien *papa_maman_camion* ne sont que quelques noms qui sont devenus iconiques au fil du montage.[5]

Le processus de postproduction était très complexe. En travaillant sur le film de Louise, j'en ai beaucoup appris sur elle.[6] Chaque image était accompagnée par un moment de sa vie qu'elle me racontait avec humilité. Elle travaille de manière méthodique, en utilisant une approche ritualiste, tout en laissant l'accident jouer un rôle important dans le processus créatif. Nous étions constamment surpris par les images que nous retrouvions. Partageant une méthodologie de travail similaire, je pouvais comprendre l'enthousiasme frénétique face à une prouesse abstraite. J'y voyais les années de recherche plastique de Louise sur pellicule 16mm.

Louise me parlait régulièrement de nouveau matériel 16mm qu'elle avait réalisé en tirage contact avec un agrandisseur photo au studio de double négatif.[7] Nous sommes finalement allés au studio pour le regarder, question de savoir si on pouvait l'ajouter au film (bien que nous étions assez avancés dans le montage et étions proche d'un rough cut). En préparant le matériel, j'ai découvert une nouvelle Louise; la personne qui s'est battue pour utiliser Adobe Premiere manie maintenant les bobines 16mm, le splicer guillotine et la Steenbeck de manière tellement impressionnante, avec précision et rapidité. La pellicule est une seconde nature pour Louise. Elle a aussi gravé le titre du film et son copyright avec tellement de doigté. Cela fut un moment magnifique et inspirant.

Nous devions trouver un leitmotiv et il nous paraissait évident que se soit des images de son père. Nous avons intégré le matériel du dossier *papa_escalier*, où l'on trouve le père de Louise assis dans un escalier. Par moment, ce matériel se présente sous forme abstraite, ou bien en noir et blanc, flashant subtilement. Ce qui est particulier avec ce matériel, c'est qu'il existe sous tellement de formes visuelles différentes, comparativement au reste. L'unicité de ces moments captés se traduit par une omniprésence de son père qui résonne tout au long du film.

Chaque coupure était littéralement un au revoir. Nous avons pouffé de rire après avoir dit au revoir à Jacques, lorsqu'on a coupé des images du dossier *Jacques_tricycle* mais étions tristes une de ces séquences magnifiques, mais non pertinente pour le film.[8] Le montage fut un dialogue constant avec l'œuvre et avec Louise. Il ne s'agissait pas de juste donner mon point de vue mais aussi de faire partie du processus créatif d'une personne. Le travail s'est fait dans un contexte de confiance et d'ouverture.

Quelques lignes sur le son du film. Louise fait généralement sa propre conception sonore pour ses œuvres. Pour *Bye Bye Now*, l'élément sonore est venu après le montage-image, car nous ne savions pas trop quoi utiliser pour la trame sonore. Au début, nous avons pensé utiliser le son des enregistrements vidéo qu'elle a fait de son père lui parlant; mais un soir, Louise a apporté un enregistrement mystérieux. Elle ne m'a pas expliqué sa provenance, ou ce que c'était.[9] L'enregistrement avait des allures cauchemardesques et dronesques. Il collait parfaitement avec les images. Louise m'a appris le montage à la microseconde, pour une forme subtile de synchronisation qui affecte le subconscient. Par exemple, à la fin de *Bye Bye Now*, lorsque le droit d'auteur est gravé sur le film, on peut entendre un train. Ce son est à la fois universel et spécifique : c'est le son d'une locomotive au loin, c'est le train qui passe souvent près de sa maison familiale à Edmundston.

Les dernières images du film ne furent pas difficiles à trouver. Un des rares plans où l'on voit Jean-Clarence Bourque marcher droit devant, qui salue la caméra avant de lui faire dos. Un au revoir à tous celles et ceux qui ont vu ces images et à sa fille, Louise.

NOTES

1. Entre parenthèses, *L'éclat du mal / The Bleeding Heart of It* (2005) est, selon moi, un des meilleurs films expérimentaux canadiens. J'ai toujours pensé que le travail de Louise est de la plus haute importance et mérite d'être davantage discuté dans un contexte académique. Ce texte est mon remerciement pour ce qu'elle nous a transmis et ce qu'elle continuera de nous transmettre.
2. Les problèmes de santé de Louise se sont développés à une époque où les processus analogiques se transformaient rapidement en processus numériques.

3. Celui qui s'appelait *Absolument* était mon préféré.
4. Dans ses films, on peut clairement voir l'amour qu'elle porte à sa famille, ainsi que son attachement à la maison de son enfance à Edmundston, au Nouveau-Brunswick. C'est la même maison que l'on voit dans *Imprint* (1997). Son histoire familiale l'accompagne visuellement. J'ai eu l'occasion de rencontrer son frère Jean-Claude et sa sœur Simone lors d'une visite chez Louise au Nouveau-Brunswick. C'était agréable d'enfin rencontrer les personnes que j'avais vues comme enfants tant de fois durant mon travail sur *Bye Bye Now*.
5. Autres noms de dossier: *Famille_aura_maison*, *Burnt_Footage*, *Louise_bébé*, *Papa_s'en_va*, et *Baigneurs*.
6. Entre autres, elle m'a fait découvrir les tranches de pomme avec de l'houmous, que vous devriez essayer si vous ne l'avez pas encore fait.
7. Le collectif double négatif est un collectif d'artistes à Montréal.
8. Vu la grande ampleur du matériel, il serait possible pour Louise d'utiliser les prises retirées pour produire un nouveau court-métrage entièrement différent.
9. Je l'ai découvert plus tard, mais cela reste entre Louise et moi.

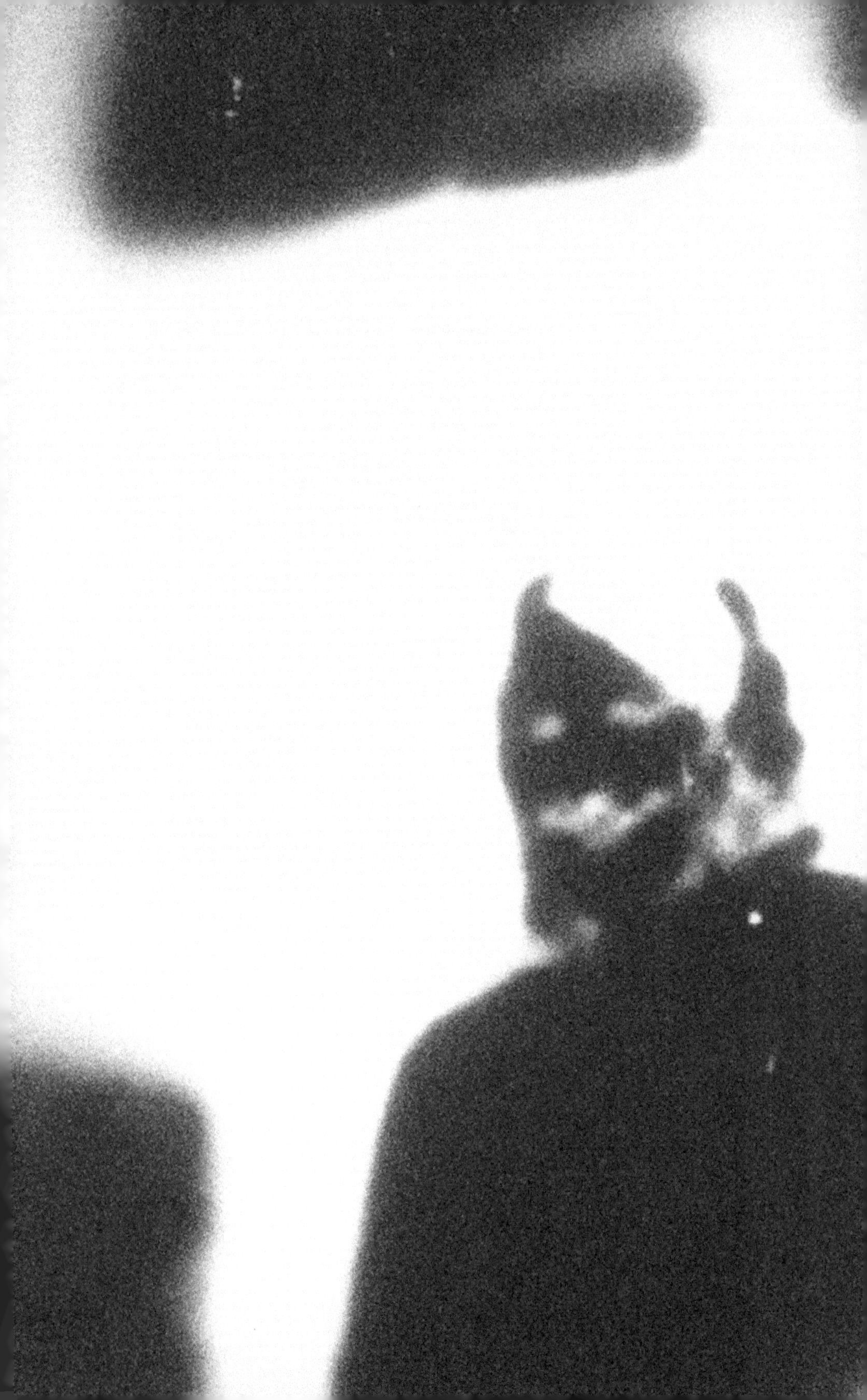

The Father Behind the Camera

A Journey Through the Bourque Family Archive

Guillaume Vallée

Translated by Kathryn Michalski

In 2018–19, I had the chance to work with Louise Bourque editing her most recent opus, *Bye Bye Now* (2021). The following are a few fragments of memories from that experience.

I first met Louise Bourque in 2014 at a symposium on experimental film at the artist-run centre DAÏMÔN in Gatineau, Quebec. It was a memorable encounter, resulting in a friendship that still inspires me to this day. Our paths crossed again in Montreal at Main Film, at a screening of *Auto Portrait / Self Portrait Post Partum* (2013), her latest work at that time. It was during this encounter that Louise shared with me that she was working on another project, one that involved looping images of children waving at the camera that were taken from her family's home movies.

Her father regularly used his 8mm camera to capture the daily life of the Bourque family, and Louise collected these family archives. At the moment, I could not imagine that four years later I would find myself digging through this material, and that I would become intimately connected to it. My initial encounter with these images was during our first collaborative hand-processing session, which took place at Main Film. The imperfect, slightly stroboscopic, black and white images were of two children sitting on a stoop waving at the camera. These images lingered with me throughout the post-production process. They functioned as a vortex, slowly sucking me into the Bourque family universe. Long before the editing process began, I had the privilege of seeing more uncut images from *Bye Bye Now* on my 16mm projector. It was at that moment that I realized something incredible was going to come out of this project.

The first of Louise's films I saw was *Self Portrait Post Mortem* (2002).[1] This was in 2007 or 2008, if my memory serves me correctly. During this period, I was obsessively interested in structural filmmaking and, among others, the work of Jürgen Reble and the Schmelzdahin ensemble of which he was a member. By integrating the decomposition of the emulsion into the creative process and opting for a materialistic approach to the film medium, the content is reinforced, resulting in a deeper aesthetic artifice. Louise's film demonstrated a symbiosis between content and form, concept and materiality. This approach is apparent in *Bye Bye Now*, revealing itself through Louise's judicious use of repetition and reinterpretation through re-photography and the chemical treatment of the images.

The post-production of *Bye Bye Now* began in 2018. Louise's health made it very difficult for her to use a computer, so I was asked to be an assistant editor.[2] Our friendship provided an environment for patience and understanding, making it easy to adapt to her needs. *Bye Bye Now* is a very subjective work that revisits her family's past, making the editing process difficult for someone who doesn't know her.

The first few minutes of *Bye Bye Now* are taken from a mysterious film that Louise often refers to as the "film puzzle." I never had the chance to see all of it, but it is a film that Louise made by splicing images together frame by frame. Using her Bolex, she re-filmed the footage off a Steenbeck while alternating the viewing speed. This same technique was used to create *Remains* (2011)—a visual poem made with light. We used only a small portion of this material. The dance between abstraction, film movement, and suggested figuration resulted in a journey through memory, Louise's memories; a re-contextualization of her family archives. The reuse of this material permitted Louise to preserve these memories or her own interpretation of the "good old days." Like her father, Louise immortalized the moments that she did not, or perhaps could not, forget. It is through these images that we reach the very heart of her memories.

A large part of the work consisted of classifying her digitized 16mm manipulations of her father's 8mm home movies. Much of the footage consisted of family members waving at the camera. In the end, there were four categories: *Absolument*, *Pas Absolument*, *Possiblement*, and *Non*.[3]

I see the film as a tribute to Louise's father, Jean-Clarence Bourque; a form of eulogy. As an outsider to these memento mori, the post-production process was quite moving, and I became absorbed in these memories. With the eye of an objective passenger, I tried to provide Louise with a new vision

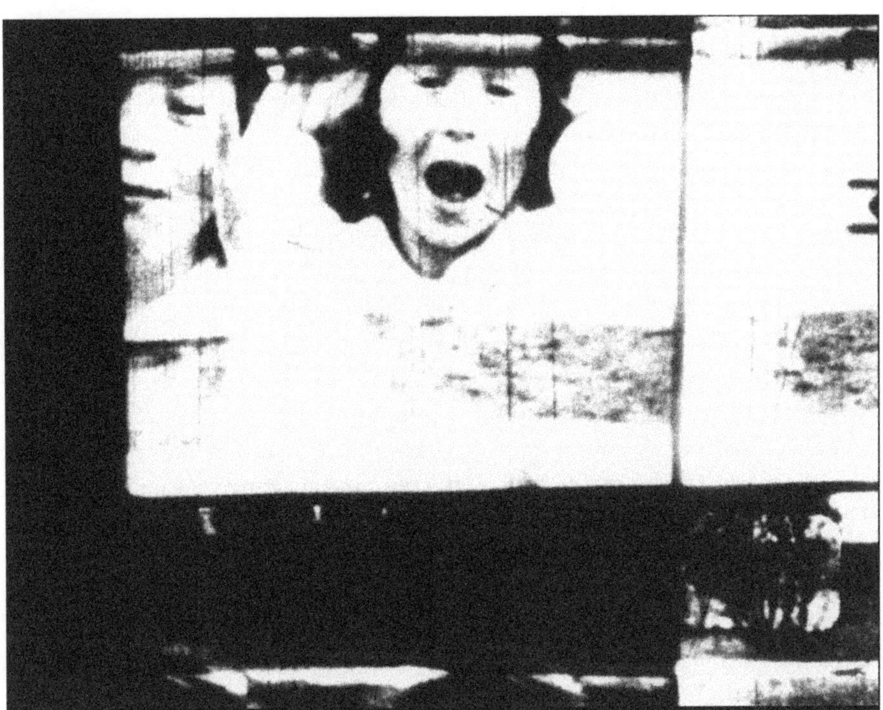

of these images, making it easier for her to make the cuts necessary for editing. Through the trivialization of this universal gesture—the wave—and through the repetition of the images, we find meaning in the goodbye: we soon will meet again, be it physically or virtually. The expertise and complexity of re-photographing the images using a Bolex, and the careful toning and chemical treatment of the footage, highlight the importance of these images for Louise. In this voluntary accumulation of material, we see the panoply of manipulated reinterpretations resulting in a coherence that greatly helped us during the assembly. Through the re-appropriation of these family films, we can see the strength of the love Louise has for her father; the images pay tribute to all those special moments he captured so long ago on 8mm.[4]

The material was organized by main themes that could easily be recognized and utilized. The folders were meticulously archived and set up in a user-friendly way. *Jacques_tricycle*, *papa_escalier*, *enfants_perron*, and *papa_maman_camion* are just a few examples of the names that became iconic through the editing progress.[5]

The post-production was a complex process. I came to learn a lot from Louise by working on her film.[6] Each image displayed a moment of her past, a moment that she shared with humility. Louise works methodically, using a ritualistic approach while accounting for the occasional accident, which plays an important role in her creative process. We were constantly surprised by the images we found. Sharing a similar working methodology, I could relate to the frenetic enthusiasm she exhibited when we encountered a surprising or unique form of abstraction. It was possible to see the years she spent experimenting with image manipulation on 16mm film.

Louise regularly told me about the new 16mm material she was working on at Double Negative's studio space[7]—contact prints made with a photo enlarger. We finally went to the studio to look at this material, wondering if it could be incorporated into the project (although at the time we were quite advanced in the editing process and close to a rough cut). While preparing the material, I discovered a new Louise; the woman who struggled to use Adobe Premiere was now handling 16mm reels, a guillotine splicer, and the Steenbeck with precision and speed. Using film is second nature to Louise. She also hand-scratched the title of the film and its copyright date with ease. This was a wonderful and inspiring moment.

We had to find a leitmotif, and we both felt that the images we found of her father would work best. We integrated images of her father sitting on a staircase from the *papa_escalier* folder. At times, these images are abstract, black and white, or appear to be subtly flashing. What is special about this material is that it exists in so many different visual forms. The uniqueness of these captured moments results in an omnipresence of Louise's father that resonates throughout the film.

Every cut was literally a goodbye. Louise and I laughed after saying goodbye to Jacques, when we cut the images from the *Jacques_tricycle* folder. We were sad to remove this beautiful but ultimately irrelevant sequence from the film.[8] The editing required a constant dialogue with both the work and with Louise. It wasn't about my point of view, but about becoming a part of someone's creative process. The work was done with trust and openness.

A little about the sound in the film. Normally, Louise creates her own soundtracks. In the case of *Bye Bye Now*, the sound component came after the picture lock, as we weren't sure what to use for sound. At first, we contemplated incorporating existing sound from video recordings she made of her father talking to her; however, one night Louise walked in with a mysterious new recording. At the time she didn't explain where it came from nor what it was.[9] The recording was drone-y, nightmarish, and fit perfectly with the images. Louise taught me about close-cutting images for a subtle form of synchronization that affects the subconscious. For instance, at the end of *Bye Bye Now*, when the copyright is scratched onto the film, you can hear a train. This sound is both universal, and specific: it is the sound of a locomotive in the distance, it is the train which often passes close to her family home in Edmundston.

The last images of the film were not difficult to find: they are one of the few times Jean-Clarence Bourque was captured on film. He walks straight ahead, waving to the camera before turning his back to it. It is a farewell to the audience and to his daughter, Louise.

NOTES

1. As an aside, *L'éclat du mal / The Bleeding Heart of It* (2005) is, in my opinion, one of the best Canadian experimental films. I have always felt that Louise's work is of utmost importance and merits more discussion within an academic context. This text is my thanks for all the moving images Louise has given us, and for all that she will continue to provide.
2. Louise's health problems developed at a time when analogue processes were rapidly transforming into digital processes.
3. The one called *Absolument* was my favourite.
4. In her films, one can clearly see the love she has for her family, as well as her attachment to her childhood home in Edmundston, New Brunswick. It is the same house that we see in *Imprint* (1997). Her family history accompanies the work. I once met her brother Jean-Claude and her sister Simone when I visited Louise in New Brunswick. It was nice to finally meet the people I had seen so many times as children while working on *Bye Bye Now*.
5. Others include: *Famille_aura_maison*, *Burnt_Footage*, *Louise_bébé*, *Papa_s'en_va*, and *Baigneurs*.
6. Among other things, she also introduced me to apple slices with hummus, which, if you haven't tried yet, you should.
7. Double Negative is an artist collective in Montreal.
8. Given the vast nature of the material, it would be possible for Louise to use the outtakes to make an entirely different short film.
9. I did find out later, but this remains between me and Louise.

Dialogues imaginés
Spectroscopie générationnelle

Louise Bourque and Herménégilde Chiasson

Originalement publié dans *Dialogues imaginés / Image Dialogues* (New Brunswick: Galerie Colline, 2014), 24–25.

Un dialogue imaginé avec Herménégilde Chiasson m'a paru, dès le départ, propice à une collaboration pour la création d'une œuvre pour ce projet. C'est en tant que poète que je l'ai d'abord rencontré il y a plus de trente ans lorsque j'étais adolescente et que je m'adonnais à l'écriture poétique. J'ai découvert son travail en arts visuels au début de ma vingtaine lorsque j'étudiais à Moncton. C'est également à cette époque que j'ai vu son cinéma. Mon invitation à cet échange s'est voulu un hommage à sa pratique en art contemporain dans diverses disciplines en tant que précurseur acadien. J'étais par ailleurs persuadée que, par sa sensibilité artistique et poétique, nous pouvions parler le même langage. Je lui ai proposé comme point de départ des reproductions numériques de photogrammes extraits de mon travail plastique en cinéma sur pellicule cinématographique. Ces images, créées à partir de films de famille tournés au Nord-Ouest dans les années cinquante, ont ensuite été reproduites et altérées par le biais d'une variété de processus photographiques non orthodoxes, mais de façon à évoquer l'évanescence des traces laissées par nos parents. Le dialogue s'est donc établi et nous avons ensemble imaginé une œuvre contemporaine, ancrée dans notre patrimoine : une seule œuvre, une collaboration, une œuvre composée de pièces jointes aux transformations multiples sur divers médiums comme autant de tissus différents dans un assemblage rappelant le travail des femmes de chez nous, dialoguant autour d'une table et imaginant ensemble la création, parfois collective, de ce qui deviendra une courtepointe.

Louise Bourque

Imagined Dialogues

Generational Spectroscopy

Originally published in *Dialogues imaginés / Imagined Dialogues* (New Brunswick: Galerie Colline, 2014), 24–25.

An "Imagined Dialogue" with Herménégilde Chiasson was for me, from the start, an ideal approach to collaborating on a work for this project. It was through art that I first met Herménégilde over thirty years ago, when I was a teenager dabbling in poetry. I discovered his work in the visual arts when I was studying in Moncton in my early twenties. My invitation to take part in this exchange was intended as a tribute to his work in several different disciplines as a forerunner of contemporary art in Acadia. I was also confident that, because of his artistic and poetic sensibilities, we would be able to speak the same language. I suggested to him, as a starting point, the digital reproduction of photograms of excerpts from films of mine in which I have painted or drawn artwork on film. These images, created from family movies made in northwestern New Brunswick in the 1950s, were then reproduced and altered by means of a variety of photographic methods that were unorthodox but chosen with a view to evoking the evanescent memories of our parents. So began the dialogue, and we imagined together a contemporary work rooted in our heritage: a single work of art, a collaboration, a work composed of pieces transformed in multiple ways on different media, like different fabrics patched together in an assemblage reminiscent of the work of women from our part of the world, in dialogue around a table and imagining together a creation, sometimes collective, that would become a quilt.

Louise Bourque

Je suis probablement à une génération de distance de Louise Bourque, mais je partage avec elle une esthétique qui nous permet de dialoguer sur une même surface et dans un même lieu. Cette œuvre est le résultat d'un dialogue entre deux disciplines qui se complètent et qui se regardent à une certaine distance à travers le temps et à travers l'espace. Entre le film et la peinture, il y a toujours eu une certaine tension; la peinture étant sans doute le plus vieux médium du monde et le cinéma ayant tout juste fêté ses cent ans. Il reste toute de même que le cinéma se retrouve de nos jours face à la vidéo et au numérique dans la même position où s'est retrouvée la peinture au siècle passé lorsque la photographie a été inventée.

Cette œuvre s'est construite par ordinateur, par téléphone et par internet. Cela n'ajoute probablement rien à sa qualité mais témoigne sans doute de l'accessibilité et de la rapidité des moyens et des structures qui transforment l'art actuel. Sa structure d'une grille où deux médiums se rejoignent fait sans doute référence à la rigueur de la science mais aussi à la ferveur des courtepointes. Elle se positionne donc entre tradition et modernité à l'image de l'Acadie actuelle qui, dans sa volonté de s'aventurer dans l'avenir, voudrait conserver l'essentiel de son identité. Cette démarche entre rupture et continuité, entre la volonté d'infuser dans les formes et les matériaux du passé un contenu contemporain, a toujours été au centre de ma démarche.

Herménégilde Chiasson

Spectroscopie générationnelle

Bourque : 8 images produites avec les logiciels Apple Final Cut Pro X et Adobe Photoshop à partir du transfert numérique de photogrammes créés sur pellicule film 16mm au moyen de manipulations chimiques et techniques inusitées de films de famille tournés en 8mm au Nord-Ouest dans les années 1950.

Chiasson : 8 images produites au moyen des pinceaux virtuels et des filtres du logiciel Adobe Photoshop dans le style expressionniste abstrait, contemporain des films originaux utilisés à la création des photogrammes.

I am probably a generation away from Louise Bourque, but I share an aesthetic with her, and this has allowed us to interact on the same surface and in the same place. This piece is the result of a dialogue between two disciplines that complement each other and view each other from a certain distance through time and through space. A certain tension always exists between film and painting; without a doubt, painting is the oldest medium in the world, while film recently celebrated its hundredth birthday. Nonetheless, film, today, is confronted with video and digital media and therefore finds itself in the same position as painting was a century ago, when photography was invented.

This piece was constructed by computer, telephone, and the Internet. That fact probably says nothing about its quality, but it does testify to the way the accessibility and rapidity of the means used to produce art and of its structures has transformed contemporary art practices. The structure of this piece is a grid on which two media come into contact; it is a reference to the precision of science, but also to the passionate energy of quilting. The piece is located between tradition and modernity, made in the image of contemporary Acadia, which, in its desire to venture into the future, still retains the essential elements of its identity. This process, between rupture and continuity, between the desire to infuse the forms and materials of the past with a contemporary content, has always been at the centre of my approach to art.

Herménégilde Chiasson

Generational Spectroscopy

Bourque: 8 images produced with Apple Final Cut Pro X and Adobe Photoshop from digital transfers of motion picture frames created on 16mm film through the unorthodox chemical and technical manipulation of 8mm home movies shot in northwestern New Brunswick in the 1950s.

Chiasson: 8 images produced with Adobe Photoshop's brushes and filters in the Abstract Expressionist style contemporaneous with the time frame of the original movie images.

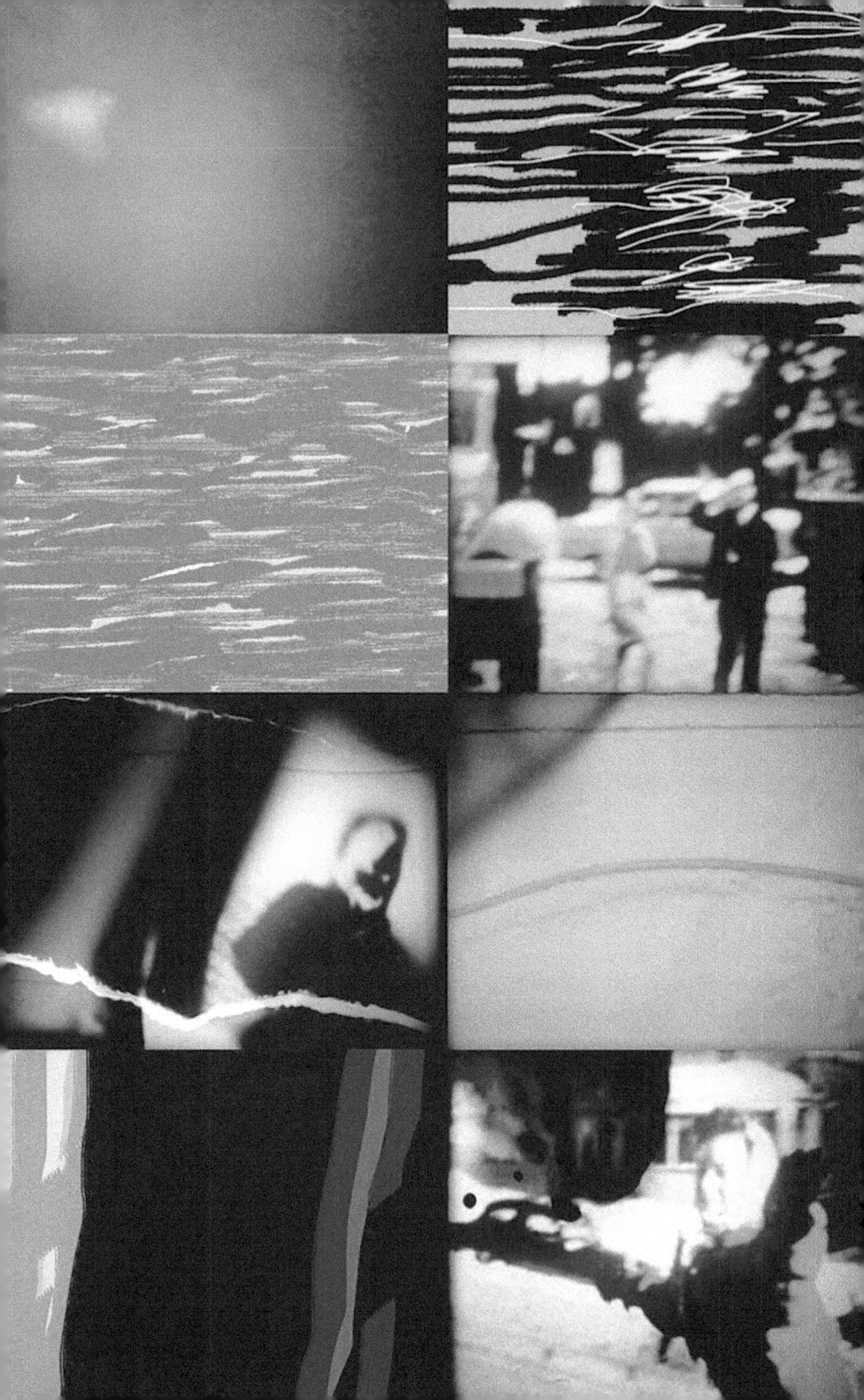

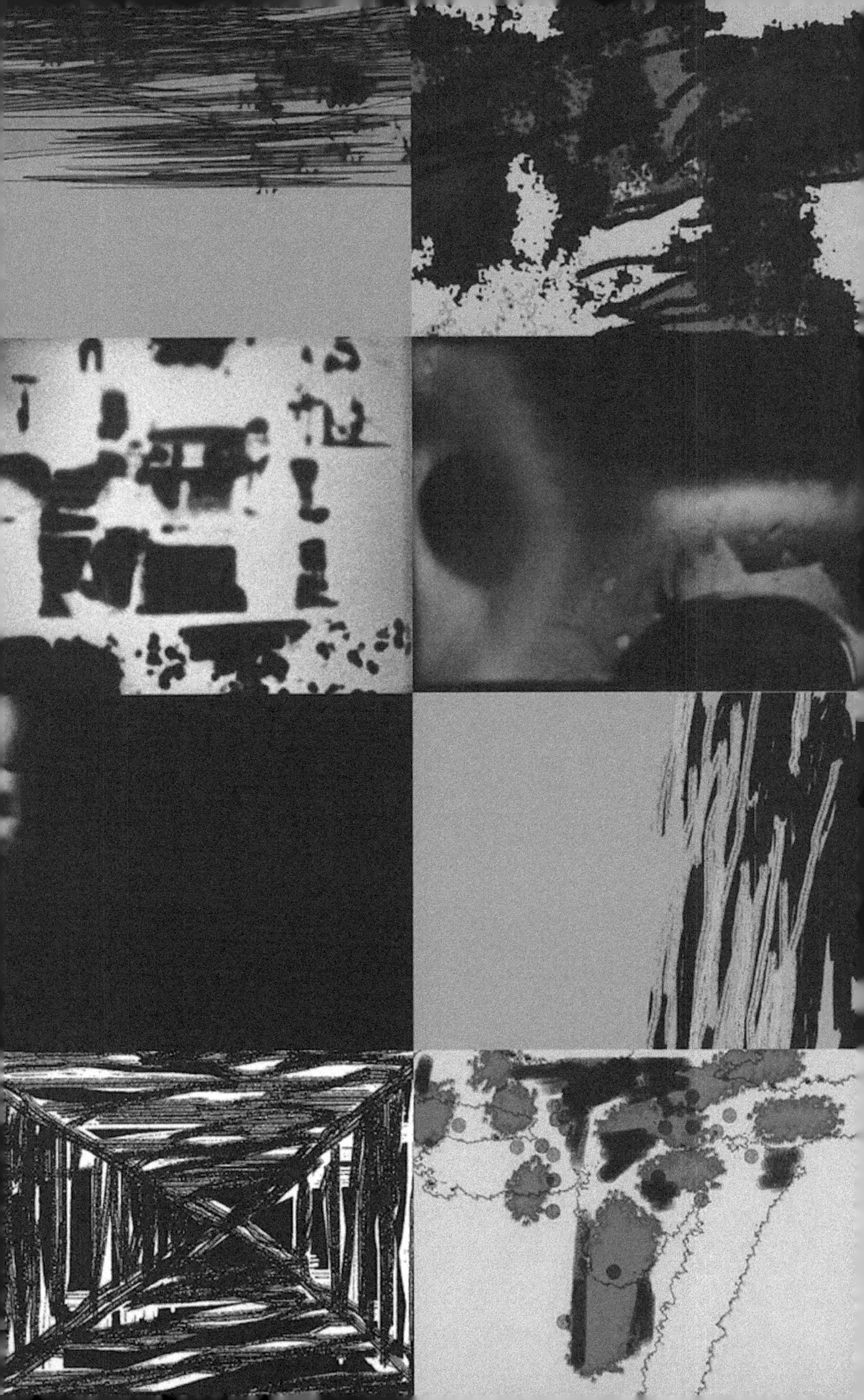

Louise!

Thank you so much for your beautiful and inspiring films!

And thankyou for supporting me, coming to my screening and talking about films with me!

I am blessed to have you in my life!!!

xo xo xo

Amanda

Precious Upheavals

Reflections on Going Back Home

Amanda Dawn Christie

I. Devastations in Gold

An uprooted house lies lopsided on its roof, as if tossed away lightly like a toy by a tornado. A large, lean dog runs across the roof of a flooded building and stops at the edge to look down at the rising water and consider its options. Large brick constructions collapse to the earth in clouds of dust. Another house—half-underwater—gently floats past the frame. A man runs feverishly across the screen as his desperate racing image reflects imperfectly on the wet street beneath his feet. We return to another overturned house, this one lying across railroad tracks as a steam engine rolls past in the distance. Through tornado, flood, fire, and earthquakes, these structures are ravaged by the elements of air, water, fire, and earth. The film is toned with gold such that the devastated domiciles become precious bodies scintillating on the screen, while the melody of an untuned toy piano lends a sense of imperfect innocence.[1]

II. Home as Origin

Louise Bourque grew up in a small town called Edmundston in the northwestern part of New Brunswick, and I grew up about five hours southeast of there, in a rural area outside of Moncton. As a woman from New Brunswick making experimental films, I feel a certain bond with Louise. I also relate to her when it comes to navigating systems in the arts (and society in general) that do not always make room for diversity when it comes to non-apparent impairment. Like invisible labour, non-apparent impairment is rarely acknowledged, and when it is, it is often either misunderstood or quickly forgotten.[2]

Unlike the rest of Canada, about half of New Brunswick's population lives in rural areas rather than in urban centres. New Brunswick is also Canada's only officially bilingual province. The Acadian population, while francophone, has a very different history and culture than the Quebecois, and is frequently overlooked in discussions regarding French-Canadian culture.

While there is a vibrant contemporary art scene in Atlantic Canada, the same cannot be said for experimental filmmaking. While the absence of an experimental film community can lead to a sense of isolation at times, it can also foster a diverse audience in which one can find poets, painters, writers, farmers, and freelancers. What is lost in terms of an audience deeply familiar with experimental film history is gained in interdisciplinary exchanges and fresh perspectives. In terms of creation, depending on one's mood or state of mind on any given day, this environment could be felt either as an isolated void or alternately as a place free from the influence of contemporary trends. There is a bit more experimental film activity south of the border, in Nova Scotia, a result of NSCAD's film program and the Atlantic Filmmakers Cooperative (AFCOOP). There are indeed media art production centres throughout the Atlantic provinces that provide equipment, facilities, and screenings, but most of them focus on mainstream production, contemporary art, or new media. Anytime a gallery or production centre gets funding to screen experimental films, it is considered a special event.

When I first encountered Louise's films, I had no idea that she was also from New Brunswick, because most of her affiliations were with the United States. I only realized that she was Acadian while putting together a program of works by women filmmakers from Atlantic Canada for the Winnipeg Cinematheque in 2010.[3] Her film *Going Back Home* (2000) fit nicely into the program because, like many other artists from the region, she and I had both moved away to study, create, and teach elsewhere. It was another two years before I met her in person, at a retrospective screening of her films in Moncton.[4]

III. Going Towards

What does it mean to go back home? When and why do we go back home? If we have moved away and built lives for ourselves elsewhere, then we often go back home to visit family or friends. One may also return home to care for, or to be cared for by, family, or alternately to settle affairs when people have passed. In many of these instances, the once-familiar childhood home may seem foreign, as so many things can change in the decades of our absence. Changes to the community or the house that don't conform to our memories can be quietly disturbing, while caring for elderly parents in their final days can be a complete upheaval.

In 2008, Louise returned home to Edmundston to visit, and ended up staying to care for her dying father, remaining to settle affairs with the house and the estate. Back home, she found herself isolated once again; however, she was also creating films in a giant homemade studio, complete with a backyard clothesline for drying film that she hand-processed in the basement sink. Although ideal for film production, by moving back home she became uprooted and isolated from the new homes she built in Boston (and elsewhere). Despite all this, she was happy to be home.

IV. Home as Lodging and Accommodations

Home can also refer to the architectural structure where one takes shelter: the house, apartment, hostel, or couch where one stays. The material lodging and accommodations where one lays one's head to rest at night include the building, the room, the pillow, the blankets, the bed, etc. Home in this material sense is closely tied to the sensory experiences of the soft, warm cocoon of the bedding, the feeling of splinters on the wooden door frame, the musty smell in the closet, the sounds of the fridge turning on and off at night, and the taste of the water from the bathroom faucet. In other words, home is a place of accommodation made of vibrant physical materials that enter into deep relationships with us over time.[5]

When discussing the materiality of film, I have long praised the scratches, imperfections, and colour shifting of celluloid over time, as it makes each print unique and distinct. I have often compared the scratches and colour shifting of celluloid to the scars and aging of the human body. Now, instead of using the analogy of aging, I would be more inclined to use the analogy of transformation, because our bodies can undergo major transformations at any stage in life, be it through the aging process, illness, or accident. These transformations apply not only to our bodies, but also to our environments, as Rosemarie Garland-Thomson writes: "Every body is in perpetual transformation not only in itself but also in its location within a constantly shifting environment."[6]

For Louise, surviving a car crash in 2006 exacerbated a previously existing illness, initiating a series of life-altering transformations. In 2015, she returned to Montreal for specialized medical care, eventually settling there a year later. In Montreal, she lives as an artist without the stability of a university teaching position or a longstanding community. Much of her time and energy are spent navigating the health care system, while continuing to make new work and attend screenings and events in a community where most people do not know the version of her before the transformations that her accident and subsequent illnesses brought. It is as if her communities in the United States know one version of her and the community in Montreal knows another.

I see an interesting parallel between the transformations that she has lived, and the way that many of her films explore the process of transformation. In *Going Back Home* she takes images of destroyed houses, and in an act of transgression, makes them beautiful through the controlled destruction of the filmic material and through chemical processes. She defiantly declares to us that decay happens by eroding and toning the image, thereby transforming these images of devastation into beautiful and lush sensory experiences.

In thinking about the material properties and transformations of celluloid, the human body, the environment, and the home, the field of Disability Studies (DS) can be a useful lens to apply, as it often explores the encounters and relationships between *bodyminds* and the material world.[7] I use the term "bodymind" because, while it is common to discuss the materiality of the body, material relationships with the mind are often viewed as intangible and immaterial. In "The Bodymind Problem and the Possibilities of Pain," Margaret Price writes that, "because mental and physical processes not only affect each other but also give rise to each other—that is, because they tend to act as one, even though they are conventionally understood as two—it makes more sense to refer to them together, in a single term."[8] Price goes on to clarify that "bodymind, the imbrication (not just the combination) of the entities usually called 'body' and 'mind,' is a materialist feminist DS concept."[9]

In "Misfits: A Feminist Materialist Disability Concept," Garland-Thomson writes that "a misfit occurs when world fails flesh in the environment one encounters."[10] She gives the example of a round peg and a square hole. There is nothing wrong with the round peg, and there is nothing wrong with the square hole; there is simply a *misfit*. Likewise, when a non-normative bodymind travels through the material world, they will encounter both misfits that are disabling and fits that are empowering. In the case of *Going Back Home*, one could argue that the houses and buildings themselves experienced misfits in their encounters with hostile environments and natural disasters.

V. Going From

Going back home can also refer to returning home from work or from an event or gathering. Since moving to Montreal in 2017, I have admired how committed Louise is to attending screenings and events, especially knowing how much of her day is spent managing physical illnesses and treatments. In my own experiences, I think of the many times I managed the labour to get my bodymind prepared to attend an art gallery opening, concert, or screening, only to have to leave halfway through, or to turn around before even arriving, to go back home due to intense pain, fatigue, or sensory overload.

One of the biggest challenges for individuals with non-normative bodyminds can be the perception of others, who may observe a highly energetic and functioning person one day, and therefore assume that this person operates on similar levels most days.[11] A common stigma surrounding non-apparent illness is the assumption that the individuals are faking it or are not working hard enough. Yet in many cases, chronic illnesses fluctuate between periods of functionality and periods of relapse and flare-ups—there are good days and bad days.

Many artists with non-normative bodyminds may actually be experiencing misfits in their encounters with systemic barriers when others mistakenly judge them as being disrespectful, uncaring, unreliable, or diva-esque. Many of these occurrences could be the result of a misfit at play. As Susan Wendell suggests, it is vital to include chronic illness in feminist politics and disability activism given that "living with pain, fatigue, nausea, unpredictable abilities and/or the imminent threat of death creates different *ways of being* that give valuable perspectives on life and the world."[12] Such lived experiences can sometimes manifest in difficulty reading and writing, delays in responding to emails, missing deadlines, difficulty moving and getting dressed, poor impulse control in conversations, or sensory overload in crowded spaces. In spite of the difficulties and challenges, these different ways of being can also present deeper perspectives on priorities as well as different perceptions of time, space, and language.

VI. Home as Comfort and Confinement

Coming back home early from events or screenings due to misfits between my bodymind and the environment, I think of how "home" in that context becomes a place of both comfort and confinement. My material home then becomes both prison and protection as I am limited by the boundaries of my safe haven. This paradoxical relationship to home is somehow consistent with *Going Back Home*'s bittersweet images of the ravaged homes in ruin that are at once terrible and lovely.

Coming back to the material structure used for lodging and accommodations, I want to flip the definition of accommodations from a physical place of lodging to the DS sense of accommodations as special adaptations supplied to satisfy a need. While accommodations are important and essential for the inclusion of non-normative bodyminds, a purely "accommodationist" approach is problematic because it works on a case-by-case basis and posits the individual as a deviant exception that needs to be adapted to, while allowing the maintenance of the dominant structure of systemic barriers, instead of addressing the actual encounter between the bodymind and the world. This is the difference between accommodation and accessibility.

When it comes to accessible design, Aimi Hamraie points out that one of the many problems is that "accommodationist strategies are often premised upon 'retrofitting' a material arrangement after the fact, rather than building a commitment to access into the process of designing a conference, event, or classroom."[13] This practice of retrofitting pre-existing structures reminds me of one of the images of an overturned house in *Going Back Home*, and I imagine a group of DS theorists and architects, flipping these houses over in a fit of frustration with the tired approaches to access as afterthought. I imagine architects of universal design setting fire to these houses and insisting on redesigning from scratch instead of retrofitting. While I am fairly certain that this was not Louise's intention with this film, a part of me delights in the idea that these overturned houses could be a metaphor for an upheaval of purely accommodationist strategies.

VII. Precious Upheavals

Coming back to *Going Back Home*, the *home* can be seen both as a point of origin—like a childhood home—and as a material structure of lodging and shelter. Home, in both senses, can be experienced as a place of both comfort and confinement when our encounters between world and flesh are filled with natural disasters: storms, floods, fires, and earthquakes. The disruption of dominant normative systems to make room for a wider variety of lived experiences can be seen as an act of empowerment, similar to the ways in which Louise took control over the celluloid material and used destruction as an act of reclamation, exerting influence over these natural disasters and transforming devastation into beauty. In the face of these overturned houses there remains the delicate melody on an untuned toy piano, as well as the glistening, gilded toning of the images that makes each one of these upheavals something precious, delicate, and provocative.

NOTES

1. The scintillating effect of the gold toning is only apparent when projected on film, less so on the video transfer.

2. While the terms "invisible disability" and "hidden disability" are still commonly used, I follow some disability activists in using "non-apparent" because "hidden" can imply intentional concealment, and the word "invisible" can be interpreted as invalidating.

3. Saltwater Bodies and Turning Tides: Women with Cameras on the East Coast screened on October 15, 2010.

4. This retrospective in Moncton was part of a tour organized by the Images Festival and co-presented by FICFA (Festival international du cinéma francophone en Acadie) and GSN (Galerie Sans Nom), where I was working at the time. In a recent conversation, Louise reminded me that I had driven to Halifax to pick up a "portable" 35mm film projector from AFCOOP for this screening. It was as I was handling and projecting her actual work on film that I first noticed the richness of the gold toning on her film *Going Back Home*.

5. See Jane Bennett, *Vibrant Matter: A Political Ecology of Things* (Duke University Press: Durham, 2010). As Bennett argues: "Humanity and nonhumanity have always performed an intricate dance with each other. There was never a time when human agency was anything other than an interfolding network of humanity and nonhumanity" (31).

6. Rosemarie Garland-Thomson, "Misfits: A Feminist Materialist Disability Concept," *Hypatia* 26, no. 3 (Summer 2011): 598.

7. Margaret Price, "The Bodymind Problem and the Possibilities of Pain," *Hypatia* 30, no. 1 (Winter 2015): 268–86. In the DS context, the term "bodymind" emerges from the field of Trauma Studies, however, as Margaret Price points out, "It should be noted that non-Western philosophies took up the subject of bodymind prior to the later trauma-oriented approach. ... Rooted in Buddhist philosophy, attunement shares with Rothschild's trauma theory the notion that we can refer meaningfully, if tentatively, to 'mind' and 'body,' but ultimately the two are so fully integrated that they should also be considered one" (280).

8. Ibid., 269.

9. Ibid., 270.

10. Garland-Thomson, 600.

11. Non-normative bodyminds are those that do not conform to the socially determined norm, which also shifts, changes, and undergoes transformations.

12. Susan Wendell, "Unhealthy Disabled: Treating Chronic Illnesses as Disabilities," in *The Disability Studies Reader*, ed. Lennard J. Davis (Routledge: New York, 2013): 171.

13. Aimi Hamraie, "Beyond Accommodation: Disability, Feminist Philosophy, and the Design of Everyday Academic Life," *philoSOPHIA* 6, no. 2 (Summer 2016): 264.

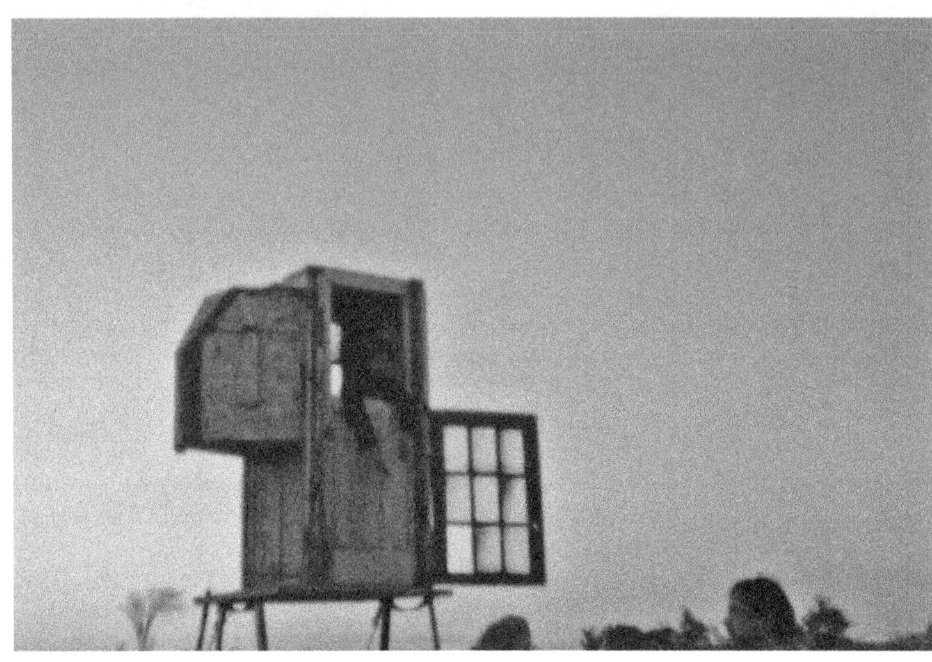

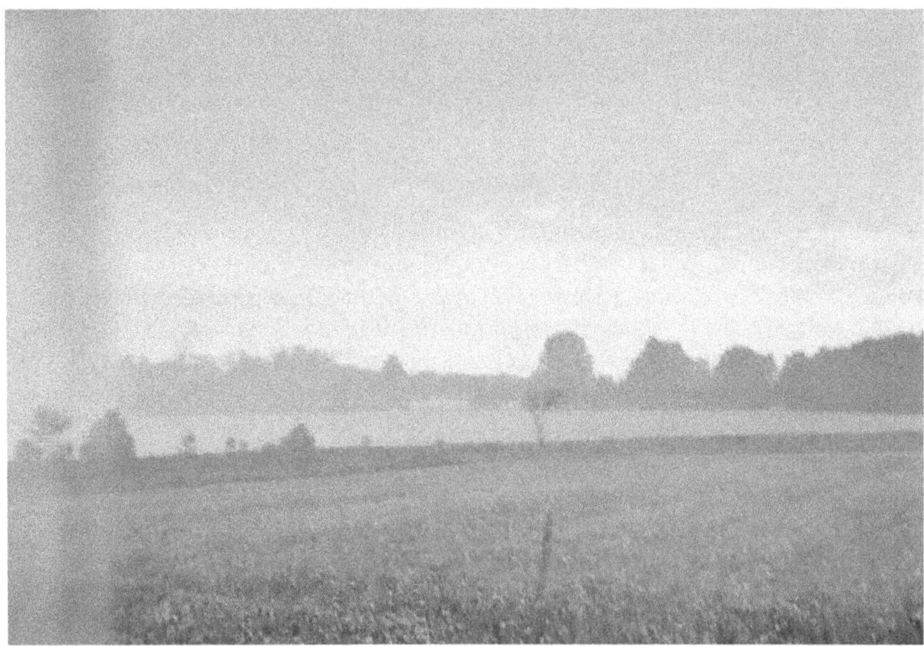

A Few In-Camera Observations about Louise Bourque

Clint Enns

This essay has been somewhat challenging to write, so perhaps I will start with a few facts that reveal why. Fact #1: I consider Louise to be a friend. I enjoy spending time with her and often wish our time weren't relegated to the brief occasions before and after screenings. Louise has many of the qualities that I seek in camaraderie, traits that I will now state as self-evident facts. Fact #2: Louise is exceptionally clever. Fact #3: Louise has both personal and artistic integrity. Fact #4: Both Louise and her work are challenging. Fact #5: Louise is generous with her time, feedback, and creative energy. Fact #6: Louise is a character. Fact #7: Louise is incredibly courageous. I feel many of these qualities allow for the production of exceptional art. Although I have presented these as self-evident facts, I will now introduce a few personal anecdotes that will solidify these claims and, perhaps more importantly, provide new insight into her work.

Let's begin with one of the things I find charming about Louise, namely, that she consistently shows up to screenings fashionably late. While she almost never entirely misses the first act, she always manages to find the most dangerous seat in the house. In particular, at la lumière, a microcinema in Montreal, there are two stools that are too high and wobbly, making them treacherous even for people who are tall enough for them. When I arrive at la lumière, I usually attempt to snag the comfiest seat in the house; however, when Louise arrives, I often silently offer her my seat, which she always graciously refuses. Given the dangerous nature of the stools, they are quite undesirable and, as such, are often left vacant in spite of the fact that they are high enough to provide an unobstructed view of the screen (and those one-inch barriers, subtitles). Out of the corner of my eye, I always watch as Louise summits the stool, ready to lend a hand if anything were to go awry. For the rest of the screening, Louise watches, teetering high above the ground, a ritual that, at least to me, functions as an apt metaphor for the cinema Louise produces, a devotional cinema that lives dangerously on the brink of falling apart while never quite toppling over.

Louise attends screenings not only to see films, but also to participate in a social gathering, in particular, one that revolves around an underground society that she has been a member of for many years. This underground society has only one condition for membership: one must engage with the experimental cinema community in some way, for instance, by facilitating screenings, writing about the work, or by actually producing new types of moving images. This is one of the main differences between commercial and experimental cinema—the latter forms a networked society in which those involved develop personal relations with each other. Since Louise has been involved with the community for many years, screenings are often a way to check in on old friends and to develop relationships with new members, since the artists will often accompany their work.

In regard to the work shown, Louise is an observant critic who, during Q&A sessions, often manages to provide new insight and readings of the work through well-informed observations and by attentively recognizing the through lines that connect seemingly disjointed films. No doubt the skills to both recognize and effectively communicate ideas hidden in difficult work were developed through her years of teaching. As observed by Michael Sicinski, the ability to transform seemingly unrelated ideas and concepts into new forms is also a trait found in Louise's art practice. Sicinski argues, "Bourque has moved through numerous strands of experimental film and video history, grounded herself in practices and traditions that once seemed incompatible, and is now pointing the way to something new."[1] Moreover, Sicinski's observation reveals Louise's familiarity with and understanding of the traditions she has devoted herself to.

Louise often expresses her gratitude for being able to attend these events. This gratitude is twofold. First, she appreciates the tremendous effort and dedication it takes to organize these types of events. Second, she is grateful that she is feeling well enough to be able to leave the house, an event that seems fairly mundane to most of us, but that with a debilitating illness can become nearly impossible.

Louise and I got to know each other at Don Blanche, an artist residency that takes place near Shelburne, Ontario. Louise was one of the artists-in-residence, and I was simply attending the public open house, a two-day art party with performances, pirate radio, art installations, and dancing. Gabrielle Moser provides a description of the residency:

> No proposals. No resumes. No deadlines. Much like the small, independent farm on which it's hosted, the Don Blanche residency is an anomaly in an increasingly globalized world. Created in 2009 by Don Miller and Christine Swintak as "a gift to artists," Don Blanche is a ten-day residency that takes place each summer near Shelburne, Ontario, a small town two hours north of Toronto.
>
> Centred in and around a huge 6,000-square-foot building that Miller constructed from century-old dismantled barns and an array of purposefully placed found window panes (Swintak has affectionately nicknamed it the "Frankenbarn"), Don Blanche hosts up to 80 artists who come from across the country to work on projects. There is no running water, and limited electricity comes from solar panels and wind turbines. Most participants camp outside or sleep in a dorm in a wing of the barn.[2]

Don Blanche is a happening straight from another era. At the farm, Louise created a film installation in a sculpture created by Felix Kalmenson. The sculpture was a small elevated room on stilts approximately seven feet above the ground, whose entrance was a small door made out of nine cut-glass panels set into a wood frame. Opposite the entrance was a window in the shape of a pyramid. In essence, entering the structure was like entering a camera with a fixed view.[3]

While at Don Blanche, Louise asked for my assistance to set up her installation. There were a few hurdles to overcome, like getting electricity to Kalmenson's structure, which was in the the middle of a field, and figuring out how to get the heavy 16mm projector into the sculpture given that it was already difficult enough simply to climb into it. Louise and I bonded while setting up her installation, a result that is worth emphasizing since this social aspect of artmaking is not often discussed. The installation was quite intelligent, beautiful, engaging, and intimate; however, the process of artmaking, although often enjoyable in and of itself, is also an opportunity to spend quality time with the people around us. Some play cards or backgammon together; others make art.

Louise's film installation at Don Blanche activated Kalmenson's sculpture, which, like a camera without a flash, was ineffective at night. The images on the loop consisted of found footage showing an unmade bed and a closeup of a woman's face moving towards the camera. On the images Louise carved the phrase "ma déchirure, ma blessure, ma suture [my tear, my wound, my suture]," one that was reused and re-contextualized in her film *Auto Portrait /*

Self Portrait Post Partum (2013). Moreover, the filmstrip had been ripped apart and sewn back together, providing the filmstrip with both a wound and a suture, one that is both visceral and cathartic. The loop was an intimate articulation of heartbreak, and Kalmenson's small room amplified the personal nature of the work. Moreover, the image was projected where the bellows once was, transforming the camera-like nature of the sculpture from one that captures images, to one that is used to transmit images.[4] Finally, given that the images were presented inside Kalmenson's camera-like structure, they can be seen as being presented "in-camera," a term used in relation to discussions in which personal or sensitive material is presented with the desire that it remain secret.

Artists Leslie Supnet and Guillaume Vallée both have had similar experiences working with Louise. Leslie spent time with Louise at the 2012 Film Farm (an analogue film residency located near Mount Forest, Ontario), helping her contact print some of the elements used in *Auto Portrait / Self Portrait Post Partum*; Guillaume co-edited Louise's film *Bye Bye Now* (2021). According to Leslie, she was quite in awe of Louise and had admired her work for many years. In the darkroom, they spent the afternoon talking while contact printing, a process that Leslie felt was "inspiring and a once-in-a-lifetime opportunity to hear from a unique storyteller"; however, she was also grateful for the opportunity to get to know Louise better.[5] Guillaume similarly described his experience working with Louise.

> We bonded quite a bit while editing, but we were close friends long before that. Working with her was interesting and inspiring. Her process is really intuitive while still remaining controlled.[6]

I contend that, in addition to enjoying the social aspects of screenings, Louise finds pleasure in the social bonds she forms through collaboration in her filmmaking practice.

Given that Louise and I first bonded over artmaking, I have attempted to focus on the social aspects of her work. Owing to the length of time that Louise has been involved with the underground film scene through teaching, curating, producing, and distributing personal, handmade films, she is deeply embedded in the scene; although it is not the sole focus of her existence, this scene is a major part of her life and social interactions. While Louise has made a significant body of work and notable contributions to Canadian cinema, the social aspects of her production, the bonds made through the production and screening of experimental works, have provided an impetus for her to continue to pursue difficult work. Fact #8: I am grateful for my time spent with Louise, and for the underground experimental film community, the antecedent of our friendship.

NOTES

1. Michael Sicinski, "Impossible Trips Back Home: The Films of Louise Bourque," *Images Festival Catalogue* (Toronto: Images Festival, 2009), 43.
2. Gabrielle Moser, "Don Blanche: House of Yes," *canadianart* 28, no. 3 (Fall 2017): 87.
3. This idea was further explored by Kalmenson in an exhibition titled Apertures, which took place in the Gallery 44 Vitrines. Kalmenson presented Internet artworks by Rosa Aiello, Matt Goerzen, and Elliot Vredenburg, which, despite being on the Internet, were only available for viewing in three wooden trapezoidal pyramids made to resemble the bellows of a camera with a view of the image at the aperture. The wooden pyramids were similar in nature to the structure constructed at Don Blanche, only inverted. That is, with the pyramids in Apertures one is on the outside looking in, and in the Don Blanche structure one is on the inside looking out.
4. This gesture is similar to the one explored by Kalmenson in Apertures.
5. From personal correspondence with Leslie Supnet.
6. From personal correspondence with Guillaume Vallée.

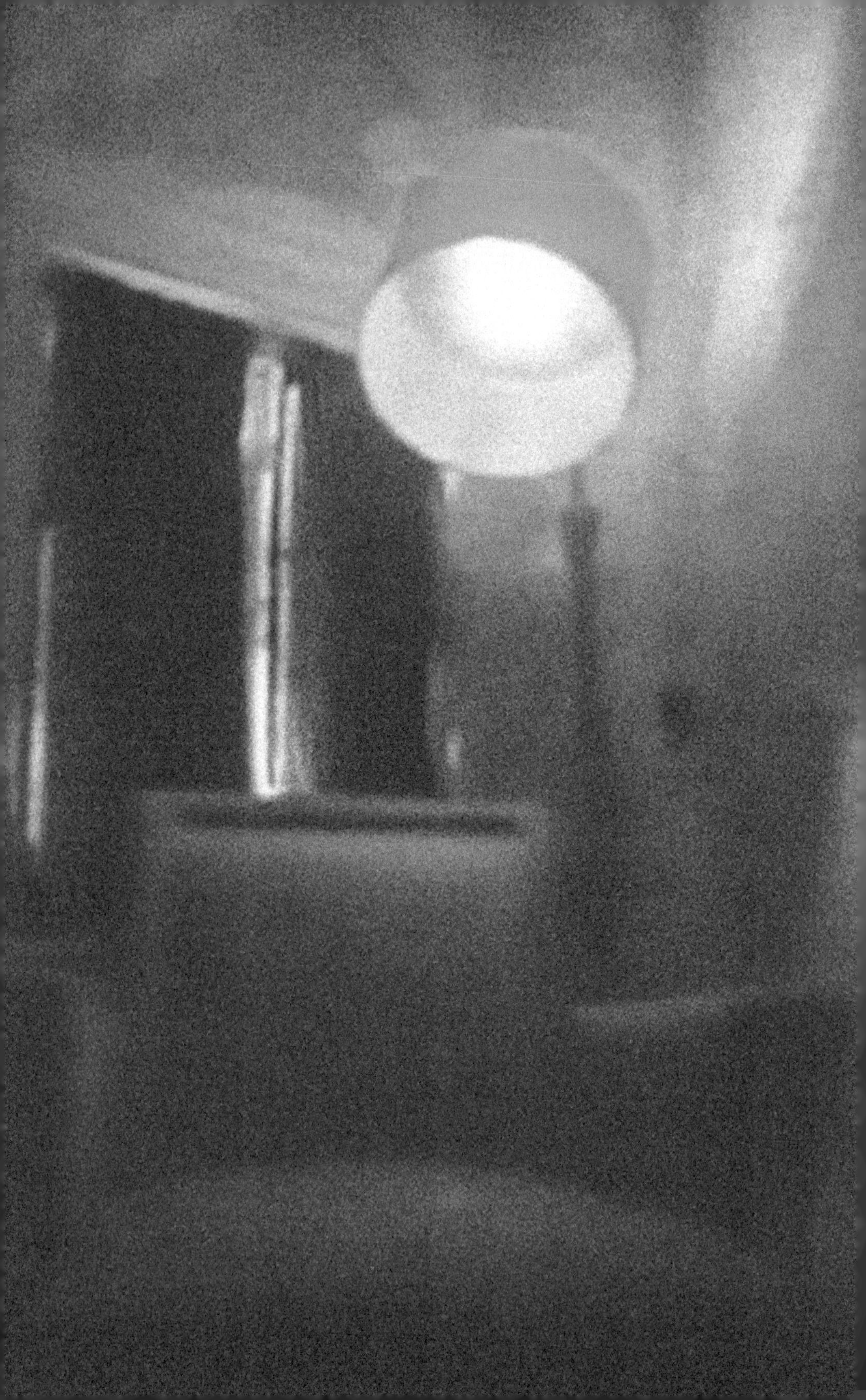

Filmography

FILM AND VIDEO WORKS

Jolicoeur Touriste, 1989, 10 min., 16mm, colour, sound

"An enclosed space, a struggle against the constraints of personal isolation explored through a fractured narrative. A man living in a broken-down rented room in a Tourist Inn travels through his inebriety, his memories and his fantasies, transcending the limits of time and space, which suddenly intertwine. A film about loss and absence." L.B.

Just Words, 1991, 10 min., 16mm, colour, sound

"In *Just Words*, Bourque intercuts footage of her mother and her sisters with a performance by actress Patricia MacGeachy of Samuel Beckett's *Not I*; the result is unnerving (as all Beckett is) yet touching (as some Beckett is not)."
Jay Scott, *The Globe and Mail*, 1992

The People in the House, 1994, 22 min., 16mm, colour, sound

"Moving indoors, *The People in the House* examines the dynamics of a family in crisis and questions the role of religious devotion in the perpetuation of dysfunction. The exterior of the house is never seen, and the family's anxiety, as is often the case, plays out within the confines of four walls. Filmed with a dreamy, surreal quality, *The People in the House* dwells within the tension between harmony and chaos."
Liz Czach, Toronto International Film Festival, 1995

Imprint, 1997, 14 min., 16mm, colour, sound

"An obsession, a fleeting image, a longing: the concept of the home as a romanticized, idealized place of intimacy, inhabiting the most private sphere, the territory of memory, dream, and fantasy. Using as source imagery personal home-movie footage of a family house reproduced multiple times, the process involves a formal and lyrical exploration in which the film image of the home is literally and symbolically treated as a material, a surface, a membrane that is manipulated directly in an attempt at reclaiming and demystifying, at finding and revealing, at capturing and letting go. The original home-movie images are affected, without the use of optical effects, through a variety of hand manipulations and chemical processes such as toning, tinting, ripping, perforating, bleaching, scratching, collaging, deterioration and lifting of the emulsion, as well as through manipulations in the contact printing and developing process. The music at the end is 'A Dream,' sung by Enrico Caruso on a 78 recorded in 1903." L.B.

"Louise Bourque's *Imprint* focuses obsessively on home-movie images of her family's house, which seems gloomily oppressive, almost filling the frame; she repeats the images with various alterations—tinted, bleached, partly scraped away—as if attacking the place, turning its darkness into light."
Fred Camper, *The Chicago Reader*, 1999

"Family portraits are frozen memories, saturated with melancholy and nostalgia. Bourque portrays her family in a very ambiguous way in her authentic 8mm home movies. By bleaching, scratching and perforating the films she creates a rawness which greatly contrasts with the actual content of the films themselves—children playing gently and the warmth associated with 'home.' The abstracted memories slowly blur into a concrete reality in the film, but the strong desire for love and tenderness still lurks apparent behind this façade of distorted images."
Annemick Engbers, Impakt Festival, 1998

Fissures, 1999, 2.5 min., 16mm, colour, sound
"A film about forgetting and remembering, about past presences and the traces they leave. In making this piece, I literally manipulated and distorted the film plane through experimentation in doing my own contact printing of personal home-movie images. The point of contact is continuously shifted so that the film plane appears warped and the images fluctuate, creating a distorted space of fleeting apparitions, like resurfacing memories. The footage was hand-processed and solarized as well as coloured by hand through toning before a final print was made at the lab." L.B.

Going Back Home, 2000, 30 sec. × 2, 35mm, colour, sound
"Turmoil of unsheltered childhood: the dwelling as self." L.B.

"Louise Bourque's *Going Back Home* conveys a sense of loss and upheaval with just a few images."
Steve Anker and Kathy Geritz, San Francisco International Film Festival, 2002

"The disasters of life can make it hard to go home. Bourque's brief, beautiful, and affecting film goes by so quickly it's printed twice on the reel, so you can get a second look."
Program notes, Images Film Festival, 2001

Self Portrait Post Mortem, 2002, 2.5 min., 35mm, colour, sound
"An unearthed time capsule consisting of footage of my youthful self—an 'exquisite corpse' with nature as collaborator. I buried random outtakes from her first three films (all staged productions dealing with my family) in the backyard of my ancestral home (adjoining the grounds of a former cemetery) with the ambivalent intentions of both safe-keeping and unloading them (I was relocating). Upon examining the footage five years later I found that the material contained images of myself captured during the making of my first film. That discovery seemed handed over like a gift and prompted the making of this film, a metaphysical pas-de-deux in which decay undermines the image and in the process engenders a transmutation." L.B.

"Rossetti's Beatrice uses Stan Brakhage as interior decorator in this through-the-glass-darkly two-way mirror moving picture of death after death."
Steve Ausbury, Cinematexas International Short Film Festival, 2002

Jours en fleurs, 2003, 4.5 min., 35mm, colour, sound
"*Jours en fleurs* is a reclamation of flower-power in which images of trees in springtime bloom are subjected to the floriferous ravages of menarcheal substance in a gestation of decay. The title is based on an expression from my coming of age in Acadian French Canada where girls would refer to having their menstrual periods as 'être dans ses fleurs.' As a result of incubation in menstrual blood for several months, the original images inscribed on the emulsion undergo violent alterations. The shedding of the unfertilized womb depredates the fertilized blossoms and substitutes its own dark beauty." L.B.

"Those few shorts that attempt something different become standouts ... such as Louise Bourque's glittering neo-feminist abstraction *Jours en fleurs*."
Ed Halter, *The Village Voice*, 2003

"I can recommend two must-sees in this year's [Toronto International Film Festival] Perspective Canada. ... Louise Bourque's short *Jours en fleurs* is an abstract series of lapping visuals that finds limitless colour and texture in a degraded image."
Cameron Bailey, *Now Magazine*, 2003

L'éclat du mal / The Bleeding Heart of It, 2005, 8 min., 35mm, colour, sound

"The house that bursts; the scene of the crime; the nucleus. A universe collapses on itself: all hell breaks loose." L.B.

"*L'éclat du mal / The Bleeding Heart of It* by Louise Bourque accesses a psychic terrain from her own childhood yet the film is much more than simply personal. Her voiceover tells us, 'In my dream there's a war going on. It's Christmastime. I'm running and I'm carrying myself as a child. It's dark in the tunnel and I'm heading towards the light, the daylight.' Her film draws upon the archives of her unconscious, images that are both personal and archetypal. Images of home abound, unspoken catastrophes, pain and loss. There is something deeply disturbing and haunting in Bourque's film. She is working at the level of those fears that lie buried in that problematic and yet compelling idea of a collective unconscious, a space that only art can truly mediate."
Phil Hoffman, Fabulous Festival of Fringe Film, 2006

"The horror of war—the fear of fire and destruction, of loss and separation—deconstructed and realigned into a haunting and rhythmic remembrance. Watching Bourque's film is like quietly watching a Christmas tree disappear, along with the house, into a delicate and shimmering cloud of smoke."
Jill Hannon, Brooklyn Underground Film Festival, 2006

Remains, 2011, 5 min., 16mm -> DV, colour, sound

"The mother figure revisited—a recurring theme in my work. A celluloid deterioration that addresses the ephemeral quality of the captured moment (the present) while revealing the insistent power of human presence in even the most deteriorated of states. The image of the mother is like a ghost that we won't let go. A lament for the inevitable loss of legibility." L.B.

The Visitation, 2011, 3 min., miniDV, colour, sound

"A statue of the Madonna from a shrine in the house where I grew up takes on an uncanny appearance as if in response to an incantation (an oft-recited prayer from my childhood)." L.B.

a little prayer (H-E-L-P), 2011, 8 min., 35mm, B&W, sound

"The images of a chained Houdini attempting to free himself; the stuttering stop-and-start (interruption-repetition) of his actions; the high-contrast of the images; the stroboscopic effect created by the open-close rhythm of the shutter; the gashes in the emulsion from the hand-processing—all combined with the multi-layered soundtrack, evoke the violence of a tortured soul in search of escape." L.B.

"Screened as a work-in-progress (although it's apparently done except for the video-to-35mm transfer), *a little prayer* marks a new direction for Bourque. Composed of re-photographed film footage of Houdini, this film employs a constant flicker that is actually quite different from any I can recall seeing in other film work. … The rhythms and brushstroke of Bourque's painted films resurface here in a different, altogether more frightening guise. This is an impressively aggressive film, and I think we'll be seeing more of it this year. Brace yourself."
Michael Sicinski, Academic Hack, 2009

Auto Portrait / Self Portrait Post Partum, 2013, 13.5 min., 35mm, colour, sound

"*SPPP* is an autobiographical experimental film exploring the ramifications of the devastating breakup of a romantic relationship. The film examines my own emotional responses in the context of how this experience is culturally represented. Painstakingly handmade, the visual and sound treatments evoke different phases of the relationship (from passionate attachment to escalating conflict to inexplicable breakup) and the various phases of the grieving process—from denial, to yearning, to anger, to final liberation: a healing release effected through the making of this film. A triptych of self-portraits—entire camera rolls, each subjected to different methods of extreme interventions on the celluloid itself—is presented in a series of tableaux punctuated by quotes reflecting on romantic love scratched into the filmstrip. These, along with the sound, are employed as a form of meta-commentary simultaneously foregrounding and deconstructing conventional representations of love, which not only represent but also influence our contemporary experience of the same." L.B.

Bye Bye Now, 2021, 10 min., 16mm -> DV, colour, sound

"In home movies, the gesture of waving provides the future viewer with the acknowledgment of a constant 'goodbye.' Yet when the film is projected, it is as if the people waving are saying 'hello' from the past in the now, the moment of the projection. This film is an homage to the man behind the camera, my father, the person who captured these fleeting moments." L.B.

SUPPLEMENTARY WORKS

People Shoot - "Home Movies," 1991, 3.5 min., 16mm, colour, silent
"Home movies shot on the set of *The People in the House*." L.B.

Days, 1999, 60 min., miniDV, colour, sound
"Shot at Days' Cottages in Cape Cod, Massachusetts. The first time I ever shot with a video camera. One sixty-minute take, the duration of a miniDV tape." L.B.

Dreams of Chaos (blind film), 2007, 7 min., super 8 -> DV, colour, sound
"Super 8 found footage edited based on graphic elements within the frame. A film made without ever projecting the original footage." L.B.

HELP, 2009, 1 min., 35mm, B&W, silent
"*HELP* is the original source material used in *a little prayer (H-E-L-P)*. It is one roll of hand-processed 35mm footage that is meant to be presented (splices and all) as a companion piece to *a little prayer*." L.B.

être été, 2013, 2 min., 16mm -> DV, colour, sound
"Punk rock direct animation with a tip of the hat to Len Lye." L.B.

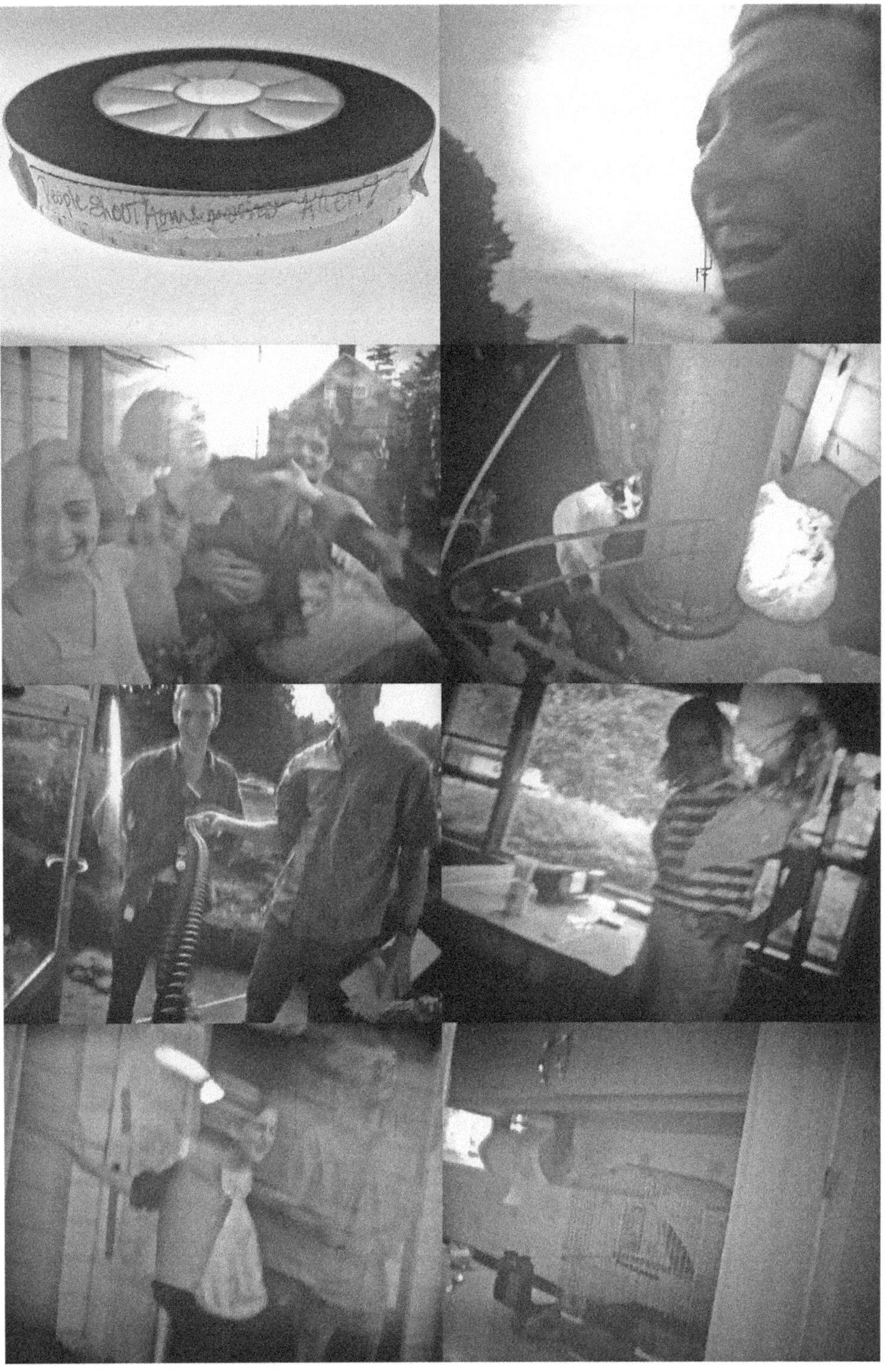
People Shoot

COLLABORATIONS

La Noce de Los Tiempos, 1985, 10 min., Portapak, colour, sound
[with Daniel Dugas and Jean-Pierre Morin]
"A video poem based on the writing of Gérald Leblanc." L.B.

The Producer, 2005, 17 min., DV, colour, sound
Rooftop Song, 2005, 3 min., DV, colour, sound
Down and Out in Buffalo, 2005, 8 min., DV, colour, sound
[with Joe Gibbons and Tony Conrad]
"Three videos made at the Lenox Hotel in Buffalo, N.Y." L.B.

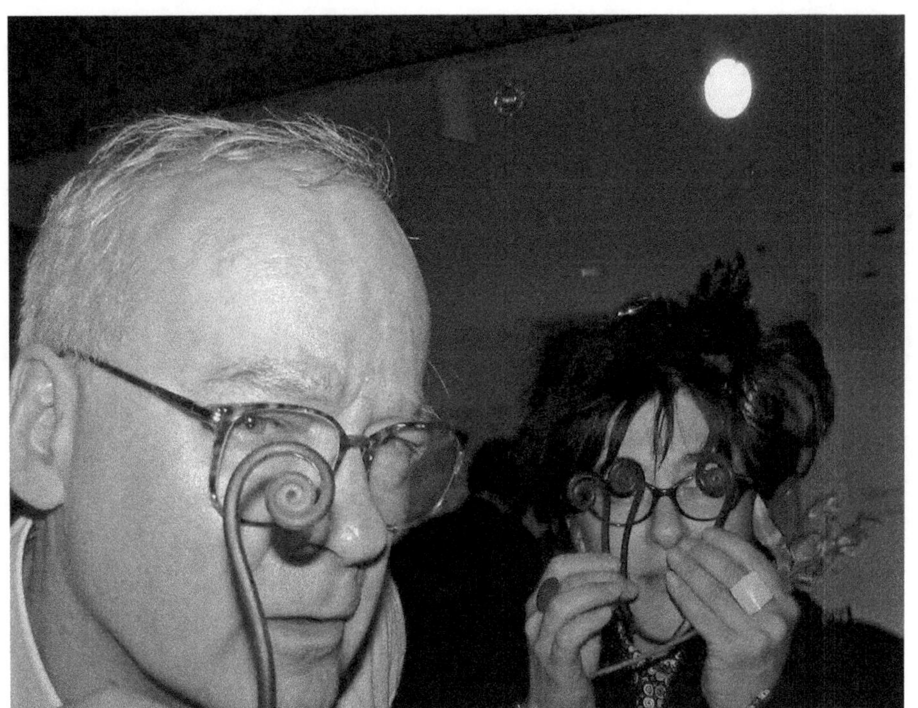

INSTALLATIONS

Going Back Home Again, 2005, 16mm installation

"To the scratchy sounds of an old music box, Louise Bourque's film *Going Back Home* weaves snippets of old reels of houses collapsing, fires and floods into a 30-second elegy. This film exerts a startling pull as it plays over and over on a postcard-size section of gallery wall. Deep within its battered places and antique sounds, the film offers the possibility of recalling something that otherwise could be lost forever."
Joanne Silver, *The Boston Herald*, 2005

À fleur de peau / Foresight Flowers, 2012, 6-channel video installation

"Un bouquet de roses coupées au bord de la fenêtre de mon appartement sur la rue Forsyth à New York que j'ai tourné en 2006 à chaque jour durant un mois avec une petite caméra-photo numérique. Par le jeu du hors-foyer, des mouvements de caméra, et du cadrage en très gros-plans, les fleurs sont transformées par moments en formes abstraites qui prennent l'apparence de la chaire humaine. Les sons de la trame sonore sont les bruits de la ville que j'entendais de ma fenêtre et enregistrais pendant que je tournais." L.B.

"A bouquet of cut roses on the window sill of my apartment on Forsyth Street in New York City that I shot every day for a month in 2006 with a small digital still camera. The play between shifting focus, camera movement, and close-up framing transfigures the flowers into abstract forms that take on the appearance of human flesh. The soundtrack is the noise of the city that I heard from my window as I recorded." L.B.

En passant / In Passing, 2013, interactive video/sound installation
[with Joe Gibbons]
"A video of an anonymous, urban head-toucher is activated by the motion of people passing by detected with a sensor aimed at the sidewalk in front of a storefront window." L.B.

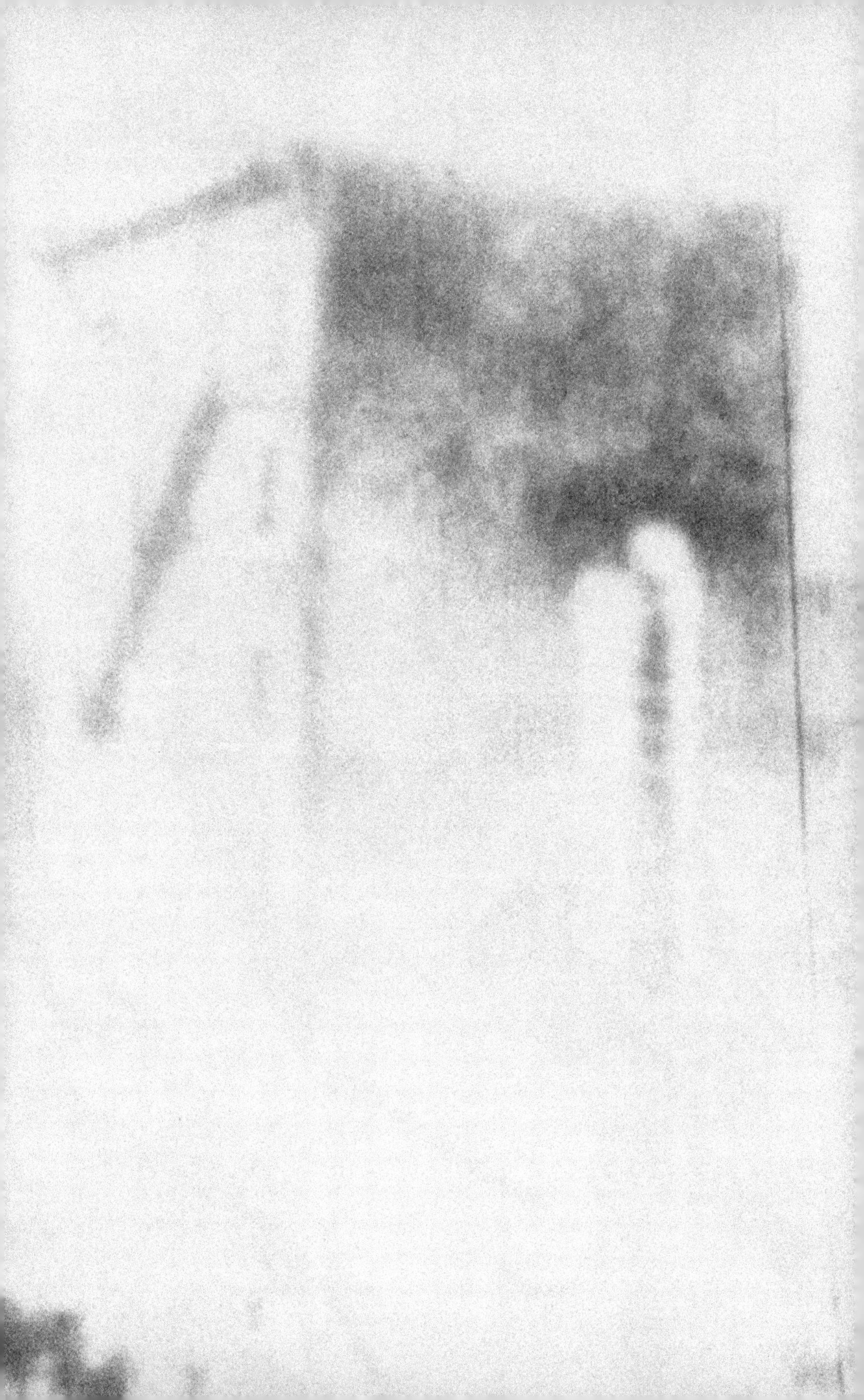

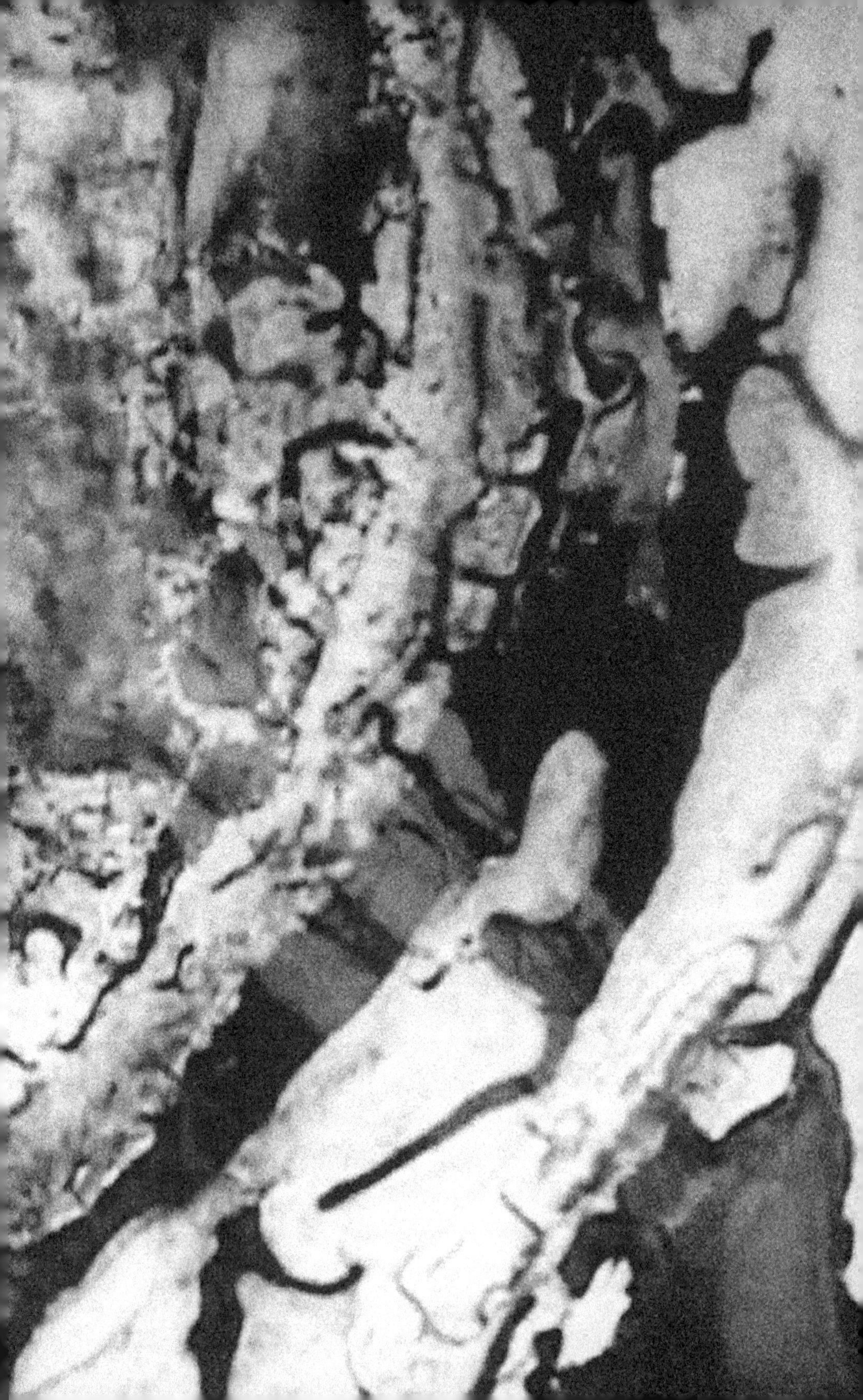

Contributors

Scott Birdwise holds a PhD in Cinema and Media Studies from York University. He has published essays on film and philosophy, experimental and documentary film, and Canadian cinema.

Stephen Broomer is a filmmaker and poet. He is the author of two monographs on Canadian experimental cinema.

Herménégilde Chiasson is a Canadian poet, playwright, and visual artist of Acadian origin. He is also currently a professor at Université de Moncton, and is a member of the Order of New Brunswick.

Amanda Dawn Christie is an interdisciplinary new media artist who makes film, installation, performance, and transmission artworks. She has an MFA from Simon Fraser University and is an assistant professor in Studio Art at Concordia University in Montreal.

Clint Enns is a writer and visual artist living in Montreal, Quebec.

Larissa Fan is a Toronto-based artist who works in 16mm and super 8 film. Fan studied at the Ontario College of Art & Design and has an MFA in Film Production from York University.

Todd Fraser is a filmmaker living in Sackville, New Brunswick.

André Habib is associate professor in the Department of Art History and Film Studies at Université de Montréal. His recent research has dealt with the aesthetics of ruins, found-footage filmmaking, cinephilia, and the archive.

Mike Hoolboom began making movies in 1980. Making as practice, a daily application. Ongoing remixology. Since 2000 there has been a steady drip of found-footage bio-docs. The animating question of community: how can I help you? Interviews with media artists for three decades. Monographs and books, written, edited, co-edited. Local ecologies. Volunteerism. Opening the door.

Nathan Lee is a visiting assistant professor in the Department of Film and Media at Emory University.

Patricia MacGeachy is a Canadian actor and retired elementary school teacher. She is originally from Scotland and currently lives near Montreal. She played the Mouth in Louise Bourque's *Just Words* (1991).

Micah J. Malone is an artist, writer, and former editor of *Big Red & Shiny*.

Sébastien Ronceray is a moving-image artist and the co-founder of the Braquage Association, an organization dedicated to experimental cinema.

José Sarmiento-Hinojosa is a film critic and curator from Lima, Peru. He is also the founder and co-director of *Desistfilm* and curator for MUTA Audiovisual Appropriation Festival.

Michael Sicinski is a writer and critic who specializes in the analysis of experimental cinema. He is a frequent contributor to *Cinema Scope*, *Cineaste*, and *Cargo*. He teaches film studies in the Art History Department at the University of Houston.

Dorottya Szalay is an art theorist and a women's rights activist, currently pursuing her PhD at the University of Theatre and Film Arts in Budapest. Her research centres around the representation of women in experimental cinema.

César Ustarroz is a writer specializing in found-footage filmmaking, re-contextualization, and appropriation. He is editor-in-chief of *Found Footage Magazine*, an independent publication based in Spain and distributed worldwide.

Guillaume Vallée is an experimental filmmaker, video artist, and independent curator. He graduated with a BFA in Film Animation and an MFA in Studio Arts from Concordia University. His work is an exploration of materiality within the creative process.

Brian Wilson has taught film production at Southern Illinois University, Carbondale, and Washington University in St. Louis. He has made many short films and videos, and has written for journals such as *Film International*, *CineAction*, and *Senses of Cinema*.

www.ingramcontent.com/pod-product-compliance
Ingram Content Group UK Ltd.
Pitfield, Milton Keynes, MK11 3LW, UK
UKHW020424250726
13967UKWH00007B/2805

9 780919 096554